THE GAME BEAT

Observations and lessons from two
decades writing about games

THE GAME BEAT

Observations and lessons from two decades writing about games

Kyle Orland

Carnegie Mellon University: ETC Press: Signature
Pittsburgh, PA

ACKNOWLEDGEMENTS

This book is dedicated to the most important women in my life: Michelle, Hannah, and Ruth. Thanks for all the support you've given me over the years...

Thanks to:

- **Simon Carless** and **David Craddock** for shepherding the book in to the Fall 2018 Video Game Story Bundle.

- **Susan Arendt** for able copy editing assistance.

- **John Harris** for general editing help and encouragement.

- **Nathan Scherer** (http://www.nathansmart.com) and **Paige Orland** (http://www.paigeorland.com) for their expert layout help.

- **Haeun Park** (https://www.instagram.com/haeunee2/) for the excellent and completely accurate depiction of me on the cover.

- The editors who've agreed to pay me for regular columns about game journalism over the years, for some reason: **David Gornoski**, **James Brightman** (two non-consecutive times), **Tor Thorsen**, and **John Keefer**.

- **Gus Mastrapa**, whose GameDaily Media Coverage column was a huge inspiration.

- My parents, **Marty** and **Ruth**, who paid for the computer and AOL access that let me start my first video game website in 1997.

- The early-2000s faculty at the Merrill College of Journalism at the University of Maryland, who taught me to take journalism seriously. Maybe too seriously.

- The friends and colleagues who looked over an early manuscript and offered promotional blurbs.

- All of the dozens of game journalists, past and present, who were quoted in this book.

- Anyone who's read and or commented on my years of blog posts and columns analyzing the game journalism landscape. I'm still a bit amazed anyone was listening.

TABLE OF CONTENTS

THE PERSONAL SIDE

THE PRACTICAL SIDE

THE ETHICAL SIDE

INTRODUCTION

> *Game journalism is young enough that we're still trying to collectively agree on the answers to some pretty fundamental questions. What makes a good review? Should we be evaluating games as consumer products or works of art? What role should scores or grades play in the review process? How should we deal with Metacritic's outsized influence?*
>
> *What can game criticism learn from existing critical theory, if anything? How close should game journalists be with the publishers and developers they cover? How can journalists get around the information control of the PR machine? How should outlets handle gifts and publisher-sponsored junkets? How are we supposed to make any money off any of this in the age of the Internet? And so on and so on.*

I wrote those words back in 2006, to introduce the relaunch of a personal blog dedicated to analyzing writing about video games. This book catalogs years of my own scattered attempts to answer those questions and many more that continue to vex the field. In the process, this book also serves as a sort of public diary of my own education in and advancement through the world of professional game journalism, from eager outsider blogger to hustling freelancer to entrenched staff writer.

I've been reading obsessively about games since I got my first *Nintendo Power* subscription at the age of 7, and regularly writing publicly about them since I started fansite Super Mario Bros. HQ at the age of 14. But I didn't start seriously analyzing (overanalyzing?) the field until college. That's when I started noticing the world of game journalism (a loaded term I use to refer to any and all writing about games) usually failed to match the lofty standards and goals being espoused in my journalism courses at The University of Maryland.

So, in 2004, I launched The Video Game Ombudsman, a pretentiously named blog where I tried to highlight the perceived failings of game journalism using nothing more than an extensive reading list, an inquisitive personality, and a huge chip on my shoulder. Since then, my shoulder-chip has largely fallen away, but my interest in writing about the people who write about games has followed me through decades of irregularly spaced blog posts and columns published on a series of professional and personal websites.

This book collects some of the best and most relevant examples of that writing, much of which is no longer available online in any form (the Internet has a short memory sometimes).

Over the years, I've been lucky enough to talk to, work with, and even befriend many colleagues who shared my interest in improving the general quality and professionalism of writing about games. The advice and viewpoints of those professionals have been been key to my continuing education about the field, and are quoted heavily in this book.

Writing about game journalism itself is a bit of peculiar niche, and I've faced plenty of accusations of excessive navel-gazing in my time. But just as honest and constructive critical analysis of games provides a way for game makers to improve, I believe honest and critical analysis of game journalism itself has helped writing about the industry improve markedly over the years.

Whether you enjoy writing about games yourself or simply reading about them, I hope the works collected here will help give you a new perspective on the video game medium and the way it's covered in the press.

HOW TO READ THIS BOOK

The Game Beat is roughly divided into four sections, each looking at game journalism from a different angle (with some admitted overlap):

- **The Analytical Side:** Pieces focused on specific issues or trends that have popped up in the game journalism space over the years.
- **The Personal Side:** Pieces focused on the particular joys and challenges of life as a video game journalist.
- **The Practical Side:** Pieces focused on how game journalists cover the industry.
- **The Ethical Side:** Pieces focused on how game journalists can maintain independence and journalistic distance from the marketing-obsessed industry they cover.

Each section is arranged chronologically, but each piece can be read individually without reading the ones preceding. Feel free to jump around as your mood dictates and skip to another section or time period if the current one isn't striking your fancy.

Careful readers who pay attention to the "Originally Published" timestamps atop each piece will be able to see my perspective on game journalism as a whole change alongside my position in the industry over the years. The game journalism world itself has also shifted significantly over the timespan covered by this book.

Back when I started my Video Game Ombudsman blog in 2004, at least a dozen monthly American video game magazines still drove the national conversation around games. Back then, a loose cadre of "professional" blogs like Kotaku and Joystiq were seen as pesky upstart competition to the IGNs and GameSpots of the online world. Today, all but a handful of those magazines are gone and even the most long-lived specialist websites and blogs are being threatened by the rise of YouTube, Twitch, Twitter, Facebook, and a general fragmentation of the monoculture that has eviscerated the media landscape, game journalism included.

This means the older pieces in this book can sometimes seem like they were practically written in a different geological epoch. That said, I've tried to include pieces where the overarching themes still apply to today's game journalism landscape, even if the particulars have changed. I've also included newly written "Author's Notes" for most older columns, to address changes in circumstance and perspective that have come since the original publication.

The ebook version of *The Game Beat* includes many links to relevant background material around the web, usually as they were included in the original published columns. In most cases, following these links isn't absolutely necessary to grasp the point of the piece, but might be useful for additional contemporary context. Many such links only work at the time of publication (in late 2018) thanks to the cataloging efforts of The Internet Archive; throw them a donation (http://archive. org/donate) if you appreciate any of those classic links.

THE ANALYTICAL SIDE

When you've been in this business long enough, you tend to see the same discussions surrounding game journalism come up again and again. Everything from "Are games art?" and "Do games cause violence?" to "Are we drowning in unrealistic pre-release hype?" and "Should a game's length affect the review?" reappear in the discourse like irregular, badly tuned clockwork.

This section revisits some of these debates in a way that hopefully still resonates today. It also covers ongoing trends in the industry like the slow, unsteady shift away from scores in game reviews, and PR efforts to get around the press filter with release-day review copies and direct-to-consumer announcements.

How Do You Pick the Best Game(s) of All Time?

Originally published on The Video Game Ombudsman, July 9, 2003

IGN says it's *Super Mario Bros.* G4 and *Entertainment Weekly* say it's *The Legend of Zelda: A Link to the Past*. *Electronic Gaming Monthly* said it was *Tetris*, then said it was *Super Metroid* just a few years later.

The varied choices gaming outlets make for "the best video game of all time," show how little consensus there can be in forming these endlessly debated lists, which these days seem to pop up at least once a year at some outlet or another.

That lack of consensus isn't necessarily a bad thing, though. A "top games of all time" list is supposed to be a product of the experiences of the writers and editors that make it, not some sort of objective ranking of every game ever made by some pre-set criteria. Too much agreement between lists could be a sign that there isn't a wide-enough set of viewpoints being considered.

Still, there are a few games that seem to show up time and time again near the top of these kinds of lists: Tetris is in the top four of all four lists mentioned above, for instance. So, are there any criteria we can all agree upon for what makes a game "the best ever"?

"Yes, of course this list is entirely objective. Just don't ask the other guy," said IGN's Peer Schneider, paraphrasing the message from the Japanese movie *Rashomon.* Schneider, who worked on IGN's top 100 list, said that objective ranking is only possible to a certain extent; much of it is just the editors' personal taste. "It's IGN's Top 100 Games—very much a collective, objective, subjective ranking of our favorite games."

EGM Executive Editor Mark MacDonald, however, thinks it is possible to rank games more objectively. "Games, as subjective as they are, there are still objective criteria to them," MacDonald said after working on *EGM*'s second list. "People who say, 'That's only your opinion,' they're wrong. It is your opinion, absolutely, but it can also be a matter of objective criteria."

MacDonald says things like awkward controls or jumpy frame rates are objective problems that most game players can agree on. "It's not always like chocolate ice cream, where you can like it or not with no evidence," MacDonald said. "Like they say in logic class: all truths are not equal."

At the same time, though, MacDonald acknowledges that "no two gamers are going to have the same list. There will never be the definitive list. You can make it as well thought out as possible, but that's pretty much all you can do."

Schneider said that comparing older games to newer games shows the difficulty in generating an objective list. "Can we really list a game like *Pitfall* alongside infinitely more complex titles, released two decades later? The creation of any ranking is a subjective process that's bound to lead to plenty of disagreements."

Video game list-makers also differ over how much credit should be given to a game that was groundbreaking and influential in its time, but has since been surpassed. Is a game that started its own genre better or worse than a newer game that improved on that base?

> *People who say, 'That's only your opinion,' they're wrong. It is your opinion, absolutely, but it can also be a matter of objective criteria.*
> **Mark MacDonald**
> **EGM Executive Editor**

MacDonald and the team at *EGM* asked a simple question of older games to help prevent the team from being blinded by nostalgia: "Would you pull it out now and play it today? If [someone brings up an old game], but they never pull it out and play it, then we'll tell them to quiet down. If they say they played it last week, then it's definitely a consideration, but not be all end all. In general, the games that revolutionized the industry are the ones you'd still pull out and play."

Schneider also said that a strong design and general "fun factor" are more important than influence or technical merits in ranking games. "If you stress technological prowess or general influence too much, you'd end up with a list devoid of charming follow-ups like *Ms. Pac-Man* or *SimCity 2000*. The reasons for a game being 'good' are manifold. A game is the sum of its parts—and sometimes more; the balance of gameplay, graphics, presentation, sound, and how well everything is wrapped up into a unified whole."

But is an intangible "fun factor" really a strong enough criterion to rank an entire medium? You don't see critics of other pop art forms like music and movies ranking works by how fun they are. For that matter, you rarely ever see top 100 lists for "higher" art like literature or painting. Is the ranking of video games itself indicative of an industry viewed merely as "an exciting form of pop-culture entertainment," as *Entertainment Weekly* put it in a press release for its own list?

"I think the things you think about for things like video games and movies... it's kind of silly when you think about it in terms of books, paintings, and sculpture," MacDonald said. "It has something to do with pop culture. Books are in [higher art], but video games and movies are only in pop culture."

MacDonald added that he thinks that the drive to rank video games might be indicative of the industry's consumer-oriented nature. "It's really consumer-driven more than something like painting or sculpture... it's much younger. As younger art forms, maybe more younger people are into them. I definitely think video games 100 years from now will be considered higher than today. As they broaden into different niches, they'll definitely be held in higher regard, but I don't know if this will affect how they're ranked."

Schneider, on the other hand, thinks video game-style rankings could be made for all art forms, as long as the ranking is done by people who know the subject matter. "Would I agree with anyone else's 'Top 100 Paintings'? No, of course not. But the whole beauty of these lists is that you will remember things you thought you'd long forgotten. I can't tell you how many games came up on other people's lists during the selection process where I sat up and went 'Oh, man! Yeah, *M.U.L.E.* was great! That has to be on there!'"

Schneider also said he thinks video games are well-suited to ranking because of the time constraints associated with playing them. "There just isn't enough to time anymore to go back and play all these games, so remembering them by writing about them is as close as we can get."

How to Spread a Fake Interview

Originally published on The Video Game Ombudsman, Sept. 12, 2003

> *Internet gaming journalism is based on one principle: If it's on a website, it must be true!*
>
> **Directrix**
> **NerdsAhoy**

Directrix is in a good position to make this statement. On the afternoon of Sept. 1, he put a now-infamous fake interview with Gabe Newell[1] up on his site. He posted a link to the article on the SomethingAwful forums, and set off an absolute firestorm of linking from sites large and small, some of which handled it skeptically and some of which did not.

Directrix said he never intended for anyone to believe the interview was real. "I'm not sure if you're familiar with those forums [at SomethingAwful]," he said, "but it is a humor site. In my opinion the people who post there are much more intelligent than what you would find in your average forum, so I didn't expect anyone to buy it. It was basically me sarcastically poking fun at the fact that any rumor, no matter how insane, can pop up on the Internet and people will believe it... or not believe it, and argue about it for pages on end."

Planet Half-Life, a member of the GameSpy network, was one of the sites that didn't totally believe it. Their post about the interview indicated that, "it could very well be a fake," but justified posting the link by explaining that "there's already a ton of inaccurate information out there." Ahem.

Kevin Bowen (a.k.a "Fragmaster"), Planet Half-Life's manager, said he doesn't regret running the story. "It was a better than average fake and the answers were somewhat amusing," he said. "We were pretty sure it was fraudulent from the start and we indicated so in the post. A lot of other sites were fooled and there's a whole bunch of other false information out there, so we wanted to give it some sort of mention to acknowledge its existence and point out that it was bogus."

But Directrix notes that, while Planet Half-Life handled the matter skeptically, they "wouldn't take an official stance on whether the interview was real or fake until [Valve Founder/ Managing Director] Gabe [Newell] himself confirmed it. They should never have even posted it."

Newell confirmed to VGO that he was contacted by numerous websites about the article, and said he felt such direct attempts at confirmation were a good way to prevent such things from happening in the future. Newell added that he didn't feel any malice towards Directrix or those that linked to his story. "It's the kind of thing that happens all the time on the Internet," he said.

Directrix, however, said he wasn't contacted by any websites seeking to confirm the veracity of his article. "I was never contacted by anyone who could string a complete sentence together," he said. He acknowledged that some of the people who linked to the article may have been in on the joke, but said the problem then was "that their audience apparently cannot distinguish between fact and sarcastic humor."

> *It's the kind of thing that happens all the time on the Internet.*
>
> *Gabe Newell*
> *Valve Founder/Managing Director*

Directrix said that other web journalists could learn a lesson from the saga of his fake article. "Don't trust one source for your information," he said, "especially a website that no one has ever heard of before." He wasn't very optimistic about the chances his advice would be followed, though. "The same thing could happen tomorrow and nothing would turn out differently... The only thing I've learned from this is that it's amusing to sit back and watch it take place. Kind of like watching sea monkeys eat each other, except you don't have to change the water."

Eliminate the Positive (or "The Only Negative Review of *Halo 2* You'll Ever Read")

Originally published on The Video Game Ombudsman, Nov. 10, 2004

"*Halo 2* isn't a perfect game."[9] It "is still a linear series of shootouts,"[5] that is "cowboys and Indians from the get-go,"[2] and features "annoying graphical hiccups" and "team AI [that] isn't always perfect."[6]

"Some will undoubtedly say that the graphics have come up a bit short."[6] "There

are occasionally some graphic hiccups, such as when a far-off texture doesn't fill in as you approach it,"[1] or when "the ground sometimes has an unrealistic ripple effect and some characters you come across look blurry."[4] One other "noticeable 'problem' is when the graphics mip-map at the beginning of nearly every scene, meaning that you first see a placeholder graphic before the more detailed version pops into place."[2] "Brutes have a very plastic appearance, and one character in particular is sloppily designed."[9]

In addition, "some of the in-engine cutscenes are kind of ugly," and "you'll actually see a little slowdown, pop-in, and LOD issues during cutscenes."[5] In fact, "you'll wonder what's going on in the cutscenes."[7] "It does detract."[8]

Besides the graphics, *Halo 2* has "a surprisingly disappointing story."[5] "The first game had a cold sense of mystery and a striking sense of loneliness that shadowed Master Chief wherever he went. This time around... *Halo 2* feels a little bit more Hollywood, a little less underdog."[2] "You spent the first game indiscriminately killing these fiends—yet now you're expected to be sympathetic to them and their hatred for humankind."[5]

"The second half tends to drag on a bit,"[3] but "easily the worst part about the story is the way it ends, insofar as it doesn't."[5] "The final battle is neither interesting while you're in the thick of it nor fulfilling once it concludes."[9] "You'll run into this game's cliffhanger ending like a compact car into a brick wall... There's little satisfaction to be found in the ending here," and "there's a good chance you'll feel emotionally betrayed by the story."[5] "More than a few people will find Bungie's [bridge] to 'Xbox 2' more than a little irritating."[2]

"I still see a bit of repetitive level design in *Halo 2*."[7] "*Halo 2*'s campaign... frequently boils down to straight-up run-and-gun corridor crawls, one after another."[5] "Bungie's ship and interior designs are almost as repetitive in both architecture and texturing as before... Given no map, you will find yourself wondering where the hell to go more often than not... More distinct texture work and asymmetrical ornamentation would've helped."[8]

"The AI has a few weaknesses, especially when it's in the driver's seat of a vehicle, where it has trouble steering around obstacles."[5] In addition, "many battles turn into strike-and-hide exercises where you take a few shots and then sneak away to let your shield recharge."[6] It certainly doesn't help that the campaign is "rather short"[5] and that "able-bodied players will probably finish the game on Normal mode in around 15 hours."[2] "I somehow expected it to take much longer."[8]

"There's no... system-link cooperative mode"[3] and "you can't play co-op online."[4] That's right, there's "no co-op play for Xbox Live or through system link."[9] "I'd have loved to see a working online co-op mode."[7] "It would have been great to play co-op online."[8] "My dream of online co-op with the Master Chief has been dashed."[7]

"*Halo 2* is not perfect."[4] "You could argue that given all the hype, *Halo 2* is disappointingly more of the same."[3] "I can't really say that the engine has been vastly improved for the sequel,"[7] "every now and then, the game goes a bit overboard with the technology,"[4] "and well, could there have been more maps?"[8] "A surprisingly disappointing story and a fairly short single-player portion are noticeable shortcomings."[5] "After all of the time we spent waiting for this product, the developers owed us something better."[9]

> *Media frenzies around games like this tend to encourage hyperbole, so this is my attempt to keep the effusive praise down to a realistic level.*

EDITOR'S NOTE: If it's not apparent yet, this "review" is simply an amalgamation of bad points from nine other mass-market reviews of *Halo 2*. All the words inside quotes were copied directly from the numbered source in parentheses immediately following (listed and linked below).

These quotes were deliberately purged of any positive context or mitigating conditionals through judicious snipping. Still, to be clear, every one of these points was intended as a negative in the original review. I did not just take random words out of context to make it look like the reviewers found flaws that didn't exist. Instead, I separated out the (often middling) negatives in these reviews from the overwhelming positives and grouped them into a semi-coherent whole.

Anyone who's still ready to send me an angry comment after that should consider that it took the relatively minor nitpicking from nine separate reviews to construct one average-length, overly-repetitive negative review of this game. Even then, that negative review still isn't very convincing. If this doesn't speak to the obvious quality of *Halo 2*, I don't know what does.

So why do this at all? First, to show that individual quotes taken from their surrounding review can be highly misleading (important to remember the next time you see a quote on the back of a game box). Second, to show that although it might seem like *Halo 2* is God's gift to gaming, it is not perfect. None of the nine reviews I read (some of which were quite lengthy and gave the game the highest possible score) claimed that it was. Some explicitly said it wasn't. Media frenzies around games like this tend to encourage hyperbole, so this is my attempt to keep the effusive praise down to a realistic level.

REVIEW SOURCES
(1) Gamespy[2]
(2) *EGM* (Mielke)[3]
(3) *EGM* (McDonald)[4]
(4) *EGM* (Leone)[5]
(5) GameSpot[6]
(6) G4TechTV[7]
(7) UGO[8]
(8) IGN[9]
(9) Gamerfeed[10]

Do Bad Games Get Shorter Reviews?

Originally published on The Video Game Ombudsman, Dec. 8, 2004

Ombudsman reader (and general Curmudgeon) Matt Matthews wrote in a while ago to ask about "the relationship between popularity of a game and the number of pages that go into a review." Specifically, Matthews pointed out that GameSpot's review[11] of the ultra-hyped *Halo 2* was four pages, while "relatively lesser-known" (but still highly rated) *Astro Boy* for GBA got a one-page review.[12] "Which factor is more important: popularity or quality?" Matthews wondered.

In GameSpot's case, the answer is supposedly neither. "We intentionally avoid rigidity when it comes to review length, because each case is at least slightly different," GameSpot Executive Editor Greg Kasavin said in an email. "There's more to say about *Halo 2*, which features a variety of modes of play, than there is to say about *Astro Boy*, which is an excellent but simple game. So why should *Halo 2* be given short shrift just because it attempts to do more than Astro Boy?"

Kasavin stressed that he has "never once imposed a word count limit or page limit on a GameSpot review," nor tried to stretch out shorter reviews to garner more page views. "Reviewers are simply expected to cover all the major bases, and when it comes to higher-profile games, there tend to be more. We include nothing in any of our reviews that we think is extraneous."

I think Kasavin's policy is, in general, the right one when it comes to review length. Each game is different, and asking different reviews to conform to the same length specifications, especially in a medium with near-unlimited space like the Web, isn't necessary or desirable. A review shouldn't be any longer or shorter than it has to be.

That being said, in my experience, reviews of large, highly-expected games tend to be a lot longer than they have to be. Consider IGN's *Halo 2* review, for one ripe example. True, any game that you're calling "the greatest Xbox game of all time" deserves a little extra space, but this monstrosity of a review repeats itself constantly over eight long pages before finally coming to its merciful conclusion.

> *In my view, a short, well-written review beats an overly-long, overly-detailed, overly-repetitive review every time.*

The IGN review spends nearly two pages pretty much listing every multi-player mode and option—information doubtless also found in the game's press release and instruction book. Another entire page is spent on different ways to say "the graphics are great." Just because there isn't a strict limit on review length doesn't mean the author shouldn't show some self-restraint.

Some might argue that reviewers are simply giving the audience what they want by providing more review space for highly anticipated games, and it's true that many eager readers want to get as much information as they can about the latest "game of the millenium." But just because there readers want a lot of information doesn't mean you have to put it all *in the review.* Separating out the nitty-gritty details and more expansive descriptions into sidebars or separate features can allow devoted followers to get all their information and more casual readers to absorb the basics in a leaner, more straightforward review. This is essentially a stylistic choice, but it's one that I feel most sites err on the wrong side of.

In my view, a short, well-written review beats an overly-long, overly-detailed, overly-repetitive review every time. Give me the essence of the experience in as few words as possible, and then let me worry about whether or not I want mountains of more detailed information.

The PSP, the DS, and Preview Bias

Originally published on The Video Game Ombudsman, Jan. 26, 2005

Ombudsman reader Benny Torres recently sent me an email airing his concerns that bias was creeping into *Electronic Gaming Monthly*'s coverage of the battle between the PSP and Nintendo DS. Torres says that recent coverage in *EGM* and on 1UP has let the "PSP get away with

awesome previews and forecasts for games ... but then on the same token shows a couple of games for the DS and makes comments like 'it remains to be seen if gamers will warm up to its innovations.'"

Torres continues, saying that "the proof is in the cover. Look at this month's [February 2005] cover. It's about 'The Year of the Portables,' not the PSP. ... The PSP is front and center on the cover, the DS is literally *behind* the PSP."

"The reason for that design is a simple one: Out of all those portables featured on our cover, the PSP is the only one anyone would consider 'the next big thing,'" responds Dan "Shoe" Hsu, *EGM*'s editor-in-chief. "We have an enthusiast-focused publication, so it's smarter for us to show a PSP up front at this point, as that's the system hardcore gamers want to read about more, as opposed to the DS, which they all already own." Hsu went on to say that Nintendo's secrecy about the DS' design made a similar DS-focused cover impossible before that system came out.

The comparison of an upcoming system to one that readers "all already own" also helps address Torres' other complaint, Hsu says. Torres argues that *EGM*'s PSP bias can be seen in the magazine's description of each system's control scheme. While the PSP is lauded for allowing you to customize your control scheme in *Coded Arms,* "the DS gets ripped in most of its reviews for lack of a specific control method in its design. *EGM* instead concentrates on the 'flexibility' of the PSP game... instead of the lack of dual sticks," Torres said.

Shoe calls this "selective reading," because Torres is comparing a review for the DS to a preview for the PSP. "In a preview, we usually don't put any final judgements on a product. Instead, we typically tell you about its features, its potential, etc. In a review, it's no-holds-barred." Hsu cites a more neutral assessment of DS controls in the *Super Mario 64 DS* preview: "As you might expect, controls are different, with the option to use the touchpad to move (and d-pad to jump, crouch, etc.) or a more standard setup where the second screen merely controls the camera."

> We have an enthusiast-focused publication, so it's smarter for us to show a PSP up front at this point, as that's the system hardcore gamers want to read about more, as opposed to the DS, which they all already own.
>
> **Dan "Shoe" Hsu**
> **EGM Editor-in-chief**

But that preview was published months ago. Comparing a preview of a PSP game to a review of a DS game can be considered "selective reading," but it's also an accurate reading of an single *EGM* issue these days. Because the PSP isn't out in the U.S. yet, all its coverage is still in the preview stage, which tends to be relatively forgiving and hopeful about upcoming games. Since the release of the Nintendo DS in the U.S., though, its coverage has shifted to generally harsher reviews that tend to focus on the flaws in final products.

The problem here—the slight 'bias' Torres is seeing—has little to do with the systems themselves and everything to do with the uncritical nature of most previews. Hsu is right to point out that comparing PSP and DS previews paints a much more balanced picture, but Torres is right that current writing about DS games (which includes some harsh reviews) might come off worse than current writing about the PSP (mainly gentle previews). Given the current absence of informed, hands-on reviews for PSP games, readers are left with no choice but to compare two very different types of writing.

This coverage will balance out over time, of course, as the PSP games face the same review standards. For now, though, an average *EGM* reader is faced with two very different coverage tones for the two different systems. The DS is being penalized for being released first, in a way.

Hsu almost acknowledges this when responding to Torres' complaint about the lack of *EGM* coverage for much-maligned PSP negatives like load times and battery life. "It's coming," Shoe says. "We're actually covering some of these things in our April 2005 issue, which comes out right before the PSP's supposed March launch. We've been waiting on a proper PSP launch guide because we're hoping to test out U.S. (not Japanese) units, and because we want to release that story right before consumers could actually buy the system itself... when that information is most useful and timely."

The question then becomes: Do readers realize the inherent tonal difference between a review and a preview? Do they incorporate this difference into their reaction to a video game feature?

I think it's fair to say that most readers do just that. It doesn't take a lot of experience with the average video game magazine to realize that—in the absence of actual play time— most previews will put the hype-building focus on what's new and exciting in a game, and leave coverage of flaws until the review. Even though this isn't usually explicitly stated, this "preview bias" is pretty much an accepted fact to people who read any significant amount of video game writing. I know a few people who won't even read previews because the hope-and-hype-filled early impressions are often completely overturned by the time a final review comes out.

If previews can't provide a predictive picture of how a game will actually end up, should we even bother writing them? Probably. Previews still provide an essential service to readers by letting them know the basic details of potentially interesting games long before they see them on store shelves. Even if previews are uniformly glowing, the publication still exercises editorial control in choosing the most promising games to feature (big marketing budgets can often influence which games merit this glowing preview coverage, but that's a topic for another time).

But is there another way to write a preview? I seem to remember *Next Generation* magazine taking a more balanced approach in their preview writing, allowing space for the game's developers to talk a game up, but also pointing out any potential flaws they see near the end of the preview. Usually these flaws were accompanied by a qualifying line, along the lines of, "hopefully the team will be able to work out these kinks before the launch." But at least early issues weren't totally ignored.

There's no one correct answer to the "preview bias" problem; how a publication deals with it depends on their audience, their writing style, and their goals for the preview section and the magazine as a whole. Some might want to publish a harsh disclaimer about the format in every preview section. Some publications may want to incorporate a more critical tone to their previews. I don't think any publication should totally ignore the issue, though. At least, they shouldn't if they want people like Mr. Torres to read their magazine.

Which Came First, the Hype or the Interest?

Originally published on the Video Game Ombudsman, March 4, 2005

AUTHOR'S NOTE

I'm reprinting this piece mainly as an illustration of how the "conventional wisdom" can coalesce among the press during that crucial hype-building pre-release period. A few anecdotal pieces of personal evidence experienced by one editor became a sign that "people are too hyped for the PSP." This drove positive coverage, which helped build more hype, which could have helped to create a self-fulfilling prophecy of success for a hot new product.

Thanks to Ombudsman reader Erik Bondurant for pointing me to a post on his blog about alleged bias towards the PSP in *EGM*. Erik argues that *EGM*'s bias lies not in a personal preference, but in an assumption of the audience's personal preference.

> *To me, it is unnecessary to predict success because too often, having the media predict serves only to influence what actually happens, or as I put it in the title, the bias of self-fulfilling prophecy. EGM thinks that Nintendo is doomed to second rank niche play while the PSP is destined to mainstream madness, well, that seems likely now that the impressionable teenagers and young adults who make up the largest and most active portion of the gaming market have been led to think the PSP is the system to own.*

Is EGM being presumptuous here? Is there any basis for assuming that "people are too hyped for the PSP," as *EGM* Editor-in-chief Dan "Shoe" Hsu said in a recent editorial? I asked Hsu this very question.

"To a Nintendo fan, or a gamer who hasn't seen PSP yet, these may seem like preconceived notions," Hsu said, "but when I see the hype around this system—not just from gaming magazines and websites but from industry people and retailers—it's incredible how much buzz is behind the machine before it's properly launched."

Hsu points to a specific example—cited in his editorial—that illustrates the buzz: "A local EB Games already has over 100 pre-orders just based on people walking in and seeing the manager's personal machine... for real."

> *When I see the hype around this system—not just from gaming magazines and websites but from industry people and retailers—it's incredible how much buzz is behind the machine before it's properly launched.*
>
> **Dan "Shoe" Hsu**
> **EGM Editor-in-chief**

Hsu also shared another anecdotal example of the the system's appeal to the mainstream public: While giving an interview to local show Stir TV, Hsu says the producer and two cameramen asked to see the system and were "blown away." Hsu cited a few other examples of his buzz perception in our chat, but none of them were very compelling, to be honest.

Altogether, these anecdotal examples don't amount to overwhelming scientific evidence that "people are too hyped for the PSP," but they certainly don't hurt. Regardless, Hsu says the buzz around the PSP has nothing to do with *EGM*'s coverage.

"People look to the gaming press as opinion leaders because we see this stuff before they do," he said. "But there's only a certain amount of reach that we have. It won't succeed just because we tell everyone to get one. Even if we don't cover the system at all, it will still be a success. The minute it's in stores, in hands, people will understand why."

Bondurant says on his blog, "It is impossible to separate sales from media coverage and decide whether the media is simply responding to the market or actually is shaping the market." He's right to an extent. It's a little pointless to speculate whether the hype or the press interest truly comes first when both are constantly feeding off each other. Still, I don't see the problem with commenting on your personal perception of buzz in an editorial, as long as you have some sort of personal evidence to back it up.

Microsoft's MTV Move

Originally published on the Video Game Ombudsman, April 11, 2005

AUTHOR'S NOTE

Looking back over a decade later, this post seems a little prescient. From corporate blogs to Nintendo's "Direct" video presentations to choreographed trailer launches, publishers these days increasingly tailor and deliver their news-making messages directly to and for their fans, rather than relying on the press as a middleman. This makes sense in an age where social media and streaming video has made everyone into a potential vector to share your marketing message.

The professional journalist still has a role in this world, both as a filter that focuses on the information worth paying attention to and as an after-the-fact check on marketing excesses. And there are still times when the press gets embargoed access to early information, which they can then contextualize and analyze before publishing.

On the whole, though, the proliferation of near-ubiquitous Internet access has given publishers a way to get around the press filter and get their messages directly to their biggest fans without even having to buy ad space. This has lessened the value of the traditional "access journalism" model of getting exclusive information first and increased the value of being able to provide good analysis after the information is out there.

If you pay attention to your news aggregation blogs, you already know that Microsoft is planning to unveil its next console on a live, half-hour MTV special May 12, days before E3 begins. Elijah Wood will host the public unveiling, which will take place at 9:30 EDT in the States.

I'm not really sure whether MTV or Microsoft benefits more from this move. MTV gets to be associated with the new Xbox, increasingly a symbol of "cool" among their target demographic. It also get to make important connections with Microsoft in advance of launching its own web-based video game channel.

Microsoft, of course, gets the coveted mindshare associated with being first to reveal its new system, effectively cutting Sony's prime E3 press conference timing. Microsoft also gets the huge MTV audience—whose target demographic neatly overlaps with Microsoft's own—and gets to take its message to the consumer without being filtered by the press.

Read that last sentence again. Savor it. Let it roll over your mind. It's enough to make an eager brand manager salivate just thinking about it.

While whole E3 press conferences have been streamed online in the past, and even been available on DVD well after the fact, most people don't get their hardware and software announcements in this unfiltered form. In the past, most people heard about the hot new system or game through those crucial "first impression" press summaries that sprout up immediately following the big conference.

But why let journalists taint the public opinion with their pretty words and potentially negative opinions of your carefully crafted event? Skip the middleman and beam your video advertorial directly to the minds of millions of potential consumers—with no pesky press commentaries until you've already had your say.

Should game journalists be worried about this move? I'd say so. If consumers take to this type of direct-mass-marketing-video-game-unveiling-event, then the game press' position as official arbiter of what's new, what's cool, and what's important in the game industry could be very highly undermined. I'm not saying the game journalist as a species would totally disappear, but their clout, as a group, could well be diminished.

Hardware makers could become even more secretive about their developments, ignoring the press entirely until they're ready to make their grand announcement from on high, leaving the rest of us to scramble for attention. Large developers, angry about negative coverage, perhaps, could deny access to the press and decide to spend their effort on their own 30-minute prime-time informercial instead. A game industry tired of dealing with a finicky press corps could circumvent them entirely.

> *Skip the middleman and beam your video advertorial directly to the minds of millions of potential consumers—with no pesky press commentaries until you've already had your say.*

I'm not saying any of this will come to pass, or is even likely. Some might say the scenario I outline isn't too different from how it is now, anyway. Regardless, I know I'll be watching closely come May 12.

It's Our Fault Games Aren't Considered Art

Originally published on The Video Game Ombudsman, Nov. 30, 2005

AUTHOR'S NOTE

The "Are games art?" debate has always been a bit silly, weighed down with too many value-laden semantic arguments and adolescent ideas about "respectability" to generate much real meaning. Years after the Supreme Court gave full First Amendment protection to video games, the whole thing feels a bit anachronistic.

That said, compared to 13 years ago, I'd say you now see many more examples of games that "provid[e] deep emotional experiences that can change the way we look at the world," as I defined the debate years ago.

The writing and discussion of games has moved along with this shift. While there are still plenty of reviews that focus primarily on a game's technical merits, there are also more and more writers offering deeply considered critiques of a game's larger meaning and message. We might not have our Roger Ebert yet, but we do have a whole generation of readers and writers more ready to take games seriously as a way to convey more than just adrenaline-soaked thrills.

When talking with friends or other journalists about the state of game criticism, I often hear the complaint that games haven't yet found their Roger Ebert—a critic who can bring semi-serious game appreciation to the masses. Many gamers wish there was someone who could similarly raise the profile of game criticism in the mainstream consciousness. Many game journalists, of course, wish to *be* that someone.

Roger Ebert himself, apparently, does not.[13]

As you might have read, the famed film critic recently stated in no uncertain terms that he knows very little about video games, and that the little he does know makes him think they are inferior to most other media in terms of artistic expression.

The question of whether or not games are art is a hotly contested one, and one I don't want to explore in depth here.

Suffice it to say I think they are, as far as they are capable of providing deep emotional experiences that can change the way we look at the world.

If you agree that games are art (or will at least grant me the premise), here's another question to consider: Have we, as critics, given people like Ebert enough reason to *believe* that games are art?

I'm reminded of a recent post[14] on Grumpy Gamer, by game designer Ron Gilbert. In the post, Gilbert partially refutes an anti-game-journalism rant by God of War designer David Jaffe (more on that in a bit) by saying, in essence, that game criticism is so bad because the games themselves are bad.

> *If you read the major gaming sites, they are mostly filled with reviews that give scores for 'Graphics' and 'Sound' and (let's be honest) come across like they are written by fanboys. They make what we do sound more like Toys than a rich emerging Art Form.*
>
> *But maybe that blame lays more in our laps than the game reviewer's, after all, what are we giving them to review? Are we just mad because they don't see Shakespeare in our Transformers?*

As I stated above, I disagree with Gilbert's implication that games aren't "a rich emerging Art Form." But even if they're not, I'm not sure that critics can get a pass for treating them as mere products to be judged purely on the craft of their graphics, sound, etc.

Art or not, games are much more than the just sums of their parts. Any idiot can write a review that simply describes a game's functionality and tells you that it is technically superior to similar games that have come before it. A good writer can take the same game and evoke for the reader the experience of playing without directly explaining the minutiae of the control scheme, for instance. They can place the game into the pantheon of the medium and the wider culture it's a part of and explain its impact, if any. This is the heart of good criticism, I feel.

Of course, this is easier for some games than others. The more derivative, generic, and mediocre a game is, the harder it is to find something interesting to say about it. But the goal or the critic should always be to find that interesting angle, that evocative turn of phrase, or that clever description of the game as experience rather than object. Anyone who is content merely describing a game and its most objectively measurable qualities ("killer graphics," "tight controls") should stop writing game criticism and start writing instruction booklets or press releases.

This gets into what I consider a fundamental split between two distinct types of evaluation: game *reviews* and game *critiques*. In my mind, game *reviews* are mainly commercial tools, meant to help consumers decide whether or not a game is worth their money and time. Game *critiques,* on the other hand, are more concerned with the totality of a game's design and what a game does to advance the state of the medium or even society as a whole. The former considers mainly whether a game is *fun,* the latter whether it is *worthwhile.*

Most of what are generally called "reviews" fall somewhere in the middle of these two extremes, and most writers probably consider both the artistic and the commercial aspects when giving their impression of a game. The way the publisher frames the game itself, through marketing and positioning, can also influence how critics consider the work.

If game journalism is to become more accessible and interesting to the mainstream, though, we need to start leaning more towards the critique side in our writing.

> *If we as game journalists are going to find our Roger Ebert, or even (dare we dream) our Pauline Kael, we're not going to do it writing reviews that simply describe a game's component parts and slap a 'buy' or 'don't buy' bottom line at the end.*

David Jaffe is at least partially right when he says that some game journalists have no business calling themselves part of the game industry. But he's right for the wrong reasons. Jaffe's argument, basically, is that writers should practice a sort of detached objectivity in our coverage because we don't affect the industry as directly as a developer or publisher. I'd say this is true of people who write game *reviews,* but not as true of people who write game *critiques.*

The objectivity and in-depth reporting Jaffe describes is absolutely essential as far as gaming news coverage is concerned, but can be absolutely deadly when it comes to game criticism. Game critics should feel *deeply* involved with the industry they cover, and this should come through in their writing. They should write as if everything they said had a direct and immediate impact on the state of the industry—as if their words might change the industry for the better (if a writer feels that everything is perfectly all right with the games industry, they should probably stick to reviews).

A critic's writing should betray deep feelings of ownership for the industry they love and study and write about. Sadly, many reviewers (and reviews) are merely interested in whether a game is bigger, faster, or stronger than what has come before. They have no business calling themselves part of the industry.

If we as game journalists are going to find our Roger Ebert, or even (dare we dream) our Pauline Kael, we're not going to do it writing reviews that simply describe a game's component parts and slap a "buy" or "don't buy" bottom line at the end. And we're not going to do it by saying that games are just toys, not worthy of serious consideration as art. We're going to do it by writing about games as the engaging, emotional, some might say *artistic* experiences that they are, and by conveying that message to readers in an interesting and concise way.

Good luck!

Rumor Report Ratings

Originally published on GameDaily, Jan. 11, 2007

Ah, rumors. The media love reporting them, the readers love reading them, and the forum trolls love prattling on about them endlessly to anyone who will listen. Unfortunately, by the time most of these rumors finally get confirmed as true or false, most journalists are busy chasing the next rumor, most readers have forgotten about the original report altogether, and most forum trolls are still trying to sell the one about Apple buying Nintendo. (It ain't gonna happen! Move on!)

At its best, reporting on rumors gives readers a valuable scoop on some important facts months before they're officially announced. At its worst, rumor reporting misleads readers with false visions of the direction the industry is heading.

Obviously, any sufficiently large sample of rumors will include plenty of examples of both types of reporting. But which type is more common? I decided to find out by looking at the granddaddy of all game rumor reporting columns: *Electronic Gaming Monthly*'s Quartermann.

Started in 1988's short-lived *Electronic Game Player* magazine, the Quartermann column moved to the pages of *EGM* starting with issue 1, where it still runs to this very day. Despite the seemingly eponymous column title, the Quartermann moniker has passed from writer to writer through the magazine's history, a semi-open secret finally confirmed in a 2004 blog post by former *EGM*-er Chris Johnston. The venerable column has gone through some slight name changes through the years, including "Q-Mann" and the current "Rumor Mill by Quartermann." Though the name has changed, the string of monthly rumor reportage remains unbroken.

THE PROCESS

For the purposes of this study, I decided to look at the rumors put forth by the Quartermann column in the 2003 issues of *EGM* (#162 - 173). Why did I go so far back? Well, I wanted to make sure that enough time had passed for all the rumors to be definitively confirmable.

Some of Quartermann's rumors were surprisingly forward-looking — for example, issue 173's report that the PS3 would play physical PSP games out of the box couldn't be confirmed as definitely false until E3 2006. Other rumors are so open-ended that their status actually changes as time passes. For a short time it may have seemed like Microsoft had actually canceled platformer *Tork,* as was alleged in issue 167, but the game did eventually limp onto store shelves in 2005. Similarly, a PSP semi-sequel to *Final Fantasy VII* (named *Crisis Core*) was finally announced at E3 2006, as predicted way back in issue 169.

Even with the waiting, some rumors remain unconfirmable because they have no theoretical end date. It seems highly likely that a *Kingdom Hearts* TV show and movie will come out some day, but almost three years after issue 164 hit the stands with the prediction, there are no concrete signs. Similarly, a sequel to 2003's *Rygar* remake, as predicted in issue 167, could still eventually come, but I wouldn't hold my breath.

Other rumors may have been technically true when reported, but are hard to confirm because nothing concrete ever came of them. Square may have indeed been planning a non-*Final Fantasy* MMO at some point, as alleged in issue 163, but since the game still hasn't come out, this information would be useless to a reader even if it was true.

> *For all practical purposes, a rumor reported in EGM is just as likely to be true as it is to be false.*

Figuring out what constituted a distinct rumor was sometimes a problem. The Q-mann's flowing writing style means conflicting predictions are often layered upon one another, sometimes within even a single sentence. The issue 166 prediction about the next *Bond* game, for instance, is actually two separate predictions—that the game will be in third-person (correct) and that the game will be a direct sequel to the N64's *Goldeneye* (wrong). Rather than parse every single sentence into individual, sometimes pointless factoids, I lumped everything that sat under one headline together as one distinct rumor.

There was also the problem of rumors that contained imprecise or subjective wording. In issue 167, Q-mann predicted a "big announcement" from Team Ninja at E3 2003. When the team announced *Dead or Alive Online*, the definition of the word "big" became relevant. Similarly, when issue 169 predicted the U.S. release of *Pokemon Box,* one had to consider whether or not a limited release in New York City's single Pokemon Center retail location really counted as a confirmation.

To combat these problems, I used a rating scale from one to five for each rumor, one being completely false, five being completely true.

Some Quartermann column items weren't really rumors, but previews or confirmed news bits that got shoehorned into the column. Other rumors were unconfirmable because they dealt exclusively with insider politics. Both of these were disregarded in the study (marked as "N/A" in the ratings below).

THE RESULTS

So after all that, how did the Q-mann do? Using the rating system described above, the 88 distinct rumors I evaluated broke down as follows:

"Truth" Ratings for 2003 Q-Mann columns

1 (completely false): 23 rumors
2: 10 rumors
3: 11 rumors
4: 14 rumors
5 (completely true): 22 rumors
N/A: 8 rumors
Mean "Truth" rating: 3.03

For all practical purposes, a rumor reported in *EGM* is just as likely to be true as it is to be false. That might not seem that impressive — after all, anyone can guess a coin flip half the time

— but considering the wide variety of completely wacky rumors that get thrown around out there, it shows relative selectiveness to publish a correct one just as often as a incorrect one.

The numbers themselves hide how ridiculous some of the actual rumors were, on both sides. Quartermann showed amazing prescience (or amazing insider sources) way back in March, 2003 when he said that Sony's then-unnamed portable was "not a portable PS1 and won't use CDs as its delivery medium." The January, 2003 prediction that the "Xbox 2" would come out before the PlayStation 3 may have seemed like a wild guess at the time, but turned out to be very true years later. The Q-mann also predicted the May, 2004 announcement of the Nintendo DS way back in August, 2003, impressive even if they simply called the system an "evolved Game Boy."

On the other side, there were some rumors that turned out to be amazingly, mind-numbingly wrong. Sequels for *Road Rash, Rygar, Splatterhouse, Pilotwings, Deception, San Francisco Rush* and *Bionic Commando* all failed to materialize (though more obvious sequels to *Metroid Prime, Metal Gear Solid, Medal of Honor* and *James Bond* did come to pass). The bottom fell out of the MMO market just in time to stop alleged plans for MMOs from Square and Rare, and alleged plans for a PS2 version of *Star Wars Galaxies* faded away with no product. And despite accurately predicting domestic ports of a variety of games based on Japanese anime (*Inuyasha, Ultimate Muscle* and *Dragon Ball Z*), the Q-Mann was thankfully wrong about *Ikaruga* staying in Japan.

But being overly ambitious in a rumor column is not necessarily a bad thing. After all, cautiously avoiding any rumor that might possibly be wrong would likely also mean leaving out some rumors that could end up being right. Besides, most readers know that there's a good chance anything they read on the rumor page will end up being false (that's what they're called rumors and not just reported as news, after all).

Hopefully, with this column, readers have a better idea of exactly what kind of chance those rumors have of eventually being confirmed.

The Blame Game

Originally published on GameDaily, April 26, 2007

> *When I hear about a mass shooting, it's like waiting for the other shoe to drop: how long will it take before someone tries to connect it to video games? How long before we learned that the Virginia Tech shooter 'trained' for his rampage with a first-person shooter?*

Video games aren't exactly the first thing that pops into one's head when hearing about a horrible tragedy like last Monday's Virginia Tech shootings. But GameLife's Chris Kohler, quoted above, captured the eventual thoughts of many gamers and game journalists in the wake of the tragedy. When will the discussion turn to video games? When is the blame game going to start? When is the other shoe going to drop?

It didn't take long. Mere hours after the shootings and a full day before the shooter would be identified, Florida lawyer and anti-violent-game crusader Jack Thompson showed up on Fox News to lay out the case for a connection. The blame game continued with daytime talk show host Dr. Phil McGraw telling Larry King that the effects of violent video games on our society in general and psychopaths in particular was "common sense."

Video game violence has been a favorite media scapegoat for real life violence at least since the days of the Columbine massacre. To this day, accounts of that 1999 shooting often mention the killers' proclivity for *Doom*. It's not uncommon to still hear the thoroughly debunked theory that one of the killers designed levels that resembled the school in preparation for the shooting. The mass media has also been quick to blame video games for other school shootings, from Paducah to Montreal.

But a funny thing happened on the way from Columbine to Virginia Tech. Video game violence is still being discussed in the wake of this latest tragedy, but generally to a more limited extent. An informal survey of the media landscape over the past two weeks shows the tired arguments about game violence just don't seem to be getting as much traction as they have in the past.

Of course, the specialist press is the first line of defense against claims of games' deleterious effects. Game-focused sites had a few interesting takes on the issue: Kotaku thoroughly dissected[15] the lies and errors in Thompson's Fox News appearance; Joystiq compiled a list of declarations[16] for gamers who want to renounce real-world violence (which I helped compile and write); and a post on 1PStart took a thoughtful look[17] at how real violence can affect our response to fake violence.

In general, though, the enthusiast press' mix of shrill defensiveness and petty name calling was pretty predictable.

The mainstream media's responses were more interesting, especially among the major commentators who refused to jump in on the video game blame bandwagon, even after the killer was named. Rush Limbaugh used his popular radio show to point out that, while millions of people play violent games, "not every video gamer goes out and murders 33 people on the college campus." Howard Stern called Dr. Phil an "idiot" for suggesting that games caused the shootings. *Hardball*'s Chris Matthews subjected Thompson to some blisteringly tough questioning, refusing to let his unsupported claims of causality go unchallenged. Two commentaries from MSNBC took the media to task for blaming games, as did a prominent opinion piece in *The San Francisco Chronicle*.

> *An informal survey of the media landscape over the past two weeks shows the tired arguments about game violence just don't seem to be getting as much traction as they have in the past.*

That's not to say there was no one in the media trying to stretch for the games connection. *Meet the Press* host Tim Russert tried to bring up the game angle with his guests, without much success. The Today Show asked visitors to its website if violent video games should be banned (the next day's poll asked a similarly pointed question about whether Alec Baldwin should lose custody of his child). An *International Herald Tribune* article on the shooter's eBay usage made the seemingly unnecessary point that a graphing calculator he sold "contained several games, most of them with mild themes." And Thompson, of course, continued to make the media rounds with varying levels of generally weak opposition from the press.

Elements of both political extremes used the media to lay blame on virtual violence, too. Former Speaker of the House Newt Gingrich included video games in the wide-ranging screed against the violent influence of "liberalism," on ABC's *This Week*. On the other side, at least one blogger on liberal clearinghouse The Huffington Post included games on a list of contributors to "our addiction to violence, which is everywhere in our culture."

These examples notwithstanding, the few mentions of video game violence seemed drowned out in the wake of the Virginia Tech shooting by the more germane talk of gun control and mental health treatment. In fact, the "games made him do it" angle sometimes seemed loudest in the echo chamber of the game-centric websites and blogs, which tend to amplify the very coverage they're trying to quash.

Why the reduced mainstream interest in the games angle? Part of it might have to do with a lack of evidentiary support. While a *Washington Post* story briefly mentioned that shooter Seung-Hui Cho had been seen playing *Counter-Strike* in high school, the anecdotal report was removed from a later version of the story. When reports surfaced that college roommates had never seen Cho playing games and a search of Cho's room found no game consoles, the media moved on to other potential scapegoats, most notably horror movies. A coincidentally well-timed report from the British Board of Film Classification on why people play games may have also muted critics in the mass media.

I think the bigger reason here, though, is the passage of time. When the Columbine massacre happened eight years ago, video games were just beginning to rise in the mainstream consciousness as something more than just kids' stuff. Today, the media increasingly acknowledges video games as the Next

Big Thing in entertainment among both children and adults. The multi-billion dollar industry is attracting dedicated beat reporters at many mainstream magazines and newspapers.

The demographics of the media as a whole are changing, too— every passing year brings those who grew up with video games closer to positions of media power and those who didn't closer to retirement. And don't discount the power of the Internet, which has given thousands of regular gamers a way to express themselves without going through the usual media filters.

All of which is to say there's reason for hope in the game industry's battle for conventional wisdom and mainstream media mindshare. The blame-the-games crowd will never go away completely in the wake of these tragedies, but as time goes on, it seems likely they will be increasingly marginalized in an increasingly open and wide-ranging media landscape. Score one for the marketplace of ideas.

Looking Back at Looking Ahead

Originally published on GameDaily, Jan. 3, 2008

The end-of-year transition is known for two things in the video game media: The "best of the past year" list and the "most anticipated games of the next year" list. While the former will be analyzed,

debated, and scrutinized for years to come, the latter is usually read and then quickly forgotten about by most readers. Does anybody bother to see if these "anticipated" games were really worth anticipating, in the end?

Now they do! I've taken the new year's break to look back at the "most anticipated" games of 2007 as chosen by CNET, IGN, *GamePro*, GameSpot, GameSpy, and Next Generation at the beginning of the year. Not surprisingly, the lists tended to differ quite a bit from the "Best of 2007" lists penned near the end of the year. Here's how the analysis shook out.

ANTICIPATE EVERYTHING!

One of the most striking things about these "most anticipated" lists is the remarkably broad definition of "anticipated" many outlets seem to have. Combined, the six outlets mentioned above made over 300 picks for over 150 distinct anticipated games. That's an average of 50 picks per list!

The average is skewed by a few sources that seemed to think a "most anticipated games" list should include practically any upcoming game that anyone has even heard of. Next Gen alone anticipated 82 distinct games coming down the pike for the PS3, Xbox 360, and Wii. How is a list that big supposed to help anyone make sense of what's hot in the coming year?

GameSpot, GamePro and CNET were a little more selective (and useful) in choosing 14, 19, and 20 games, respectively.

SEQUELITIS

In looking to the future, we inevitably look to the past as a guide. So perhaps it shouldn't be surprising that a full 64 percent of the games picked on the above lists were sequels or games based on existing licenses.

This is not entirely the fault of the media outlets making the lists. An increasingly risk-averse game industry means a large proportion of games released these days are attached to an established franchise or license. Still, the amount of space on these lists devoted to "no duh" anticipated sequels is pretty staggering. Is any reader going to be shocked by an "anticipated" pick for *Super Mario Galaxy, Halo 3,* or *The Orange Box*? Anticipating a sequel to a big-name franchise is a safe bet, but not really one that's likely to be all that helpful to readers.

To be fair, new franchises like *BioShock, Assassin's Creed, Crysis,* and *Mass Effect* appeared on plenty of anticipation lists. But even the new franchise picks were largely limited to big-name companies with proven track records. There's nothing inherently wrong with that—these companies have a good track record for a reason. Still, it would still be nice to see a separate list of anticipated games that we haven't all heard of—potential sleepers by that haven't gotten blanket coverage because they're from smaller companies with smaller marketing budgets. Such a list would be harder to make, but immensely more useful to many readers.

WAIT ANOTHER YEAR

One of the most striking things about the "anticipated games of 2007" lists is how many of the games didn't actually come out in 2007. A full 31 percent of the picks from the above lists still haven't been released as of the first week of 2008. A few aren't even anywhere close to release—*Dragon Age,* which 1UP and IGN were looking forward to in early 2007, is currently scheduled for release in late 2008.

> *Trying to predict the year's hottest games in January is a fool's errand.*

Again, this isn't entirely the media's fault—game companies are hyping new releases earlier than ever these days. But to have nearly a third of "2007's most anticipated games" not even make it out in 2007 is pretty depressing. Of course, the 2007 no-show hasn't stopped these games from reappearing on many "most anticipated games of 2008" lists. Apparently the expectations for games like *Super Smash Bros. Brawl, Grand Theft Auto IV, Army of Two, Alan Wake, Metal Gear Solid 4,* and *Spore* are high enough to keep the media on pins and needles year after year...

FIRST QUARTER BIAS

Looking a whole year into the future can be tough. Luckily, looking just a few months ahead is a lot easier. A full 21 percent of games picked for 2007's "most anticipated" lists were released in the first quarter of 2007 (23 percent of distinct games). That might sound low, considering the first quarter by definition makes up 25 percent of the calendar year. But it sounds high when you consider that relatively few games come out in the first quarter, and that most critically-acclaimed and/or best-selling games tend to come in the fourth quarter, when over half of all releases for the year are squeezed together in a holiday blitz. The "Most Anticipated" lists by-and-large don't reflect this.

So why are first-quarter games disproportionately represented here? Simply because they're almost done when the lists are written. Journalists have probably seen close-to-complete versions of these early-in-the-year games, which are therefore fresher in journalists' minds than far-off, pre-beta releases.

Just because these games are almost done doesn't mean they're good, though. This was especially true for the Wii in 2007: First-quarter games like *Mortal Kombat Armageddon, Medal of Honor: Vanguard, Wii Play*, and *Sonic and the Secret Rings* were eagerly anticipated in January, only to be critically panned by the end of March. Granted, some early 2007 games were deserving of the anticipation: *Virtua Fighter 5, Motorstorm*, and *God of War II* among them. For the most part, though, be wary of early "anticipation" for games that are only a few weeks from release.

WHERE DID *THAT* GAME COME FROM?

On the others side of the coin, there were many excellent, well-received games that were absent from the "most anticipated" lists simply because they weren't well-known in January of 2007. *Call of Duty 4, Uncharted: Drake's Fortune*, and *Rock Band* were the most notable "anticipation list" no-shows, but smaller games like *Puzzle Quest, Skate*, and *Jeanne D'Arc* were also absent at the beginning of the year. Many of these games didn't make their big media splash until E3 2007, which makes IGN's decision to revisit its "anticipated" lists in July seem like a good one.

WHAT TO ANTICIPATE FROM ANTICIPATION

So what's the takeaway from this analysis? Simple: Trying to predict the year's hottest games in January is a fool's errand. Sure, there are some no-brainers, but between delays, sleepers and far-off, still unannounced titles, you're likely to miss as many as you hit. Despite this, I'm going to end the column with my own bold prediction: Most "most anticipated lists" aren't going anywhere anytime soon.

The Top Ten Game Journalism Clichés

Originally published on GameSpot, March 28, 2008

Every writer knows that they should avoid clichés like the plague. But writers are busy little beavers, and since a stitch in time saves nine, even the best writers occasionally find that slipping into familiar clichés is as easy as shooting fish in a barrel. This is true in game journalism too, where bad clichés can destroy good writing like a bull in a china shop. Since the proof is in the pudding, as they say, I now present, without further ado, my personal list of dumb-as-a-doorknob clichés that tend to be particular to video game journalism.

10) THE TOP TEN LIST

Humans, in general, like to make sense of the world by organizing things into lists, so it's not surprising that "Top games of all time" and "Top games of the year" lists are staples for game journalists. Outlets could even be forgiven for the occasional quirky one-off list of trivia. But still, the top twelve video game toilets?[18] The top ten butts in gaming?[19] The top ten Pokemon we'd like to eat?[20] Eventually we will run out of things to list and have to start listing our favorite lists.

(Yes, I do realize the irony of using a list to decry the cliché of list-making, so don't bother pointing that out!)

9) THE HISTORICAL OPEN

How many game reviews have you read that start something like this: "The [Series X] series has always been known for frenetic action, witty writing, and lots of references to pickles. [Game Y], the 17th game in the series, doesn't change up this winning formula, but it has just enough new things to keep fans happy."

Sure, these openers are a good way to familiarize readers who don't know about the series (both of them). Through overuse, though, this type of opening has become stale and predictable. I know figuring out how to start off a review of yet another *Tom Clancy* game is hard, but writers should at least *try* to come up with something unique.

8) HEADLINES WITH A "?" AT THE END

Here's a fun game to play: Any time you see a headline with a question mark in it, assume the answer is "No." All right, this isn't so much a game as it is a time-saving device. The fact of the matter is that the large majority of headlines that require a question mark will end up being proven false in due time. Sometimes the writer even knows they're false as they write the headline.

So why do we see these interrogative headers so often? Because we journalists often get paid by the post (or the click), and writing about speculation pays as well or better than writing about established fact. In the long run, the benefits of promoting the rare, true rumor probably isn't worth the dashed hopes and misinformation caused by the vast majority of inquisitive headlines.

7) 7/10 REVIEW SCORES

The 7/10 review score has become something of a joke in game journalism circles, connoting a game (and, often, a review) that is wholly unremarkable and barely worth the words used to describe it. Even review scales that allegedly rate an "average" game as a 5/10 often see the practical scoring average creeping ever closer to 7/10 as time goes on.

This doesn't mean a 7/10 score should be outlawed or anything, just that reviewers should be more willing to utilize the entire review scale—from 0 all the way up to 10—and not just clump most all of their reviews around a safe, inoffensive mean.

6) "REALISTIC GRAPHICS"

This isn't an entirely meaningless cliché, and is usually used as a shorthand for games that approach "photorealism." But it's a little ridiculous to see this phrase bandied about for games populated by ogres and demons, or aliens and spaceships for that matter. When a reviewer says graphics are "realistic," they usually actually mean the game has detailed character models, smooth animation, and a consistent art direction. The fact that those same graphics will look ridiculously dated in just a couple of years won't stop the clichéd writer from calling the next generation of gaming graphics equally "realistic."

> *Yes, I do realize the irony of using a list to decry the cliché of list-making, so don't bother pointing that out!*

5) "QUIRKY"

These days, any game that isn't a first-person shooter or by-the-numbers action-fest gets this backhanded compliment assigned to it. Games can have quirky gameplay, quirky graphics, quirky controls, or even a quirky plot, but all this all-purpose adjective does is tell the reader that the writer really doesn't know how to pigeonhole the aspect in question. Instead of explaining whether the "quirkiness" in question as a good or bad thing, many reviewers will throw the term out almost as a pejorative and move on to explaining other, more conventional parts of the game. Don't fall prey. Explain your quirks.

4) "FANS OF [X] WILL ENJOY IT"

As in: "This game isn't great but fans of the genre/the series/the license it's based on might be able to overlook the flaws and enjoy it." Here's a news flash: fans, by definition, tend to show a slavish devotion to the subject of their fandom, frequently overlooking flaws that get in the way of unquestioning appreciation. This can go without saying, and generally should.

3) "ONLY TIME WILL TELL"

The ultimate finisher to news stories and previews alike, "Only time will tell" is the tautological gift that keeps on giving. Wondering whether a "quirky" title can compete with the well-established franchises? Will those bugs be fixed in time for the release like the publisher promises? Will I be able to fit in this dress for the wedding? "Only time will tell" applies to every single one! It's a phrase that's almost always technically accurate, but also almost always a useless space filler. Then again, it does provide a nice, simple way to close out a piece.

Will this lazy phrase ever fall out of favor? I think you know the answer to that.

2) REVIEWS BROKEN UP INTO STANDARDIZED SECTIONS

This has become a bit of an anachronism in major outlets in recent years, but reviews that get broken into distinct sections like "graphics," "sound," "gameplay," and "fun factor," still manage to hold on in some corners of the game journalism landscape.

This phenomenon seems unique to game journalism as far as I can tell: I've never seen a movie review broken down explicitly into "acting," "cinematography" and "set design;" or a book review separated out into "plot," "grammar," and "punctuation" sections.

Even if the review isn't broken up, sometimes the final score will be split into a few specific sub-scores. Either way, the format actually transforms a game into less than the sum of its parts—a random assortment of attributes that never come together into a greater, cohesive whole. It's a lazy, overly simplistic way to organize things that should be excised from game journalism by any means possible.

1) "FUN"

The most overused word in gaming is the one that's the hardest to quantify. Entire books have been written about what makes games fun, yet many reviewers will often say that an important game element is "extremely fun" with no elaboration or even a second thought. The maxim of "show, don't tell" comes to mind here—show the reader why the game is fun instead of simply telling them that it is. This doesn't mean you can't use the word "fun" anywhere in your review, but it does mean you should try to justify the designation with a description of the experience that makes the adjective self-evident to the reader.

Do Sports Games Have a Sporting Chance?

Originally published on Crispy Gamer, Oct. 9, 2008

In August, 2008, four separate versions of a single game took up four of the top 10 spaces in NPD's monthly game sales report, including the three top spots. In the previous month, a similar game in the same genre took two of the top 10 sales rankings spots, including the top spot. During the summer release doldrums, you'd think that such sales domination would merit blanket coverage in the gaming media—coverage of the sort seen for marquee releases like *Halo 3* or *Super Smash Bros. Brawl.*

For one reason or another, though, the specialist gaming press largely ignored top-sellers *Madden NFL 09* and *NCAA Football 09* this summer. For the most part, it focused instead on yet another fighting game sequel, a long-expected, arguably overhyped role-playing game and, of course, the upcoming holiday releases.

The press' cold shoulder for this year's football releases is just the latest example of a consistent pattern of neglect that the big name publications routinely have for sports games. Despite better-than-healthy sales and a huge fan base, sports games, for some reason, can't seem to get any respect from the gaming press.

"Sports games have a huge audience—thus, they should be covered hugely. Yet, they aren't. They're covered decently, at best." So says Todd Zuniga, a freelancer and host of 1UP's Sports Anomaly podcast. Part of the reason for this lack of coverage, Zuniga says, is that the people who make up the gaming press by and large aren't sports fans. "I think in large part, the people in power at gaming websites and, before that, magazines, weren't 'sports guys,' and few have had the foresight to acknowledge sports as a viable income-maker. I also think there's this nerd versus sporto mentality that's pervasive, and unfortunate—like the people who like sports games are going to beat up the RPG lovers or something."

It's not like a gaming publication can throw just anyone onto the sports game beat. Covering sports games requires detailed knowledge of not just the games, but also the history and strategy of the sports themselves. "Being a flight [simulation] critic requires some know-how, [and] I'd never review a flight sim because I have no idea what I'm doing," says longtime freelancer and sports gaming specialist Bill Abner. "Just watching *SportsCenter* once a week and playing in your office fantasy football league isn't enough. I think you need to have a grasp on some of the finer points of the sport you are critiquing."

Unfortunately, many gaming publications just don't feel that it's worth devoting time or effort to this kind of specialized coverage. "Sports can't really be denied as a viable moneymaker for these venues," Zuniga argues, "[but] the idea on the inside is sports games are going to sell anyway, so there's no sense in promoting them. Most sites are already stretched desperately thin providing the content they provide. To add a sports element into the mix is more work, and if it's not an area of expertise, then that's even more effort."

The resistance is so strong that Zuniga at first had to record his Sports Anomaly podcast on his own time, just to prove that there was a market for sports-centric content in the video game world. "One day I just decided to record one, under the radar, and it went live. It ticked some people off, but now it's listened to by a growing audience. We were at 5,000 downloads weekly a few months ago. So it really just took initiative, because there's so much going on to cover the big games."

> *I think in large part, the people in power at gaming websites and, before that, magazines, weren't 'sports guys,' and few have had the foresight to acknowledge sports as a viable income-maker.*
>
> **Todd Zuniga**
> **Host of 1UP's Sports Anomaly podcast**

Part of this resistance might come from the perceived gulf of separation between sports gaming fans and fans of other games. "I think sports games are looked at [as] being a bit outside of the hobby," Abner says. "You have sports gamers who play nothing *but* sports games. It's one of the genres that brought in the mainstream player. I think that is why they are looked at a bit differently, and why it's also hard at times to find a critic who can review them properly."

Whatever the reason, sports gaming fans definitely notice when an outlet isn't giving their genre enough attention. "To a lot of folks, those [general gaming] sites are run by 'geeks' who know nothing about sports," says Chris Sanner, an editor at sports gaming megasite Operation Sports. "It is getting better as time goes on, but the hardcore community as a whole just doesn't trust reviews from anyone, really."

And why should they? When general gaming publications do cover a sports game, the results are often incomprehensible to those who really follow the genre. "Sports games by and large get a free pass with critics," says Abner. "You can pretty much guess what the review scores will be before the game even ships. ... The reviews for *NCAA 09* and *[NFL] Head Coach 09* are prime examples. Some of those reviews literally make no sense to me."

Of course, some of the problems affecting sports game critics are the same ones that affect all game critics. "So few sports reviewers take the time to play these games over the long haul to see if they have staying power," Abner says. "There are good sports critics out there; I don't mean to imply everyone is a hack. But we need more people to really test these games and not just play them for a few hours and write a review. ... I just wish critics would take these games to task more than they do. I want sports games to be reviewed like any other genre and right now it's not the case. ... It makes us all look bad."

For some sports gaming fans, though, treating sports just like "any other genre" isn't sufficient. "I think game sites that try to lump all games into one pot and score them on the same scales and on the same basis just [don't] work," Sanner says. "Sports gaming fans are looking for something completely different than RPG fans. Trying to lump everything into five or six categories [that act] as a catchall for games will not give you the most accurate reviews going forward. You have to treat each genre differently if you want to give each game the most accurate score possible."

"To me, the perception really soured after several of the top gaming sites gave *Madden NFL 06* a good review," Sanner continued, "when nearly everyone in the hardcore crowd thought the game was an absolute mess. Some sites gave the game a score of 80 or higher, which was just way off base. ... When you take into account the lack of atmosphere and presentation and the only average gameplay, the game just didn't feel quality at all. It would be like shipping *Call of Duty* with a single-player campaign that was missing half of the levels. The game would still technically play fine, but you would not like the fact you only got half of the game."

In the end, this sort of tone deaf undercoverage for sports games could be a missed opportunity for gaming publications. "I would love to see 1UP create a space for a daily update that features sports games," Zuniga said. "I think there's enough out there, and EA and others are savvy enough about promoting their games to give that kind of content daily. I think the most important thing for people to recognize is that there are opportunities out there to create sites and cover sports games in new and inventive ways."

How Hype Helps (and Hurts) High-Profile Hits

Originally published on Crispy Gamer, Oct. 23, 2008

Sometimes it seems like the game industry is drowning in pre-release hype. Before a major game hits store shelves these days, potential players can look forward to months (or sometimes years) of slow drips of information, screenshots, trailers, interviews, gameplay videos, demos, developer

diaries, blogs, events, flashy print and TV ads, and more. It's all designed to breed enough familiarity among the target audience so that, by the time the game finally hits shelves, those gamers will already feel intimately comfortable with its look, its feel and, most importantly, with the idea of owning it.

But while the end consumer is the main target of all this promotion, the critics are definitely an important secondary audience for promotionally-minded game publishers. Even the most secluded reviewer can't help but be exposed to the deafening roar of pre-release hype for the biggest releases. But does this hype have any effect on the final critical reception for a game? And if so, is the net result good or bad?

The press-influencing power of pre-release hype is far from new. "I still remember *Earthworm Jim* from 1994," said game journalism veteran and game historian Steven Kent. "When other journalists are buying into the hype and calling a title 'The best game of the decade,' it takes guts to give a game a C or a D. Look, two years after *Earthworm Jim,* Nintendo released *Super Mario 64.* I think 1994 may have been a bit early for best of decade accolades."

It seems hype hasn't lost its effectiveness as a press-swaying tool in the new millennium, either. "There are definitely cases where pre-release hype has helped games score somewhat unrealistically high scores," said freelancer Tim Stevens. "*Halo 3* comes to mind; great game, but I think the prevalence of 10/10 reviews was at least somewhat driven by a bunch of reviewers getting a little too excited about getting early access to that holiday's hot release."

Halo 3 wasn't the only recent game some journalists felt received a hype-inflated score. "I think *Grand Theft Auto IV* was generally given a higher score than it deserved even on my own publication, Gamer 2.0,' said Executive Editor Anthony Perez. "The franchise carries so much clout in both the industry and amongst gamers that there is an initial 'wow' factor that comes from its presentation."

Another game journalist, who asked to remain anonymous to protect his relationship with Rockstar, called the company's crime simulator the "one shameless, ultimate example of hype influencing review scores... Virtually every publication—print and online—rubber-stamped *GTA IV* with a perfect score, and once the dust settled, it became increasingly clear that *GTA IV* was actually fairly disappointing."

And even without a big marketing push, some franchises get hyped in the press based on name recognition alone. "Trying to review a game when it's [part] of a revered series is something where hype dodging becomes a real problem," said freelancer

Kris Rosado. "You want the game to be good because of its pedigree, but sometimes you're faced with something that just doesn't live up to it."

And critics often aren't too eager to burst the hype-bubble that develops among fans of some high-profile games and series. "Nobody wants to get the 'Nintendites' mad by criticizing a *Mario* or a *Zelda*," Kent said. "Nobody is going to feel comfortable dousing Little Big Planet, Heavy Rain, or Halo. That is the lonely part of the job. It's also the most important part of the job."

But pre-release hype isn't an automatic ticket to a perfect review score. In many cases, all that hype raises unrealistic expectations about games that can't live up to their promise. "One thing I have seen with regard to reviewers is their attitude toward the game where the publisher starts hyping it *too* soon," said venerable game journalist Bill Kunkel. "When you're looking at a game at conferences and trade expos for the third or fourth year, you can begin to smell panic at some level of its development cycle. I think reviewers become wary of games that are hyped for too long before delivery."

> *Nobody is going to feel comfortable dousing* Little Big Planet, Heavy Rain, *or* Halo. *That is the lonely part of the job. It's also the most important part of the job.*
>
> **Steven Kent**
> **Video Game Historian**

Many journalists pointed to Will Wright's *Spore* as a game that suffered from an overly long and overly ambitious build up. "After all of the hype, *Spore* was destined to either walk on water or get slammed," as Kent put it. And while *Spore* didn't exactly get slammed in the reviews, many reviewers seemed to punish the game for not living up to its promise. "I've talked to *Spore* reviewers who said that if you don't expect anything—especially from the build up in recent years—then it's a great game," said one anonymous critic. "Did *Spore* not achieve every bullet point Will Wright ever noted? Who cares? That's not a review, that's a postmortem."

It seems that, at some point, too much hype can be harmful to a game, a fact that some at EA may have noticed before *Spore*'s release. "I remember when I went to check out a hands-on of *Spore* this Spring, I was startled by it," Gamer 2.0's Perez said. "The EA rep continuously harped on that point by basically saying repeatedly that 'it's not a very deep game.'"

But while the hype can hurt a good game, most journalists seem to agree that it can't help the reviews for a truly bad game. "When *Enter the Matrix* came out and didn't live up to expectations, everybody knew it," said *Official Xbox Magazine*'s Dan Amrich. "But I didn't hear anybody saying, 'Well, I was looking forward to this, so I guess it's okay.' I think advance hype for under-performing titles only does damage; the game is more likely to become a punchline."

What hype can do, though, is force an outlet to pay attention to a game. "I object to big marketing campaigns because they effectively tell us what to cover in the first place," said game blogger Rachel Webster. "If enough money backs a title, and if the fans and publicity force it onto our radar, then we have to review it prominently, even if it's *Too Human*. ... The press should always have the power to ignore. Even when we deal with blockbusters."

In the end, while pre-release hype can't carry or sink a game on its own, its presence can change the nature of the race for attention. "If a publisher is hyping up a game and it fails to succeed in terms of delivering upon that hype, the game is basically going to run a 40-yard dash and burst out of the gate, then come to a stop almost immediately after," said GamerNode Editor-in-Chief Brendon Lindsey. "On the other hand, if a game isn't hyped that much and then surpasses any and all expectations, it will usually run a marathon and start off really slow, then finish with a burst."

The Top 10 Good Things the Internet Has Brought to Game Journalism

Originally published on Crispy Gamer, July 16, 2009

AUTHOR'S NOTE

It's a bit weird to read this story today, when the Internet is the ocean we all swim in 24 hours a day and game magazines are all but extinct in the US. At the time, though, some members of the old guard were lamenting what was being lost in the transition away from dead tree media.

I took a more optimistic view here. For all the warts inherent to Internet journalism, I wouldn't want to go back to paying excessive printing and delivery costs for a once-a-month shot of gaming news and views.

I was bit surprised to see last week that Bitmob's Dan Hsu (formerly of *Electronic Gaming Monthly* fame) had compiled a list of The Top 10 Bad Things the Internet Brought to Gaming Journalism.[21] Yes, the list made some good points, and was generally fair about considering opposing points of view. But overall, focusing a list solely on the problems caused by the Internet presents a pretty skewed picture of how the shift away from magazines has changed the game journalism landscape over the last decade or two.

The simplest way to correct this skewed picture is obvious: A similar list of the top ten *good* things the Internet has brought to game journalism. And here it is:

10) COMMUNITY

While two *EGM* readers have very little chance of interacting with each other (unless they happen to meet in real life), two readers of a video game site can easily connect and share their common interests through comment threads and message boards. Sites like Destructoid and 1UP (and Bitmob itself!) work hard to cultivate this kind of community and make themselves into places people come not just to get information, but to share their passion with like-minded people.

On the other hand: The "communities" surrounding many sites are either eerily silent or filled with trolls and fanboys that seem unable to carry on a serious conversation.

9) RESEARCH AIDS

This point is largely invisible to readers, but behind the scenes the Internet has made being a game journalist immeasurably easier. Reaching out to a developer via e-mail or instant messenger is much easier than catching them on the phone, and telecommuting has allowed many journalists to work effectively from well outside the usual L.A. and New York media hubs. Then there are tools like RSS feeds, Google News searches, and electronic press release archives that have made it incredibly easy for journalists to get background information, cross reference related stories, and add context to their pieces.

On the other hand: The Internet has also made it easier for lazy journalists to simply copy and paste press releases with minor touch ups, discouraging the shoe-leather reporting that can break important stories.

8) JOURNALIST ACCESSIBILITY

In the pre-Internet days, the primary way for readers to getting in touch with journalists was a plain old snail mail letter. If you were lucky, you might get a response a week or two later. If you were really lucky, your missive would show up in the magazine's letters page for the entire readership to see... a month or more in the future.

Compare that to today's landscape, where Internet journalists are accessible via email or social media instantaneously. And any reader can instantly add their two cents to a comment thread right below the story, helping to guide the continuing conversation. Besides giving journalists crucial context for what the readers are actually interested in, these feedback mechanisms can also help those journalists catch and correct mistakes quickly.

On the other hand: Most readers are idiots, and their comments often involve baseless charges of "bias reporting [sic]." Some sites might also give too much deference to commenters, posting ginned up, "controversial" stories just to get the readers chattering.

7) PEOPLE

Shoe cited this as the No. 1 "Bad Thing" the Internet has brought to game journalism, saying "some people never need to be heard from again, period." While that's undoubtedly true, there are some people who definitely *do* need to be heard from—people that only have a chance to speak their minds because of the Internet.

In the old world of print-only gaming journalism, there was a very limited set of voices that could affect the debate—if you weren't one of a few dozen staffers or freelancer at a major magazine, you were effectively left out of the conversation. The Internet has opened up the conversation to the masses, allowing regular Joes to post everything from intelligent commentary to awkward personal YouTube reviews and everything in between.

Sure, separating the wheat from the chaff is tough, but that doesn't mean there isn't any interesting wheat to be found out there on the Internet. More importantly, most of that wheat would have gone totally unreaped in the more limited magazine era.

On the other hand: Most gaming forums quickly devolve into wretched hives of scum and villainy (see: NeoGAF).

6) DEPTH

In the magazine-only era, most outlets had the same types of consumer-focused content—surface-level news stories, short reviews with number/letter grades; hyperbolic previews—with little space for deeper critical consideration of games or issues that affect the industry at large. There's nothing wrong with this per se—gaming is a consumer-driven medium—but the Internet has shown there's also a market for more thoughtful writing about games and the industry.

Sites like The Gamers Quarter, The Escapist, and countless others look at gaming from original perspectives that by and large weren't represented by the mass market game magazines. Some of this change has been driven by the slow maturation of gaming itself, no doubt. But a lot of it has come from the Internet and its ability to bring together the smaller audience of people who want more thoughtful analysis of games and gaming without having to worry about the space and economic constraints of magazines.

On the other hand: Most Internet game journalism is shallow, consumer-driven pap that resembles the content of most of the magazines that came before it.

> *In the old world of print-only gaming journalism, there was a very limited set of voices that could affect the debate—if you weren't one of a few dozen staffers or freelancer at a major magazine, you were effectively left out of the conversation.*

5) BREADTH

Because of space constraints, most game magazines can only cover the biggest releases every month. On the Internet, sites like GameSpot and IGN can write a review for practically every game that comes out on every platform. This isn't just good for lovers of *Barbie's Horse Adventures* but also for fans of indie games and releases from smaller publishers that would have had trouble finding space in magazines. These types of games have a much better chance of getting coverage and breaking out through Internet coverage.

On the other hand: By trying to cover everything, some sites don't cover anything particularly well.

4) SPECIALIZATION

Can you imagine an entire magazine devoted to adventure games succeeding in today's market? Seems hard to believe. But a site like Adventure Gamers can thrive off a small community of devoted fans thanks to the power of the Internet.

Name any popular genre or series, in fact, and you'll find similar communities sprouting up on the internet, from *Grand Theft Auto* to *Dance Dance Revolution*, from RPGs to, um, my own Mario fansite.[22] These sites can dig deeply and passionately into these niches within a niche and provide a specific focus that general interest magazines never could.

Not only that, but the Internet has allowed for outlets that target demographic niches outside the usual young male target of gaming magazines. It's hard to imagine sites like What They Play, GirlGamer, TheGayGamer, and countless others being able to sustain a costly magazine on their own. Online, though, you can find a niche community that caters not just to your taste in games but to your personality and/or lifestyle as well.

On the other hand: How many *Pokémon* sites do we, as a species, really need? I mean, really!

3) PODCASTS

The worst thing about written game journalism is that you have to decide between reading it and actually playing a game. Not so with podcasts. Now you can mute the game soundtrack and listen to your favorite journalists yakking about games while you grind through *Fallout 3*. It's just like having a bunch of friends chatting in the room while you play, except without the pesky need for human interaction.

Podcasts are also useful when you're working out, doing errands, working a desk job, or any other situation where you want to catch up on video game chatter but can't easily read a website or watch a video.

On the other hand: Most video game podcasts are poorly edited, hours-long non sequiturs where the hosts seem more interested in the sound of their own voices/laughter than imparting any interesting information.

2) VIDEO

I'll never forget the first time I downloaded a game video, wasting four hours on the old AOL dial-up to get a 30-second, postage-stamp sized, grainy, shakycam video of *Super Mario 64* direct from Nintendo's Space World 1995 show half a world away. In the nearly 15 years since then, we've advanced to instantly-streaming, full-HD video trailers for most big releases and live streams of E3 press conferences beamed out to the entire world.

Screenshots and fancy layouts are nice, but there's simply no way a magazine can provide an experience comparable to seeing a game in motion. These videos help put a vivid picture of a game in the viewer's head and give new life to the accompanying words we write. And who needs printed words at all when video is also providing original reviews and analysis of popular games?

On the other hand: OK, Angry Video Game Nerd, we get it: old video games sucked and you enjoy cursing.

1) TIMELINESS

When Sega shocked the world by announcing an immediate surprise launch for the Saturn at E3 1995, you were more likely to see the system on the shelves before reading about the news in a magazine. Today, you'd be able to follow the press conference through a liveblog and line up at your nearest Gamestop immediately.

When it comes to news, there's just no way magazines can compete with the immediacy of the Internet. By the time you read about something in a game magazine, that information is at least two to four weeks old and may very well be outdated or inaccurate. With the Internet, not only do you get the news as soon as it breaks, but you can follow a story as it develops and evolves in real time. In an industry where so much can change day to day, this is crucial.

On the other hand: The fight for timeliness leads many sites to focus on getting it first rather than getting it right, and rewards quick blurbs rather than deep analysis.

Should Game Journalism Be More Tabloidy?

Originally published on The Game Beat, April 22, 2010

Yeah, I know the IGN feature imagining what a "Video Game Celebrity Trash Mag" would be like[23] is meant as a joke, and that virtual characters don't get into real-world scandals like flesh-and-blood celebrities. Still, it brought to mind a long-standing question I've had rolling around my head about the proper role of celebrity coverage in game journalism.

AUTHOR'S NOTE

The rise of indie games, social media, YouTube, and fan-focused conventions has helped the "Q rating" of some of the names and faces behind popular games. That said, I don't think most players could tell you the name of a single member of the team behind *Red Dead Redemption 2* or *Spider-Man,* two of the biggest games of the season. As I discuss below, this is both a good thing and a bad thing.

For the most part, one of the things I like about game journalism (as compared to other forms of entertainment journalism) is the overall dearth of the kind of trashy, voyeuristic, stars-behaving-badly tabloid stories exemplified in the IGN parody. Even the higher quality, consumer-focused movie, music, and TV rags occasionally descend into this kind of lowest-common-denominator story for a very simple reason—it sells. Game journalism, on the other hand, does a pretty good job of keeping the focus on the games and the business/culture that surrounds them, which is nice.

On the other hand, the reason the game industry doesn't have celebrity tabloid journalism is because, by and large, we don't have celebrities (I mean real life celebrities, not digital celebrities like Mario or Lara Croft). Tons of people know the director behind *Saving Private Ryan* or the producer behind *Lost,* but last year you'd be hard pressed to find 1 in 10,000 players who could have named the creative heads behind *Modern Warfare 2,* the best-selling game of 2009.

What did it take to turn Jason West and Vince Zampella into well-known names in gaming circles? A tabloid-ready scandal[24] surrounding their defection from *Call of Duty* developer Infinity Ward and to Activision.

> *Let's face it, Shigeru Miyamoto will never have the 'star power' or magazine-cover-carrying power of Angelina Jolie.*

With very few exceptions, the people who make games are complete strangers to the vast majority of the people who play and enjoy them. This is partly due to the nature of the medium— the superstars of game development don't appear on millions of screens the way TV and movie actors do. But partly I think this is the fault of us journalists, who often don't give enough attention to the human side of game development.

Sure, we'll publish interviews with the developers behind a hot new game, but the focus of the interview is usually the game itself, not the personal, human story of the developer behind that game. The exceptions to this rule tend to be the most outrageous and outspoken developers—the Kojimas, the CliffyB's, etc. These are the developers that, by and large, get their names out via controversial statements that push game journalism that much closer to the tabloid end of the spectrum.

On the *other* other hand, maybe the lack of a human focus in game journalism has to do with the unmarketable nature of most game developers. Let's face it, Shigeru Miyamoto will never have the "star power" or magazine-cover-carrying power of Angelina Jolie. Plus, game developers tend to be a pretty homogeneous and unexciting lot—you can only ask a developer's outside interests and get back the answer "comic books and anime" so many times before you just give up.

And besides, game developers tend to be way too busy with work to spend time getting into the really juicy tabloid-style scandals. As Chris Grant memorably put it at our PAX East panel, "we're not writing about Will Wright murdering some guy" (though very occasionally we are writing about game executives crashing Ferarris).[25]

David Jaffe is a Liar. Do We Care?

Originally published on The Game Beat, June 24, 2010

> *[W]e are not making a new Twisted Metal altho [sic] I think doing one WOULD be fun...but we simply are not. Also a game by Eat Sleep Play will NOT be at E3 2010.*
>
> **David Jaffe**
> **to Joystiq, May 24**

> *Hey everybody, I'm David Jaffe and this is Scott Campbell and we're the co-founders of Eat Sleep Play, and we're really excited to show you guys the next edition of the* Twisted Metal *franchise [for the PS3].*
>
> **David Jaffe**
> **on stage at Sony's E3**
> **press conference, today**

The above quotes prove David Jaffe is a liar. This is not up for debate. There is no way he could show this game off today and truthfully say he was not working on it on May 24. The lie is a fact.

Given that fact, how should we, as journalists, respond?

My first instinct is to respond with anger. Our goal as journalists, first and foremost, is to report the truth, and Jaffe's lie forced us away from this goal. I suppose technically you could argue we still told the truth (when we said that *Jaffe said* he wasn't working on *Twisted Metal,* that was true... he did *say* it!') but in effect Jaffe's lie made us complicit in misleading our readers regarding the game's existence.

In general, when a journalist catches a source in a lie (especially about something big), it's a story in and of itself. If a politician is caught lying, it can lead to resignation or even impeachment. If an executive is caught lying about his business dealings, it can lead to criminal proceedings. If a journalist is caught lying about the source of their writing, their credibility is forever ruined.

I know Jaffe's lie doesn't quite rise to these level of a lying politician or high-powered business tycoon, but even if we just hold him to the standards of our own profession, shouldn't we at least have the decency to never believe another word out of his lying mouth?

In a subsequent PlayStation blog post,[26] Jaffe defends his lie by arguing it was all in service of the surprise reveal at the show. He wasn't trying to maliciously lead us off the trail of his game's existence, you see... he was just trying to maintain the "sense of surprise and discovery [that] has all but vanished from the E3 experience." (The post also suggests Sony urged him to lie to maintain the surprise, making the company at least somewhat complicit in all this.)

That argument doesn't hold water for me. It's possible to maintain secrecy about a project without outright lying about it. How many gamers knew about Retro's *Donkey Kong Country* revival before it was revealed today? How many knew Harmonix was working on a dancing game for Kinect before it was revealed yesterday?

Sure, there were rumors suggesting both of these revelations, but there are rumors about all sorts of crazy things in the lead up to E3, and most members of the public have no idea which ones are going to turn out to be true and which one are just so much hot air. There have been rumors about a *Kirby* game on the Wii for years, but they didn't turn out to be true until *this year.*

> It's possible to maintain secrecy about a project without outright lying about it.

Other companies, when asked to address rumors, almost invariably offer up a curt "no comment." They don't actively lie to the questioner (and, by extension, the readers). Instead, they just shrug it off and let everyone continue to do their job without active obstruction. I know Jaffe knows how to do this— he did it with regard to this very question back in 2008, even adding an expletive for good measure. A "no comment" might be frustrating, as a journalist, but it's definitely better than an outright lie.

Yes, Jaffe's lie did help tamp down the recent rumors of the PS3 *Twisted Metal* game (rumors Jaffe himself helped start with his loose lips at this year's DICE, I might add). But the lie didn't remove the very question from all recorded history. Addressing a rumor with a lie is not a permanent solution. All lying does, in essence, is take the small problem of an inconveniently timed rumor and trade it in for the big problem of a plain-as-day lie in the very near future. Did Jaffe think we'd just forget about his previous statements? Did he think we wouldn't care?

Maybe he did. And maybe we shouldn't care. Maybe I'm being too sensitive. After all, Spong said they "expected that of [Jaffe]" after his lie was revealed. G4's Andrew Pfister predicted Jaffe was lying just before the press conference started.

Maybe it's my fault for not being skeptical enough about Jaffe's denial. You could argue the journalists covering this announcement shouldn't have merely taken Jaffe at his word, and dug deep into their own insider sources to confirm or deny his direct denial. That seems impractical for such an anodyne (and usually straightforward) statement, but it's definitely a standard we should take for Jaffe's statements going forward.

In any case, I'm not particularly happy about our profession being used to willfully mislead people, even if it's just in the service of "the sense of surprise and discovery." I didn't get into journalism to help maintain the timing of a company's marketing plan. I got into it to report the truth. So I still get a little mad when liars prevent me from doing that.

What's in a Length?

Originally published on Gamasutra, July 27, 2010

Without a doubt, Xbox Live Arcade's *Limbo* is an instant classic. The reviews are near-unanimous in their praise. *Limbo* is "bleak and beautiful." It's "haunting." It's "elegant and minimalistic." It's "clever." It's "gorgeously constructed." It "will stay with you for a very long time." Some are already calling it "a masterpiece." Others are breaking out the dreaded A-word: "Art."

AUTHOR'S NOTE

In the years since *Limbo* came out, indie games that can be completed in one or two sittings have become much more common. Plenty of critics will still focus on a short length as a negative in their reviews, but plenty more seem willing to judge these self-contained games on their own merits (and lengths).

Some busy critics might even appreciate a review assignment they can complete with a bit less time investment. See "Game Critics Face Their Own 'Crunch Time'" in The Practical Side section for more on this.

But there's one other thing *Limbo* reviewers are almost equally unanimous about. Some seem almost reluctant to bring it up. Others seem proud that they were able to find some flaw to balance out an otherwise glowing review.

The critical consensus seems to be that Limbo is excellent but, well... it's kind of *short.*

THE LENGTH COMPLAINT

"The only real complaint I have of this game is that it is so short," writes Gaming Age. "Probably the only flaws that I can think of with *Limbo* are that the game is sadly shorter than it should be..." writes Planet Xbox 360. "If you are concerned about the game's length, you might want to see how low the price can go," writes Cheap Ass Gamer, living up to its name by complaining about the value of a high-quality $15 game.

Perhaps nothing speaks better of *Limbo*'s essential quality than the fact that the only negative most reviewers could come up with is that they want to play *more* of it. Still, it seems a bit gauche to bring up the game's length when everyone seems to agree the game is almost perfectly crafted in every other respect. It's like whining that the Mona Lisa wasn't painted on a bigger canvas, or that *Casablanca* wasn't padded out with more fight scenes.

But many critics seem to agree that *Limbo*'s length is lacking, even if they can't agree what that length is exactly. "Four hours" seems to be the number most commonly cited in reviews, but plenty of critics claim it only took them three. Plenty more mention getting stuck in *Limbo* (HA!) for five or even six hours.

My personal favorite quote on *Limbo*'s length might come from The Review Crew, who say the game took them three to four hours, but "of course it will take you longer if you get stuck on the numerous puzzles." I mentally inserted the unwritten subtext: "Note: This game may take you a while if you are not as awesome at video games as we are."

A RELATIVE MATTER

This brings us to one of the maddening facts that makes video game criticism different than criticism of most any other medium: length is not an absolute fact. Different players play at different paces—a game that's a two-hour breeze to some might be a ten-hour slog for others. The very idea of a set length doesn't even make sense for many games. How long does it take to complete *The Sims*? *Tetris*? The Multiplayer mode in *Modern Warfare 2*? These games only last as long as you are willing to keep playing them.

This should be the critical length benchmark for every game: not "How long until I reach the end?" (Are we theeeeere yet?) but "How long do I *want* to play?" Yet publishers constantly describe the "number of hours" for upcoming games as if that was a feature as concrete as "number of players." What usually goes unsaid in these inflated marketing claims of "hundreds of hours" of longevity is that 90% of those hours will be spent mindlessly grinding for experience points, or repeating endlessly similar escort missions, or chasing down hidden doodads that have long-since ceased being interesting to collect, all in pursuit of some quasi-mythical and utterly pointless "100%" on some statistics screen.

> *The critical consensus seems to be that* Limbo *is excellent but, well... it's kind of short.*

Perhaps this marketing push is why many critics seem fixated on length. Or perhaps they're just used to judging games less as carefully constructed works of art (or even craft) and more as mere value propositions. "Give me X hours of gameplay for every Y dollars of my investment" is the unspoken context of this type of review.

The relative quality of those hours—and whether all those hours eventually come together into some sort of satisfying whole—don't seem to matter as much to these critics. As long as the game is suitably distracting from the essential emptiness of everyday living then more quantity equals more quality, as far as they're concerned. And hey, if that game only costs $20, that leaves $40 extra in the budget left over to take the family out to a thoroughly enjoyable two-hour movie. Er, wait a minute...

THE VALUE OF AN HOUR

This value-based approach to reviewing seems ill-suited for a game as carefully constructed and self-contained as *Limbo*. Heck, it seems inappropriate for any game, especially considering that reviewers often rush through their single, straightforward playthrough of a game as quickly as possible in order to meet some very tight deadlines. How are these reviewers supposed to judge replay value when they're expected to move on to the next game on their review pile almost immediately? In fact, you'd think most reviewers would *appreciate* a shorter game, given the mountains of unplayed games sitting unloved on their shelves (poor babies).

Still, it seems wrong to totally ignore the issue of game length. Games are consumer products as well as works of art, and sometimes even a good game doesn't provide sufficient value for the money. One of the most elegant solutions to this problem I've seen came from the sadly short-lived *Game Buyer* magazine, a Future publication which ran for four months in late 1998.

Each review in *Game Buyer* came with a horribly unscientific graph with time on the X axis and the game's "tilt level" on the Y axis. So a game that started slow but had tons of replay value would have an upward curve, while a game that started with a bang but fizzled out would curve downwards. Bang! The value proposition in a handy visual format—you don't even have to waste any words in the review text!

To be fair, many reviewers seem to be handling the problem of *Limbo*'s length appropriately, even without the aid of graphs. *The Telegraph* review mentioned a "perfectly formed running time of around four hours," while 7outof10 pointed out that the game "packs more spine-tingling wonder and horror into its opening hour as [other] games manage in eight or more." Some reviews, most notably *Paste*'s and Eurogamer's, even managed to capture the game elegantly without mentioning the completion time at all (or, in the case of Eurogamer, downplaying it).

But perhaps the most elegant statement on the matter of Limbo's length came, surprisingly (to me at least), from IGN's review of the game: "While [five or six hours] may sound short, it's better for a game to leave us wanting more than to overstay its welcome."

Amen.

Who's Really Hurt By a Review-free Launch?

Originally published on The Game Beat, July 28, 2010

As I begin writing this, *Starcraft II* has been out for over a day and has exactly one review listed on GameRankings.

This is practically unprecedented for a major, modern video game release. *Mass Effect 2* had 27 online reviews listed on GameRankings by its Jan. 26 release date. Curious *Super Mario Galaxy 2* shoppers had at least 15 different professional critical opinions guiding them on launch day. Even reclusive Rockstar Games allowed 11 reviews of *Red Dead Redemption* to hit the presses in time for that game's release. You get the idea.

> **AUTHOR'S NOTE**
>
> The situation described in this piece has only become more common as the years have gone by. In some cases, particularly centralized online games, there are technical reasons why a pre-release build wouldn't give critics an accurate view of the game.
>
> Then there are publishers like Bethesda, which made an explicit policy out of withholding games from early reviews starting with *Doom* back in 2016. Bethesda quietly reversed that policy in 2018, though, telling VG247 "we were tired of reading reviews where the first paragraph spent more time talking about our review policy than the game."
>
> Hey, maybe the publishers care about what we write after all!

This dearth of reviews wasn't an accident—it happened by design. While journalists have had access to *Starcraft II*'s multiplayer beta since February, they only got access to the final retail build of the single-player campaign when the Battle.net servers were turned on for consumers yesterday. Blizzard isn't officially commenting on the move, but Eurogamer's on-background sources have them comfortable enough to say "the new Battle.net service and its online features are so integral to the game that it would be both impractical and undesirable for press to review it before servers go live." Of course that doesn't fully explain why journalists couldn't have access to those servers a little earlier than consumers, but it is what it is.

As it stands, dozens of critics are currently dashing through their copies of *Starcraft II,* rushing to put together some coherent impressions before the launch-window attention dries up (and before competitors get *their* reviews into the vacuum). Quite a few sites felt the need to specifically tell their readers about the lack of early review access, perhaps none more amusingly than Rock Paper Shotgun.[27]

IGN was almost apologetic about it: "The goal is to get you a review as quickly as possible, but we'll also be taking to time to see all there is to see in *StarCraft II.* Because of that, there's no specific date when the review might show up. We are working on it, though, so don't think we've forgotten about what's arguably the biggest game of the year."

It seems obvious why this isn't an ideal state of affairs for everyone involved. Gamers who want to buy the game on release day will essentially be going in blind, basing their purchase decisions on incomplete previews and a prequel that was released 11 years ago. Blizzard will be losing out on media attention and consumer mindshare that launch day reviews generate. And critics, of course, lose out on all the traffic and attention surrounding the game's launch, which will likely never be higher than it is on release day.

But maybe these negatives aren't really negatives. After all, reviews obviously aren't very important to the more than 800,000 people that pre-ordered the game without reading a single "10 out of 10." Analysts are already predicting the game will sell 7 million units over its lifetime, suggesting Blizzard won't be paying any significant long term price for the small dip in release day media attention. As for the critics... well, they kind of get the short end of the stick here, don't they?

When you think about it, it's kind of surprising that publishers let reviewers have early access to *any* big-name sequels. *Starcraft II*'s impressive pre-order numbers seem to show that, absent any first day reviews, consumers are comfortable coming out in droves for a game (and a developer) that has a sufficiently impressive pedigree.

Now think about how the equation changes if reviews are available on day one. If the reviews are good (as they almost always are for such big-franchise releases), it will just confirm consumers' expectations and probably not lead to a significant bump in launch day sales. But if the reviews are somehow worse than expected, potential first-day purchasers might hesitate, holding their money until they get confirmation from a friend, or even moving on to another game entirely.

> *As for the critics... well, they kind of get the short end of the stick here, don't they?*

For smaller games, the risk of bad early reviews is worth the opportunity to capture more media attention and consumer mindshare. But for the biggest titles, where consumer mindshare is already saturated by release day, surely the potential risks outweigh the potential rewards.

There's a reason film studios increasingly don't allow early press screenings of some of their most heavily marketed movies—they want to buy their way into a decent opening weekend before the critical world (and word of mouth) potentially breaks the marketing bubble they've created. I'm increasingly afraid that *Starcraft II*'s review-free launch will prove that the same strategy will soon become the standard for the video game market as well.

Our On-again, Off-again Love Affair with *No Man's Sky*

Originally published on The Game Beat, Aug. 26, 2016

If you write about games for any length of time, you get intimately acquainted with the fact that many, if not most games, don't fully live up to their pre-release hype. But the release of No Man's Sky, coming as it has after years of sky-high expectations, seems to have caused a particular bit of soul searching on this point among some in the press.

Rock Paper Shotgun's Brendan Caldwell put a pretty fine point on it, asking more or less directly whether we in the press expect to be lied to in pre-release marketing,[28] and, if so, why we seem to be so OK with it.

> *In the videogames industry we are used to scripted marketing material being shown at E3 or GDC or Gamescom, packed with interesting stuff that changes radically by the time of the a game's release. We all remember BioShock Infinite's fake trailers, which seemed like 'gameplay' but were really only thinly-veiled first-person cinematics, none of which ended up in the final version. And because we have grown used to this type of advertising, a lot of people are shrugging when it comes to Hello Games' space-faring survival game. It is no different, you could say.*
>
> *This is a narrow-minded and anti-consumer attitude. Just because every game developer under the quintillion suns does the same thing, does not make it OK. The right question to ask is: Why do we think this is an acceptable thing within our industry? Why are we prepared to buy into a intergalactic spectacle and then shrug off the discrepancies when that spectacle turns out to be only spectacle?*

Some consumers over at Reddit were definitely not OK with those discrepancies. In a widely circulated image,[29] Redditor rationalcomment juxtaposed laudatory previews for *No Man's Sky* with middling reviews for the final game from those same outlets.

This is a ridiculous argument, in some ways. Expecting every review to match up with the tone of the preview is, in essence, expecting every review to be a rave (more on that in a bit). There's a reason previews are labeled previews, and why any critic worth their salt will tell you to wait for the final review(s) before making a decision (remember kids: never pre-order).

The reason for the differences between preview hype and review realism get back to Caldwell's question: before we have a final review build in hand, we as critics can't fully tell how much of what we're seeing for the preview is, essentially, a lie. Even the best previews are based on small, early slices of the game as a whole that give an incomplete and often effectively misleading view of the final product. It's like trying to review a movie based on the trailer, in a lot of ways.

That said, all too often we in the press often seem much too willing to take developers at their word during pre-release demos. This is understandable, in a way: no one wants to be too critical of a work-in-progress, especially when the developers promise up and down that any current and/or future problems will be addressed before the release. No one wants to give a high-and-mighty denunciation of a game they only played for 30 minutes. No one wants to be the guy who points out every typo in an early rough draft ('I haven't run spell check yet, just tell me what you think of the *ideas*').

And no one wants to be the sore thumb sticking out in an ocean of hype, shitting on a game that the audience is primed to *want* to love. As USGamer's Kat Bailey put it on Twitter, "All the people complaining about *NMS* and complaining about the media were [downvoting] skeptics into oblivion six months ago."

So we, as previewers, generally tend to give the developers the benefit of the doubt early on. We take the easy route, relaying the promise of that shining orb of perfection the developers describe while holding our tongues at anything that might give us pause in an early pre-release build. This isn't true of 100% of all previews, but it's still the case an overwhelming majority of the time, especially for high-profile games with large marketing budgets.

> *All too often we in the press often seem much too willing to take developers at their word during pre-release demos.*

If the developer's early vision later ends up being impossible, or unfeasible given time and budget constraints, most critics and readers won't hear about that until the final review hits. At preview time, wide swathes of the game press seem to forget a simple fact that Kotaku's Jason Schreier pointed out in his own hype-analysis piece:[30] things change during game development.

"When a developer makes claims about features in their game, how can video game fans tell if they're guarantees or just hopes?" Schreier asks. Well... ideally, it's the job of the previewer to evaluate which of those "hopes" seem most likely to become "guarantees," and which have a good chance of being dashed to bits. But that can be tough when the time with a game (and the scope of what you can see) are so limited at preview time. It doesn't help that many critics have a limited understanding of the realities of game development, and might not actually know what's a feasible promise and what's just smoke (for more on this, see this Andrew Groen Twitter thread).[31]

Schreier lays the blame for this state of affairs at least partially on overly secretive PR departments:

> I certainly hope the lesson for game developers here isn't to stay quiet or lean on strict PR-controlled messages for their games. If anything, they should have the opposite takeaway. Have to cut cool features you've talked about in the press? Fine! Video games change. We get it. The solution isn't to stay silent about it, but to explain to fans why they can't, say, see one another when they're on the same planet. Or why the No Man's Sky described in 2014 looks so much different than the one we're playing in 2016.

There's something to that, but it's not PR's job to call attention to the things about a game that might be potentially worrisome. If the press in general was more willing to write cautiously or even skeptically about those preview presentations, maybe readers wouldn't be so blindsided when a game doesn't live up to the always sky-high promises.

Brendan Keogh summed up this point nicely[32] in his analysis of how the press should handle "aspirational" early promises from developers and PR people while their games are still in the works:

> *Marketers inflate the truth and tell untruths and stay conveniently quiet about less sexy truths. We know this. When video games aren't involved, we're pretty good at being critical about this. When Apple says I can buy a new Macbook 'from $500' I know that the $500 model is going to be the most bare-bones, smallest, shittiest model and most of the models will be $2000. Because that is how marketing works. There are pro-consumer regulations in place to prevent marketers telling outright lies, sure. That is good. That doesn't mean consumers don't still need to be critical and cynical in how they interpret the information marketers say to them.*
>
> *Core game demographics are not very good at being critical of game marketing. Preview material is typically read as factual information about what a game will be and not content that exists exclusively for marketing purposes to make people spend money on a thing.*
>
> *But that's not simply because videogame consumers are gullible idiots. It's because the pre-release marketing hype of publishers is super integrated into the day-to-day reporting of game journalism and how videogames are talked about generally. We always want to talk about the next big thing. The next final videogame that will, finally, be the one. Marketers sell us that myth because they know we have always lapped it up. Being excited by the next thing is the treadmill that all of gamer culture has been running on since the mid-'80s.*

It's easy sometimes to feel like it's our job to be excited about every big new game coming down the pike; to reflect back the hopes and dreams of both the readers and the aspirational developers we're covering. Often, though, the job is just the opposite. A review shouldn't be the first time a reader has a chance to potentially hear our collective worries about a game. That's especially true of a game that's being heavily hyped for years before its release.

Reporting on a Console That Doesn't Exist (Yet)

Originally published on The Game Beat, Sept. 2, 2016

In my long years covering and following gaming news closely, I've seen a lot of product news leak out before the product maker was quite ready to announce it. That said, I don't think I've ever seen anything quite like the current situation surrounding the PlayStation 4 Slim model, which has leaked

AUTHOR'S NOTE

One thing I wish I'd focused on more here is the marketing and PR pressure a corporation like Sony can bring to bear here. Is reporting on the PS4 Slim before Sony is ready worth being left off the early review hardware list for every subsequent Sony game and console? It's the kind of call that would make any website publisher anxious.

so heavily and so widely that you could argue the console has been launched before it has even been officially announced.

A quick tick-tock of the developments over the past few weeks:

- **Aug. 21:** Online auctions for the PS4 Slim appear in England (apparently via retail sources in the UAE, filtering through the UK). Some guy on Twitter says he has the unannounced console.
- **Aug. 22:** Eurogamer physically tracks down the guy and takes photos and videos[33] of his system. Eurogamer then takes down the video "upon taking legal advice," but leaves up the picture (which I guess is more legally defensible than the video, somehow?)
- **Aug. 23:** Another guy on Twitter gets the system, and posts a video of it. He then takes down the video, citing "copyrights from Sony" but plenty of mirrors are still available.[34]

- **Aug. 29:** Laura Dale from Let's Play Video Games gets the system and does a massive unboxing/review.[35] This video has yet to be taken down.

Amidst all this, I can tell you that I've heard from a few major outlets that have direct access to this system, but are wary to write about it for legal reasons. Dale also notes on Twitter that a few "major gaming sites" backed down from offers to have her review the unit.

This is somewhat understandable, since the press protections in this case aren't quite as robust in the UK as they are in the US. My understanding is that you'd have to be able to argue a compelling public interest to get over Sony's potential objection of "IP theft," and that is a tough road to climb, legally. For bigger outlets, often owned by major conglomerates with a lot to lose, even the risk of paying for a winnable lawsuit might not be worth the limited news value of reporting on a system whose details have already been fully leaked online.

This is one case where being smaller actually turns into an advantage, journalistically. Random people on Twitter don't have nearly as much to worry about just talking about a system they bought legally. A small site like Let's Play Video Games has a little more risk (including potential blacklisting—Hi, Kotaku), but is a bit more insulated from the pressure. Dale tweets that "Patreon funding is what allows us to take these kinds of risks."

In any case, every major and minor tech and gaming news site has been able to cite the leaks that have happened as proof that the PS4 Slim does exist. Despite all this, *Sony continues to refuse to publicly acknowledge the system.* The company is apparently waiting for a Sept. 7 event where it will announce the system officially, and quite possibly put it on sale immediately, based on rumors that other retailers already have them in their possession.

I suppose there's some good reason for Sony to publicly keep on pretending these leaks never happened (legal threats notwithstanding). If people know a new PS4 Slim is coming out in just a few weeks, they probably aren't going to buy the current PS4 right now, which could piss off retailers trying to clear out stock. On the other hand, if Sony announced the Slim early, those purchases would probably still happen, just deferred by a few weeks.

Regardless, the cat is out of the bag now. The bell can't be unrung. You can't unhear a song. And other such clichés. Perhaps Sony realizes this, to some extent, since it hasn't brought the same legal pressure on Dale's review that it did on the newsier leaks the week prior. Dale, for her part, thinks her review is still up because of "the number of sites that reported on my review and the Twitter trending. It got too big too fast."

At this point, though, this news is out there for anyone paying even cursory attention to the world of games. Sony pretending that it isn't just makes them look kind of out of touch. Maybe this feigned ignorance will be worth it when Sony tries to makes its "big splash" with an "available right now!" announcement next week. More likely, though, that announcement is going to echo with a dull thud after week's of Sony acting like it isn't reading the same news leaks we all are.

The Press Spoils Nintendo's Switch Surprise

Originally published on The Game Beat, Oct. 23, 2016

The most surprising thing about Nintendo's big reveal of the Nintendo Switch late this week might have been just how unsurprising it was.

Sure, Nintendo got to make a splashy reveal of the new name for what had previously been known as "NX" (branding-wise, Switch is a big step up from Wii/Wii U, in my book). Nintendo also got to reveal small details like the massive list of development/publishing partners, and show off a few seconds of a new Mario game (by the by, GameXplain's 11-minute analysis of that six seconds of footage[36] is everything I love and hate about game journalism rolled into one).

Aside from those small tidbits, anyone paying attention could have told you the basic outline of Nintendo's new system months ago. Nintendo waited 19 whole months between first mentioning the NX publicly and giving any details on its design. During that time, the press stepped up and filled in those details via leaks that ended up being extremely accurate.

A quick trip down the memory lane of NX leaks, all of which turned out to be 100% true:

- **October 2015:** The Wall Street Journal describes[37] NX dev kits with "at least one mobile unit that could either be used in conjunction with the console or taken on the road for separate use."
- **May 2016:** Reports suggest[38] the system will use "cartridge" media instead of discs.

- **July 2016:** A detailed Eurogamer report[39] confirms the portable/console hybrid idea, mentions detachable controllers on the side of a tablet screen, and suggests and an Nvidia Tegra-based processor.
- **September 2016:** The Pokemon Company president Tsunekazu Ishihara lets slip[40] additional confirmation that the system will "change the concept of what it means to be *a home console device or a hand-held device* [emphasis added]."

The extreme leakiness of the console's basics is especially ironic given that Nintendo's Shigeru Miyamoto said in June that he was "worried about imitators" if they revealed the NX concept too early. Thanks to diligent work by the press, those imitators have had months to copy the basics on the NX design well before the official unveiling this week, if they wanted.

> *It's hard to say if the press is actually getting better at uncovering these console details before they're officially announced, if the console makers are getting worse about containing leaks, or some combination of the two.*

The lack of drama in the Switch reveal mirrors a few other recent, high-profile hardware launches whose details leaked way ahead of time. Kotaku broke word of the "PlayStation 4.5" back in March, broadly describing the system that would officially become the PS4 Pro in September (other outlets were able to confirm Kotaku's report in the following weeks and months). Word of Microsoft's upgraded "Project Scorpio" stayed secret a little longer, but leaked out to the press in May, a few weeks before that system's E3 announcement.

Broadly speaking, these kind of widespread pre-reveal leaks are not standard for the game industry. There were certainly plenty of rumors floating around about Nintendo's "Revolution" console throughout 2005, but when Nintendo finally unveiled the Wii and its motion sensing Remote at September's Tokyo Game Show that year, the larger gaming press was thrown for a loop. Early rumors surrounding the Wii U focused on the system's potential for HD graphics, and not on the out-of-the-blue touchscreen tablet controller that was first shown at E3 2011.

Then again, by 2012, a massive leak of Microsoft internal documents gave a lot of early information that ended up being directly relevant to the Xbox One's 2013 unveiling (then called the Xbox 720). And well before the PS4's early 2013 unveiling, we had what turned out to be reliable rumors on the system's chip architecture and relative processing power.

It's hard to say if the press is actually getting better at uncovering these console details before they're officially announced, if the console makers are getting worse about containing leaks, or some combination of the two. In any case, the situation begins to approach farce when major companies continue to officially deny any knowledge of products that have been completely and accurately described in public reports (see "Reporting on a Console that Doesn't Exist (Yet)" for an extreme example of this). If this kind of leaking continues, hardware makers are probably going to have to get a little more flexible with their marketing schedules.

Tell Me a Story (or "The Play's the Thing")

Originally published on The Game Beat, April 28, 2017

If you are connected to video games professionally, this week you probably heard some sort of discussion over Ian Bogost's provocatively headlined *Atlantic* piece Video Games Are Better Without Stories. The actual piece is a bit more restrained than the headline implies, more arguing that games should get past the "cinema envy" that is driving a lot of linear character vignettes these days. The argument nonetheless got a bit of pushback from across the industry.

The whole brouhaha got me thinking about how we, as journalists and critics, handle the presence of story in games. It's been said that a story in a video game is like a story in pornography—it doesn't matter how good it is, but you notice if it isn't there. That might be a bit glib, but it's also probably true of the way most people play the most popular games these days. For a lot of players, the story is just meaningless context that can largely be ignored.

On this subject, I often think back to a 2015 Ben Kuchera piece[41] that argues we should all "stop pretending *Halo 5*'s story matters:"

> *After so many games of nearly incomprehensible stories and lore that requires terminals and study outside of the core gaming experience I've decided to give up on the story of Halo. Not that it ever showed anything interesting outside of a few neat, big ideas that no one seemed to know how to develop into a working narrative. If you want a great story and interesting characters let's stop pretending the game starring a faceless, gravelly voiced super-soldier is going to provide it. Even Nathan Fillion, who punches well above his weight class when struggling under bad scripts, only makes a slight impression here.*
>
> *It's not that I'm not upset Halo 5 couldn't deliver a workable story with a beginning, middle, and end. I am. It's just that between the fun to be had in the pure expression of play within Halo 5 and the many multiplayer options the lack of story is a very small detail in a very large package that's being sold for $60. You're going to get your money's worth, and my personal journey with the game has only begun. I can't wait to play more, and to master the higher level tactics and the interesting Warzone mode.*

In short, Kuchera's argument boils down to:
1. The story in *Halo 5* is really bad;
2. That doesn't matter at all;
3. *Halo 5* is still a great game.

You may disagree on the specifics in this case, but it's probably not too hard for you to think of a game that you similarly love despite it having a horribly written and/or forgettable story.

Think about the implications of this argument. If even a horrible story can't destroy a game that's otherwise good, what does that say about the value of storytelling in games? What does that say about how much we should even bother talking about the story when reviewing a game like *Halo 5*? Do the readers even care, or should we really just focus on how the new weapons affect the balance of Team Deathmatch mode? Would *Halo 5* be just as good if it just gave up and didn't even bother trying to tell a story at all?

Looking from the other side, can a well-told story redeem a game that's otherwise boring or a chore to actually play? This question can lead to a lot of debate among gamers, especially when well-known "walking simulators" like *Dear Esther* and *Gone Home* or text-based interactive writing like *Depression Quest* come up. These games are almost 100% story, with only the slightest hint of interesting interactivity.

It can be hard to anchor a traditional review of these types of games without the ability to fall back on the technical crutch of describing and critiquing mere mechanics. If I wanted to talk about plot and character development I'd have been a film critic, right?

Back at the opposite end of the spectrum, it often seems that games that *completely* lack an explicit story struggle to get traction with the critical establishment. While titles like *Rocket League* or *Threes* might occasionally become media darlings, the vast majority of titles that get coverage are ones rooted in *some* sort of narrative.

Story-free games probably get less attention partly because they come from genres (puzzle) or platforms (mobile phones) that are considered unserious. Sometimes, games that are too purely about play get labeled as mere "toys," without the structure and goals that make games "meaningful" (compare the reception of *Katamari Damacy* and *Noby Noby Boy* for some idea of what I'm talking about).

Partly, though, I think many critics struggle to get a handle on a game that doesn't have some sort of narrative hook to ground the description. "A game may not 'need' a story, but 'who am I & why do I care' is absolutely the first question you'll get from many, many people," as Zak McClendon points out on Twitter. If writing about video games is like dancing about architecture, then writing about narrative-free games is like dancing about blueprints; there's nothing solid there that forms a base to build on top of.

Then there are the games that are so open-ended that it's nearly impossible to write about the story in a universal way. How do you describe the narrative of a game like *The Sims* when every emergent playthrough can develop in a million different storylines depending on player choice? What good is my description of a single path through a *Mass Effect* game when the reader's playthrough could contain significantly different plot decisions?

And let's not forget the extreme spoiler-phobia that limits a lot of the public discussion of video game narrative. At or before a game's release, when reviews are most in demand, some readers can be paranoid about having even the tiniest plot details ruined for them by a casual mention in a review. By the time enough people have played through the game and are ready to talk about the story in depth, those readers have probably moved on to looking forward to the next big game. The temporal window to get serious narrative discussion around games that merit it can be vanishingly small.

The main takeaway here (if there is one) is that explicit stories in games have very different levels of value to different people, and a story that you find incredibly crucial to a game's value might be meaningless filler to someone else. If we can't even agree if stories in video games are important, how are we going to start discussing whether a specific video game story is good?

Penny Arcade's Tycho has a line about two distinct types of gamers that has stuck with me, and which you should keep in mind when considering your audience:

> *I play games to enter a trance state and experience other lives, [Robert] plays them to defeat the designer of the game by proxy. That's a significant distinction.*

"Courting" Controversy

Originally published on The Game Beat, May 4, 2018

Is there such a thing as a game that's too controversial to cover? How should we handle games that are obviously playing up their worst qualities to attract hateful coverage? If we ignore the most ignoble games out there, will they just go away?

These are the kinds of questions I've been asking myself in the wake of the March release of *Super Seducer*, a game in which "world-renowned dating coach Richard La Ruina... teaches players the secret psychological tricks of attraction experts, accumulated from over 20 years of live workshops," according to its own press materials.

Among the gaming press, there seems to be widespread agreement that this is a horrible, creepy, amoral game that arguablyencouragesharassmentofwomen.It'sagamethatpress reports unanimously agree deserves to be ignored by players.

At the same time, it also seems to be a game that much of the gaming press itself is largely unable to ignore. Myself included.

A selection of somewhat ironic quotes from coverage that heaped attention on *Super Seducer* while essentially asking players to pay no attention to the game:

> *We need to hide this game under a rock and starve it—and the whole PUA [pick-up artist] culture—of light and oxygen until it dies. PUA culture is what society tells men to be, and it starves men of options and different ways of being in the world."*
>
> *Vice Motherboard*[42]

> Super Seducer *is clearly intended to be part of the PR exercise, an attempt to portray PUAs as just guys looking for ways to convince girls to like them, albeit through techniques that are primarily focused around lying and manipulation. It's an attempt to put a friendly mask on an ugly face.*
>
> **Rock Paper Shotgun**[43]

> *I could probably bend your ear for hours at a stretch explaining how women aren't Rubik's Cubes, solvable with the correct series of intricate twists made while thinking five steps ahead of yourself... But I don't even need to go that far to turn you off of the game. All I need to tell you is— are you sitting down?—it's a full-motion video (FMV) game.*
>
> **TheNextWeb**[44]

Was this all part of the plan for *Super Seducer*? Negative attention is still attention after all, and there's some merit to the argument that there's no such thing as bad press. In a modern gaming market that's absolutely flooded with games (see "Sipping from the Fire Hose" in The Practical Side for more on this), *Super Seducer* is getting more attention than 99.9 percent of all available titles (almost all of which surely deserve more playtime than this travesty). Giving *Super Seducer* any attention could be akin to feeding the trolls.

The counter-argument is that ignoring the worst games out there doesn't stop those games from existing, or stop people from hearing about them from sources that could be more sympathetic to the game's message. With no pushback from culture at large, and the press that's supposed to represent it, developers and players might start to normalize these games as just another valid (if niche) part of the industry that's largely ignored by "the discourse."

> It's a game that press reports unanimously agree deserves to be ignored by players. At the same time, it also seems to be a game that much of the gaming press itself is largely unable to ignore.

Generally, I think the the former argument has the better end of it for unknown games. That's because highlighting bad ideas in order to attack them can often have the opposite of the desired effect.

Consider a hypothetical audience of 10,000 readers that first hear about *Super Seducer* by reading your article about it. Say an overwhelming 90 percent of them are horrified by the very idea of the game while only two percent think it's a compelling idea they might want to check out (the other eight percent are relatively neutral). That two percent represents at least 200 interested potential customers you introduced to a game that you think rightly deserves zero customers.

You can fiddle with the assumed percentages a bit, if you want, and maybe some of those readers would have heard about the game anyway, or already read competing coverage of the same title (the calculus changes substantially for widely publicized games that "everyone" already knows about). But this is the kind of math you have to do when you have a big audience that you're ready to train on an unknown title, even to trash it. As *Wired* noted recently, "Psychologically speaking, elevating chicanery and those who propagate it—even to debunk the lie—only spreads their nonsense."

THE "NEWSWORTHINESS" LINE

For me, what can often override this kind of argument is newsworthiness. When *Super Seducer* was just a trashy game trying to gin up controversial attention, I leaned towards ignoring it. When Sony decided to block the game's planned PS4 release, though, it became part of a bigger story on where platform holders should draw the line for what's allowed on their platforms. That's a story I decided was worth covering,[45] even if it meant giving some attention to an otherwise ignorable title.

A similar situation popped up a few years ago, when Destructive Creations' *Hatred* tried to gin up attention by featuring over-the-top levels of ultra-violent gore. The game started gaining a lot of (largely negative) buzz from the moment its first trailer hit in October 2014, but it still wasn't that hard for a gaming news outlet to ignore an obviously sensationalized game from an unknown studio.

When Steam Greenlight barred (and then reinstated) the game in December, though, it became much harder to ignore a story about how PC gaming's largest distributor conducted itself. *Hatred* got a few more cycles of "legitimate news" when it received a rare AO rating from the ESRB (blocking the game from console release in the process) and then again when the game was refused a listing by online retailer GOG. By that point, though, the game had already achieved such infamy in the press (and the larger game industry consciousness) that further coverage probably didn't raise its profile all that much

Today, a slightly different coverage controversy is brewing over the upcoming release of *Detroit: Become Human*. When French developer Quantic Dream sued a number of media outlets over reports of a toxic work environment, some in the press and development communities felt like it was time to start ignoring the studio and the game altogether.

"I'm going to be pretty fucking pissed if anyone covers Quantic Dream games ever again," freelancer Eric Smith stated bluntly on Twitter in response to the suit. "Were I still in the press, I'd have trouble covering Cage's shitty games with the knowledge he hates a free press," former game journalist Henry Gilbert noted a bit more diplomatically.

There is some argument that journalists should show solidarity with their sued brethren here and not lend their voice to Quantic Dream's work. But here I think the press deciding to ignore the game could be counterproductive. *Detroit* is being backed by a massive marketing campaign from Sony and has already received years of intense coverage from all corners of the gaming press. Ignoring the game at this point is going to do little to nothing to lessen overall awareness of one of the the PlayStation 4's key exclusives this year.

On the contrary, a review of the game can provide a good opportunity to highlight the controversy surrounding Quantic Dream in a context that might be of more interest to casual readers. Deciding to ignore what is obviously an important release, on the other hand, could come off as a churlish and futile protest borne of personal animosity rather than a true desire to "serve the readers" by... protecting them from a problematic studio's work?

I'm reminded somewhat of the Huffington Post's 2015 decision to cover Donald Trump's presidential campaign in the "Entertainment" section, rather than "Politics," an attempt to make a point about what they saw at the time as a "sideshow." When they were forced to reverse that decision months later, as Trump continued to rise in the polls, the move ended up looking like a petty fit of pique. Like it or not, some controversial figures are just too big to not cover seriously.

Surrendering the Score Wars

Originally published on The Game Beat, May 25, 2018

A quick glance at review aggregators like Metacritic and OpenCritic shows an abnormally wide range of reviews for today's release of *Detroit: Become Human,* with scores going from 40/100 to 95/100 on those sites' standardized scales. But there's another divergence hiding in the critical discourse over this game: that between the scored and unscored reviews.

Some of the most scathing professional commentary currently available for *Detroit: Become Human* isn't reflected in the game's respective and relatively healthy average scores of 79 and 80 (out of 100) on the review aggregation sites. Consider some of the punishingly negative (but unscored) takes that aren't accounted for in those averages:

- "The biggest crime a piece of media can make is to be boring and *Detroit* is as guilty as can be." -VG247
- "In *Detroit,* androids can dream. But the game's creators can't seem to dream of anything new to say." -The Verge
- "[The self-serious introduction] is the first hint at how profoundly, confidently ignorant Quantic Dream is about how the future, history, society, oppression, and even human beings work." -Mashable
- "*Detroit: Become Human* is like something my Alexa would come up with, were I to ask her to write a story about androids with feelings." -Kotaku
- "...there's very little soul staring out at you from behind *Detroit*'s pretty, almost-human eyes." -The AV Club

- "...that underlying story ends up so fragmented, so poorly executed, and so clunkily written that it's very difficult to appreciate the narrative playspace." -Ars Technica (by yours truly)

Of the 77 scored reviews for *Detroit* currently on Metacritic, 57 qualify as "positive" compared to only two as "negative." Of the eight unscored reviews listed (not including those "in progress"), six out of eight are overwhelmingly negative (including my own). The other two unscored reviews could charitably be called "mixed."

Let's assume these eight unscored reviews were suddenly given scores, and averaged out to a 60/100 rating (which, if anything, is generous based on the negative thrust of the text). That alone would be enough to lower *Detroit*'s Metacritic average from 79 to 77 in one stroke. And that assumes the previously unscored outlets were given equal weighting to the scored ones. Metacritic says its secret outlet weighting algorithm takes "quality and overall stature" into account, and most of the non-scoring outlets for *Detroit* would seem to have that in spades over many of the outlets giving the game a high review score.

The yawning disparity between scored and unscored reviews, in this case, is enough to make me wonder if the very process of scoring a review can skew the way critics consider a game (this Tyler Treese tweet got me started thinking along these lines). Critics writing a scored review go in knowing (on some level, at least) that the score at the end will be the only thing some large proportion of "readers" will ever see. That's especially true given just how many consumers rely exclusively on aggregators like Metacritic to help them make their buying decisions.

Scored reviewers also know that any score that stands out too much from the crowd will likely be dogpiled by fanboys of one stripe or another, ready to shout that a dissenting opinion is inherently "teh bias." That's doubly true for a heavily marketed, high-profile game that happens to be a major exclusive for a major console. The intense public focus on the score increases the subtle (and not-so-subtle) pressure for a critic to give an opinion that stays in line with the crowd (See "The Pressure to Stay in Line" in The Practical Side section for more on this).

> *The yawning disparity between scored and unscored reviews, in this case, is enough to make me wonder if the very process of scoring a review can skew the way critics consider a game.*

Reviewers not giving a score don't have to deal with that kind of pressure, consciously or unconsciously, which could be enough to sway their collective takes. Maybe it's easier to give an unvarnished negative review of a game if you know that review isn't going to be blamed for "bringing down the average" and ruining some poor developer's Metacritic-linked bonus payment.[46]

This isn't the only explanation for the scored/unscored disparity for *Detroit*, of course. It could just be a coincidence that the reviewers at unscored outlets tended towards the negative end of a very polarized consensus this time around. I don't have the data or the time to examine if such scored/unscored splits exist across other games on Metacritic, but I wouldn't exactly be surprised if they did.

These kinds of complaints about review scoring and aggregation are not new, but I'll admit they felt newly relevant thanks to a Twitter conversation I had Thursday with former Gamasutra journalist (and current indie game publisher) Mike Rose. I was surprised he had come away with the impression that the *Detroit* reviews were overall "good," since the ones I had read at that point had largely been negative. When I pointed to my own review for a "not good" take, he admitted he "didn't see it cos it's not on metacritic."

It is on Metacritic, of course. But it's in the unscored section at the bottom, where some savvy, industry-connected readers don't even bother to look, it seems.

I'm not trying to pick on Mike (whom I consider a friend) or project some sort of personal offense that my own brilliant review is being ignored by the masses because of Metacritic's bias towards reviews with scores. And while I personally push for scores to stay off of Ars' game reviews, I don't think scored reviews are inherently worse than those without a number at the end.

Looking at *Detroit*'s critical split, though, I do wonder if non-scoring outlets are engaging in a sort of unilateral disarmament in the discourse over game quality. Is forgoing a score worth risking virtual invisibility among a significant portion of the potential audience? I still lean towards yes (for most of the usual reasons, well outlined here)[47] but some days I'm not so sure.

THE PERSONAL SIDE

"The worst part about being a game journalist is that you can't complain about it."

I forget where I first heard this truism, but it's stuck with me over the years. Writing about the game industry is a great job, of course, but it's still a job. And if you want to make it a full-time career, it's a far cry from the popular image of sitting around in your pajamas, playing games all day.

Sometimes you also get to check Twitter.

Seriously, though, this section takes a look at what it's really like to live the life of a professional game journalist. That includes a lot of discussion of how to make a career in the business work both professionally and financially. It also includes many interviews with gaming editors (past and present) reflecting on their work from a perch at the top of the game, including many magazine editors reflecting on the near-extinction of game journalism printed monthly on dead trees (in the U.S., at least).

There's also a fun story about convincing your romantic partner that writing about games is a real job, so check that out.

Meet the Game Press: Francesca Reyes

Originally published on The Video Game Ombudsman, Jan. 16, 2006

In 1995, Francesca Reyes was just another English major at San Francisco State University. In her free time, she worked at a coffee shop, played as many video games as she could get her hands on, and read up on her hobby in her favorite magazines, *GameFan* and *Game Players.* One day, a friend alerted Reyes to an open position at Sony's consumer services desk, which eventually led her to editorial positions at *Ultra Game Players, Next Generation, PSM,* and *Official Dreamcast Magazine.*

Over ten years later, after being named as editor-in-chief of the U.S. *Official Xbox Magazine (OXM)*, Reyes admits she "kind of got sidetracked" from her plans to be an English professor.

Reyes' promotion from executive editor to editor-in-chief puts her at the head of the largest "official" video game magazine in the country and makes her the only woman currently serving at the top editorial spot for a U.S. game magazine. Previous *OXM* EIC Rob Smith will become associate publisher for Future USA, taking with him some of the more business-focused responsibilities previously belonging to the editor-in-chief, Reyes says.

Reyes says the promotion doesn't represent a drastic change in her job responsibilities, but it is quite different from the days when she could do five or six reviews for a magazine in a month.

"As you move up the food chain, you get a lot busier and you're a lot more hands off," Reyes says. "You have responsibilities that take you away from your desk. The onus is on you to make sure you still have that connection to the games. It's tough, it's a balancing act."

Even as one of the rare women to head a major video game magazine, Reyes says she's "always kind of nervous to speak as the representative for half the population." Reyes says her gender might bring some new perspectives to the magazine, but it's not an overwhelming part of her editorial voice. "It doesn't inform every decision I make," Reyes says. "My gender is my gender."

In her experience, Reyes says she hasn't run into any real adversity as a woman trying to break into the overwhelmingly male field of game journalism. She attributes the proportional lack of women writing about games to a lack of women who view writing about games as a viable choice for a career.

Reyes speculates that the ranks of qualified female applicants to gaming magazines will start to increase as the girls who grew up in the PlayStation generation start to see other women in higher editorial positions, like hers. "With gaming permeating every aspect of of pop culture these days, this generation of gamers—females, males, young, old—they'll be entering media without ties to how it was done before," she says.

Many assume that working for an official magazine brings with it many benefits and constraints of cozy access with the hardware maker. But besides the ability to have a demo disc, Reyes says working for an "official" magazine is not that different from working for any other magazine. The biggest difference, Reyes says, is in the readers' perceptions.

"It goes both ways," she says. "Some people see 'official' and think that means it's automatically true. On the flipside, a lot of people think everything you have to say is biased." Reyes thinks that most readers are savvy enough to understand that their editorial is independent, adding that the scores the *OXM* staff gives games are tough enough to show they aren't in Microsoft's pocket.

> *Some people see 'official' and think that means it's automatically true. On the flipside, a lot of people think everything you have to say is biased.*

As for the demo disc, Reyes says she "wouldn't be surprised" to hear that some people buy the magazine just for the demos, and she wouldn't be hurt either. "[The demo disc is] a tangible thing. It lets you play the games right then and there. You don't have to read about them. I'm not doubting [the appeal of that]," Reyes says. "My hope is that the editorial is compelling enough that people would buy on its own. It's a package, the disc and the magazine."

Reyes acknowledges that, in some areas, magazines these days face tough competition from the Internet. "We're going to have to figure out a way to refocus," Reyes says. "Online will always have 24/7 news feed... print magazines will have to find a way to be more creative in how we cover games by filtering out all the noise and giving the gamers what really matters to them."

Still, Reyes is confident that printed coverage of video games isn't going anywhere. "In ten years, there will still be game magazines," she says. "It's hard to replace the actual tangible feeling of having a magazine."

Whether or not game magazines continue, Reyes says she has no idea where she'll be in a decade's time. "If you asked me ten years ago [where I would be today], I never would have picked this," she says. "It's a day-to-day thing. I don't want to dominate the world. I just want to have fun, write good stuff, and make a good magazine."

Mind the Gap

Originally published on GameDaily, Feb. 8, 2007

In a review of the 2005 box office bomb *Bewitched,* Roger Ebert off-handedly mentions that he watches over 500 movies a year. The admission was by way of explanation for Ebert's lack of knowledge of the TV sitcom of the same name. When you spend hundreds of hours in front of a movie screen in the course of your work, Ebert explains, you devote your free time to "more human pursuits" rather than TV sitcoms or sports teams and the like.

This throwaway quote in a throwaway movie review has stuck with me, and helped me realize the utter futility of trying to have a truly comprehensive grip on video gaming as a medium. While a movie critic can easily watch hundreds of movies a year—keeping up with the major releases and finding new appreciation for the classics in the process—video games tend to demand a more significant time commitment.

While a new movie, CD, or TV episode usually takes only an hour or two to complete, video games can routinely eat up

AUTHOR'S NOTE

If anything, the problems of breadth described in this article have only gotten worse in recent years, as the number of commercial and experimental game releases has exploded. A critic that spends 40 hours a week simply playing games—a second full time job on top of the writing and other responsibilities—would be lucky to finish a few hundred of the thousands and thousands of titles released every year.

Only a small handful of a year's releases probably count as "must play" titles for a knowledgeable critic, of course. But curating your own playlist to focus on these important games is an important skill that game critics have to learn if they want to maintain any semblance of an outside life.

For another perspective on this problem, see "Sipping from the Fire Hose" elsewhere in this book.

dozens of hours before the player reaches "the end" (if there even is a "the end"). Assuming a very conservative average of five hours each, completing 500 games would take up over 312 eight-hour days. Don't worry though, you could crank the gameplay out in 108 days if you didn't stop for other activities like eating and sleeping. Even then, you'd still have barely made a dent in the thousand or so commercial games released in an average year these days.

Given the near-impossible task of playing everything, practically any video game journalist is bound to have some major gaps in their play experience. *Wired* columnist Clive Thompson put this issue front and center when he recently admitted to having never played a single *Final Fantasy* game before picking up *Final Fantasy XII*. Thompson's mea culpa made me wonder: what other major games or series have other game journalists neglected, and how did they deal with the gaps in the course of their jobs?

WHAT DID I MISS?

In an informal poll of a large group of game journalists, I found only a few who were cocky enough to declare that they had no significant gaming gaps whatsoever. *Game Informer* Editor-in-chief Andy McNamara said he didn't feel like he missed anything in gaming because he "spends most of my waking hours in some video game or another... if anything, I need to spend more time with my wife and dog." GameDaily's own PC Editor Steven Wong came close to the same declaration, saying he had "played just about every big PC title out there to a reasonable degree ... I'm not sure what the amount of time I spend gaming actually says about me as a person, but I like being informed about what's out there." Other journalists may have shared these sentiments, but they were probably too busy playing games to get back to me by press time.

Many journalists that responded to my inquiry found they just didn't have the time to really get into certain epic games. CMP's Simon Carless lamented that he'd probably "have to take a holiday" to put aside his current pile of games and finally get through *Twilight Princess.* GameDaily's Robert Workman is waiting for "a lazy summer day" to finally give *Oblivion* another go.

Others find deadline and life pressures prevent them from finishing many games. "Doing game reviews on a weekly basis usually means not finishing a game," said Harrisburg (Pa.) *Patriot News* game reviewer Chris Mautner, adding that free-time game playing "often competes with things like family, housework, getting drunk, etc."

World of Warcraft was a surprisingly common omission from many journalist's playlists, given its popularity among millions of registered players. *St. Petersburg Times* game reviewer and blogger Josh Korr resisted the game's immense popularity because "for everything I've read about *WoW,* nobody has satisfactorily explained what's so great about it."

Denver Post game columnist Dave Thomas was put off by "the bleary eyes of *WoW* players as they try to turn their endless hours of grind into some interesting conversation." But some are not so strong—Gamasutra podcast host Tom Kim finally decided to stop being "that guy who doesn't play *World of Warcraft*" among his friends because, as he puts it, "there comes a point where, due to critical mass, certain things become nigh unavoidable."

Some gaming gaps come about because journalists missed out on the games when they were impressionable kids with too much free time. *Computer Games* Editor-in-chief Steve Bauman sees his childhood without a Nintendo-made system as somewhat beneficial. "This helps me to look at the company with a bit more of a critical eye than those who seem to treat the company with kid gloves and parrot everything it says," he said.

Freelancer Gus Mastrapa was unfortunate enough to grow up in "one of those backwards clans that didn't [even] get a VCR until the (very) late '80s, so I missed out on a bunch of NES and SNES classics." Destructoid Executive Editor Robert Summa admits he never developed a taste for *Final Fantasy* during his formative years because "my circle of friends growing up, that's just not the kind of games we played. We played sports games, *Mario,* and all the other classics."

Other gaming gaps come by choice. Curmudgeon Gamer's Matt Matthews notes "there are far more games out there that I want to play than games I feel I ought to play out of some misguided sense of being well-rounded. We are fortunate that the video game market is so rich that you can get lost studying the intricacies of a single genre and never run out of interesting things to see and write about."

Slashdot Games' Michael Zenke agrees, asking, "Why would I want to play 'Dragonball Z Budokai Senwhatever 2' when there are better games available? Sometimes the creative stagnation in the games industry can be a busy journalist's best friend."

> *There are far more games out there that I want to play than games I feel I ought to play out of some misguided sense of being well-rounded.*
>
> **Matt Matthews**
> **Curmudgeon Gamer**

WHADDYA KNOW?

While most game journalists admit to some major gaps in their gaming knowledge, most also suggested that it doesn't matter as much as you might think. *Electronic Gaming Monthly* Editor-in-chief Dan "Shoe" Hsu says that while all his reviewers need to have some baseline skill and familiarity with all genres, having a big team means that most any game can be reviewed by an expert in that genre. "We cater to a more hardcore audience ... [so we don't need] to explain *Final Fantasy XII* to someone who has never played it," he said.

Even journalists that tend to focus on one genre can get away with having a few gaps in their area of expertise. Freelancer and self-described strategy game expert Troy Goodfellow doesn't feel too bad about never having played ultra-popular RTS *Total Annihilation* because, he says, it didn't really influence the games that came after it. "You can be well versed in the evolution of the RTS and still skip a major title since the most important games remain *Starcraft, Age of Empires* and *Warcraft*... Very few games, I think, fit in the 'Professional Duty to Play' category."

Indeed, while an extensive playlist helps, a game journalist can probably get by with a deep understanding of just a few key titles in the vast gaming canon. Mautner probably put it best: "Being a good writer, being insightful, having a unique point of view... these are more valuable traits to me than merely being a video game know-it-all. Being knowledgeable is not necessarily a prerequisite to being a good critic."

Meet the Game Press: Bill Kunkel

Originally published on GameDaily, March 1, 2007

Video games as a medium are so young that describing anyone as a "grandfather" of the industry comes off as a little bit of a misnomer. That being said, Bill Kunkel is unquestionably the grandfather of video game journalism. After writing the first regular American game review column for *Video* magazine in the late '70s,

he helped start the first American consumer magazine for gaming, *Electronic Games,* in 1981.

Kunkel has meandered a bit since those days, writing for comics and wrestling magazines, and even working as a game developer and design consultant for a time. But he's always come back to game journalism, bouncing between a variety of print and online outlets before recently becoming the editor-in-chief of *Tips & Tricks* magazine starting with the January 2007 issue. I caught up with Kunkel at his Michigan home and talked to him about his career, his new magazine, and his thoughts on the industry. Here are some highlights of our conversation.

ON THE INTERNET'S IMPACT ON GAME JOURNALISM

"They like to say 9/11 changed everything. Well, the Internet changed everything for game journalism. In the '80s right through the '90s it was all about the magazines, they held sway completely. Once the Internet got established, basically magazines started dying because so much of game journalism had become about news—the signing, the specs for the next generation system that hasn't come out in Japan yet. That kind of obsession—everything here is kind of OK and boring, but everything that's coming is infinitely more exciting—when you get readers conditioned to think that's what it's all about, magazines don't stand a chance in hell against the Internet."

> *Love of the game is never enough. ... People can tell you they like something or they don't like something, but it's very rare they can tell you why.*
>
> **Bill Kunkel**

ON THE CHANGING FACE OF
TIPS & TRICKS MAGAZINE

"With *Tips & Tricks,* we're trying things that nobody else has tried. We're doing a magazine that has traditionally been exclusively about strategy—either extended strategy guides or cheat codes—and we're adding our own lifestyle content to it. Lots of columns covering everything from game-based movies, music in games, to columns on things like *World of Warcraft* and feature articles.

"The major problem that we've had is that, up until the January issue, we didn't have an email address. Right away, that turns off computer literate readers. I felt we had to re-establish our credibility, give them a reason to contact us by email. Only 10- and 11-year-olds actually sit down and take out a lined notebook and write letters to comment. They would get a lot of them, but as a result our top demographic was hitting like twelve years old... It's been a process of basically trying to attract new readers.

"It used to be up to half the back of the book would be cheat codes... I'd like for this to be a magazine that someone who has no interest in any of the three games being strategized in-depth could still pick it up and find enough content in it to make it an interesting read for them."

ON THE USEFULNESS OF PRINTED STRATEGY VS. THE INTERNET

"Let's say I want strategy for *Virtua Fighter 5.* Do I want to go to GameFAQs which is gonna have 20 strategy guides in ASCII, unedited, written by god-knows-who, or would I rather have one that was correct, that had nice pictures, that had maps, that used streaming video to show people rather than tell people. With the web, it's like a quantity over quality issue. I'd rather have one good guide than 20 done by chimpanzees."

ADVICE FOR JOURNALISTS JUST STARTING THEIR CAREERS

"Love of the game is never enough. ... People can tell you they like something or they don't like something, but it's very rare they can tell you why. When young writers come up to me and say, 'I want to get into game journalism, what should I do,' well, the fact that they tell me they want to get into game journalism means they're obviously interested in games. Well, everybody else here is interested in games, too. How about the journalism end. Study journalism, learn the rules, learn how to proofread, learn how to do research. Search engines are one of the most marvelous gifts given to writers, and so few know how to use them."

AUTHOR'S NOTE

This interview was conducted during the era when the ESA was scaling back E3 and the future of the annual trade show seemed in doubt.

ON THE POST-E3 CONFERENCE SCENE

"Eventually you're going to see the model of the auto show and the boat show, where game shows are being put on regionally, around the country. They don't all get the big guys—nobody gets Microsoft, Sony, Nintendo, EA—but maybe you get one or two of them.

"I think the biggest problem is the fact that these shows have been hidden from the public for so long. You've had these gigantic events for the media, and for the game companies the booths were becoming more and more expensive. If you were a smaller publisher you got sent off to the Warsaw ghetto of Kentia Hall, which had really become a joke in the last year.

"If there is [another single, dominant show like E3] it will have to be open to the public. When all three hardware companies tell you 'this doesn't work for us,' that pretty much settles the issue... It's a pain in the ass for journalists, but the industry isn't really designed to make the journalists happy, it's designed to make the consumers happy."

ON JUNKETS AND THE VALUE OF PR

"The danger of the junket has always been that you have impressionable young writers going out to visit people who are like mythological beings to them. When these people interact with them and pretend to bond with them and start showing them sketches and stuff, it's very, very difficult to remain impartial, especially for these young writers who are not trained journalists, who don't know it's supposed to be adversarial.

Of course you smile and you shake their hand, but you have to be looking for the hard questions. I don't care whether you're paid to get there or not, if you're going to be influenced by that, you're going to be influenced by that."

ON WORKING IN THE INDUSTRY

"In wrestling, you hear it all the time: 'Until you've been in the ring, you don't know what it's like. You can't criticize.' Bullshit. I know a good match when I see it and I know a bad match when I see it because I've been watching since I was six.

"[That said,] if you're writing about wrestling and you do have a chance to get in the ring, you should definitely take it. You don't have to have had cancer to cure cancer... but it certainly can't hurt you. Just about anything you can do to make money in this industry I've done, except programming, and every one of those elements, I believe, has made me a better game writer."

ON HIS CAREER ARC

"I know how lucky I am. I know there are not a lot of 56-year-old writers in this business that are getting phone calls. I could easily work on a film magazine, a children's magazine, almost any magazine, but in the games business there's this assumption that once you hit 30, it's all downhill from there, you can't understand what makes a good game anymore.

"Writers retire when they get buried... As long as I can keep playing games, as long as I can keep writing, what's to retire? I'm having a ball. I have no desire to spend my days watching the TV shows I've recorded on Tivo. It's a nice break at the end of the day, but day in, day out, I'm much happier working."

Meet the Game Press: Steve Bauman

Originally published on GameDaily, March 22, 2007

Until recently, I knew *Computer Games* Editor-in-chief Steve Bauman chiefly through a series of somewhat spirited debates conducted through comment threads on my Video Game Media Watch blog. Through these debates I got to know Bauman as a devoted, opinionated, and intelligent journalist and a great guy to have arguing the other side of an issue.

I didn't actually meet Bauman face-to-face until the last day of this year's Game Developers Conference, where we continued our spirited debating without delay. Little did I know Bauman would get a phone call later that day letting him know the magazine he'd worked at full time since October of 1994 was no more.

Unlike the *Official PlayStation Magazine,* which got a lot of attention for its recent shutdown (**AUTHOR'S NOTE:** *OPM* was subsequently relaunched after this piece was written) *Computer Games* and sister magazine *MMO* (previously named *Massive*) were shuttered rather unceremoniously. Rather than an official announcement, the news just sort of trickled out through forum posts, the odd quick-hit news brief and one touching online remembrance.[48] Surprisingly enough, the magazines were brought down not by declining interest in print or PC gaming, but by a costly summary judgement in an anti-spam lawsuit brought by MySpace against parent company TheGlobe.com.

I talked to Bauman via email about his career, his magazine, and the future.

ON GETTING THE NEWS

I got a phone call about it mid-day on Friday, [March 9], while at GDC. The wonderful irony about the timing is that I got the word at the tail end of the show. Had I been told two days earlier, I would have been in an ideal position to find a new job (Hello, there's a freakin' job fair there). Or at least better than I am sitting in my apartment collecting unemployment and sending out resumes.

I was a little numb, but I wasn't shocked. A part of me was surprised we lasted as long as we did. On a personal and career level, I'll probably regret sticking it out this long. I loved my job, but unlike others at the magazine, I never profited from its sale/acquisition or was paid what I was worth. But at least I got one week of severance pay—plus a few days of unpaid vacation—for my 13 years of employment. I suppose I should be thankful for that.

ON WHAT MADE *COMPUTER GAMES* MAGAZINE DIFFERENT

Most game magazines/sites use first-person a lot and I reserved its use for columns or specific features. My feeling was that while it may increase the connection readers feel to the writer, it also made it seem more anecdotal and less definitive. It's the difference between writing, "I think it's the best game ever" vs. "It's the best game ever."

I think it also had something to do with our decision to have a more serious tone than others. We didn't have silly nicknames, we didn't share details of our personal lives, we didn't put a lot of in-jokes on each page. We didn't treat everything like it was a joke, even though the issues were full of humor. We just kept everything separate.

ON CREATING *MMO* AS AN OFFLINE MAGAZINE FOCUSED ON ONLINE GAMES

It was an interesting challenge. First off, it was quarterly. This forced us to think about articles that would last for three months. But after the second issue, I realized that MMO players only want to read about their MMO. We'd assumed general interest features were the way to go, and while the ones we did got (mostly) positive responses, ones that focused on a single game—even when what was being discussed was relevant to other games— were typically criticized by players of those other games.

So, moving forward, it was obvious everyone still wanted to know more about "the next big thing" despite their lack of interest in other MMOs currently available. I hate previews myself—I'm not entirely sure why everyone wants to know everything about the games they're going to be playing, don't you ever want to be surprised?—but I'd resigned myself to figuring out new and different ways to approach them. More interviews, fewer feature lists, more detail about specific aspects of the games, simple things like that.

ON GAME MAGAZINES' UNEARNED NEGATIVE REPUTATION

A lot of people will say, "I'm not paying $4.99 for old news in a magazine." I get that—magazine are old and busted, blogs are the new hotness—but I can't tell you how many times people have given reasons they stopped reading magazines that were no longer relevant. The magazines have changed a lot, but people still perceive them as being full of fluff and old, useless content. While it's our fault that we were unable to convince them otherwise, those seekers of amazing, high-quality content should consider making some effort to actually find it. And maybe they should also consider spending a few pennies to reward those who are at least trying to produce it.

> *We didn't have silly nicknames, we didn't share details of our personal lives, we didn't put a lot of in-jokes on each page. We didn't treat everything like it was a joke, even though the issues were full of humor.*
>
> **Steve Bauman**
> **Computer Games Editor-in-chief**

I want to believe there's a market for better game writing, though most evidence points to people choosing "free and fast, regardless of quality" over "paid and slow, but good." Most people would rather have that review or news right now—even if it sucks—than wait a few days or weeks for better or more informed opinions.

And I get that. I'd rather have "fast and good" too. But those two are often at odds with each other.

ON THE CHANGING FACE OF GAME JOURNALISM

There's a lot more coverage, but there's just as much good coverage. Which is to say, there's a lot more crap out there. The coverage has gotten a lot more professional and amateurish at the same time. There are a lot more people doing amazing things, and a lot more people doing horrible things. Coverage has gotten more superficial and even more fetishistically detailed. And if you think everything is superficial now, just wait until more text—yes, even online—is replaced with video. Everyone better get started on that Zone diet and start saving up for those veneers. Why read a thousand words of text when you can watch a five-minute video?

ON THE FUTURE OF *COMPUTER GAMES* AND *MMO*

I can't mention any specifics. A few people expressed interest [in a buyout], but at least one backed out when news broke of the magazine's closure.

If given the opportunity, I'd want to continue producing the magazines. But at this point in my life, I probably couldn't take the financial hit of joining a poorly-funded startup.

Despite some of the problems we had, there was always the sense that every issue was better than the previous one. We had so many good ideas for interesting feature stories bubbling around; I'll regret not being able to work those out with our writers.

It seems contradictory to want to produce these kinds of pieces despite some of my previous comments, but I was selfish; I was producing a magazine and articles for me, ones that I dug. I hoped enough people shared my tastes.

Start Me Up

Originally published on GameDaily, April 19, 2007

"HOW DO I GET YOUR JOB?"
It's a question that any game journalist should be familiar with, and one that's not trivial to answer. Sure, it's easy enough to recite your personal career path (In my case, fansite editor to college paper game reviewer to game media critic to semi-pro blogger and freelancer). But there are so many ways into this business that looking at just one journalist's experience for guidance is a little myopic. What's more, talking to a variety of game journalists reveals some pretty big disagreements out there over exactly what it takes to make it in this business.

One thing most all game journalists agree on is the primary importance of knowing how to write well and quickly. "All the video game experience in the world doesn't mean jack if you can't put a decent sentence together," said (Harrisburg, Pa.) *Patriot-News* columnist Chris Mautner. "Being able to write coherently and effectively is worth more than your prowess at *Counter-Strike*."

What's less agreed upon is the importance of formal education in developing those skills. CNN/Money's Chris Morris said that "the best way to learn [how to craft a story] is to study English or journalism in college." Destructoid's Robert Summa also recommended that potential game journalists "get out of college with an English or journalism degree."

But others don't see a college degree as an absolute requirement. IGN Editor-in-chief Peer Schneider contends that a journalism degree is "a plus, but not as essential as a firm knowledge of—and passion for—the subject matter itself." *Wired* Associate Editor Chris Baker agreed that "you can still break into journalism without a journalism degree" by educating yourself about the ethical and professional standards of the industry.

Other journalists found that a non-journalism education helped them stand out from the crowd. "My knowledge of history and systems means that I can bring insights to the table that could bring a review or interview to life if I have the leeway to do so," said freelancer Troy Goodfellow, who holds a doctorate in political science.

Some journalists found that getting their foot in the door depended on luck as much as education or skill. Freelancer Tim Stevens said he got his first job writing Saturn reviews for a website partly because "nobody else had bothered to buy the console." *EGM* editor Crispin Boyer said he got his first job at the magazine because he was lucky enough to stumble across an ad for a job opening while waiting to cover a health department meeting for his local paper.

Others think that luck has nothing to do with it. "I don't believe in luck. I do believe in working hard and taking advantage of opportunities when they present themselves," said Gamasutra Podcast Executive Producer Tom Kim. "I believe that the recognition in the field is still ...somewhat of a meritocracy. The game journalists who work to be relevant, incisive, and entertaining will continue to maintain or grow their audience."

> With so many talented writers out there doing their things in personal blogs and smallish sites, it seems you have to bring something special to the table to get noticed.
>
> **Tim Stevens**
> **Freelancer**

Lucky or not, once you do stumble across that first gig, it can be easier to get further work. "It's harder to get that first bite than it is to get nibbles afterwards," Goodfellow said. "Editors like to know that they have a stable they can rely on, and if you don't screw up whatever chance they give you, there's a good chance of it leading to future work."

Or maybe it actually gets harder after your big break. "There are too many people today who assume that getting the job is the hard part," said Morris. "There are writing gigs around, but if you don't know how to craft a story or how to listen and follow-up on questions, you won't get another assignment from that outlet."

But there are always other outlets, right? Some think the explosion of games writing on the Internet and mainstream publications has made it easier than ever to break into the field these days. "There are a lot more outlets for video game writers now," Baker said. "There may be tons of competition to write for *EGM* and GameDaily, but your hometown newspaper may be open to pitches."

But Schneider thinks that breaking in today is harder because games are "more than just the little brother of the movie biz. ... Even though the means of publishing things online have become more accessible thanks to video-sharing sites and blogs, it's tougher for a hopeful candidate to stand out as games and entertainment journalism are now much more in the public eye."

The truth is probably somewhere in the middle. Stevens probably put it best in saying that it's "definitely easier to get into the fringes of the gaming industry today" but it's also harder to get to the prestigious, well-paying jobs. "With so many talented writers out there doing their things in personal blogs and smallish sites, it seems you have to bring something special to the table to get noticed," he said.

Many journalists echoed Stevens' sentiment that being unique pays off. Schneider urged wannabe writers to "come up with unique ideas, find content niches, and do something different." Baker agreed that "people will always take notice of someone who has a strong voice, well-developed critical faculties and something original to say." Boyer encouraged writers to pitch him original ideas regardless of experience. "If you come out of nowhere and hit me with an interesting feature pitch and your writing doesn't suck, I'm more than likely to give you a shot writing for *EGM* on a freelance basis."

But more than uniqueness, in the end the key to getting a job writing about games might just be writing about games, in any capacity possible. "Writing for a tiny website won't help as much, but it's still best to get clips wherever and however you can," Morris said. "The best advice I can give anyone starting out is to just write. The more you write, the better you will get," Kim said.

Again, though, Stevens may have put it best. "When people ask me how to get started I always tell them to just get started," he said.

Going to the Dark Side

Originally published on GameDaily, May 10, 2007

AUTHOR'S NOTE

If I started counting the number of working game journalists I know personally who have moved on to game industry positions since I wrote this piece, I would quickly run out of fingers and toes. If anything, the seeming conveyor belt from observer to participant is only speeding up as the number of stable, long-term, full-time game journalist positions shrinks in the modern media rat race.

There are a handful of "lifers" in the business today that I think have the skill and drive to stick to game journalism for their entire careers (Totilo, quoted in this piece hoping for more long-term journalism career paths, is among them). Still, it's weird to be in my mid-thirties, with just over a decade of full-time experience in the game journalism business, and feel like I'm one of the few over-the-hill "old timers" that hasn't moved on to doing something else.

"THEY'RE DROPPING LIKE FLIES."

That was my immediate reaction when I heard that IGN's Doug Perry, GameSpot's Curt Feldman, and 1UP's Luke Smith were all quitting the game journalism business to go on to work in the larger game industry. Add in the recent high-profile departure of GameSpot Editor-in-chief Greg Kasavin and we've got a veritable game journalist exodus on our hands.

Of course, this is just the latest wave in a trend that's nearly as old as game journalism itself. Bill Kunkel, America's original game journalist, has bounced back and forth between game development and game journalism throughout his career. "Working as a game journalist was a massive help in terms of game design because, unlike most developers, we got to see every game that came out," Kunkel said. "That perspective is invaluable—you know what works, what doesn't and you don't have to reinvent the wheel."

Other journalists that have made the jump agree that journalism experience helps in the game-making world. Former *Game Informer* editor Lisa Mason said reviewing games was "basically on-the-job training [for a development position]—play a ton of games, talk about them to death, and explain to other people why the title in question was successful or not." She describes her current designer job at Destineer as the same process, just backwards: "I imagine the game, plan it out, and try to figure out where it could go wrong."

Still, a journalist's understanding of the industry is often incomplete. "I probably learned more about the game industry in three weeks of making games than in six years at Future," said Chris Charla, who worked at *Next Generation* and other Future magazines for four years before becoming a developer at Digital Eclipse. "I learned a lot more about the nuts and bolts and that was really satisfying to learn."

With all the cross-pollination, it's easy to picture game journalists using their positions as temporary stepping stones into the larger industry. There's some truth to the impression. "I wanted to get into development at some point, I think most professional game journalists do," said Greg Sewart, who worked at *Electronic Gaming Monthly* for four years before joining developer Vicious Cycle in 2003. "The thing to remember is that, especially in the old days, game journalism was pretty easy to get into without a lot of schooling or even that much experience, so it was a great place to build up your stock and become a known commodity," he said.

Others agreed with the journalism-as-education sentiment. "I wanted to transition from games as a lifelong hobby to games as a career, and I knew that writing about games would give me lots of opportunity to learn," said Vladmir Cole, a former Joystiq blogger who went to work at Microsoft this year.

Others see the move to the industry more as a convenient out than a lifelong goal. "I think most people who get into games journalism realize that if they make good contacts and friends, going into development is going to be an option at some point," Charla said. "But most of the journalists I know are pretty passionate about the journalism part of it, so I wouldn't say everyone has a secret plan. I don't think people with good career planning skills do anything related to games in the first place so I don't see secret machinations there."

> *I probably learned more about the game industry in three weeks of making games than in six years at Future.*
>
> **Chris Charla**

Others are a little more irked over losing skilled writers to the so-called dark side. "Talented reporters taking jobs in the fields they cover is nothing new, but it seems to happen so often, with so many of gaming's brightest reporters and critics, that I can't help but feel a reflex reaction against it," said MTV game columnist Stephen Totilo. "I ... cheer for the day when writing about games will be a rewarding enough experience— creatively, personally, and financially—that more people will be able to stick with it."

Oddly enough, many former journalists who made the transition to development said they did find writing about games extremely rewarding. "I was really spoiled working at

Next Gen. It was such a great job, it was difficult to think of anything else I would want to do in game journalism," Charla said. Still, staying in one place for too long has its hazards. "I think you run the risk of getting stuck in a rut, unless you are a very special kind of person, and I'm not that special."

Long-time critics also often find a desire to prove that they can create art as well as they cut it down—just look at Roger Ebert and his brief stint as the screenplay author for *Beyond the Valley of the Dolls.* "I was at a huge, successful gaming magazine having a great time, [but joining a developer] is really putting my money where my mouth is, to use a huge cliché," Mason said. Charla agreed: "I guess in the back of my head there was always a notion of, 'put up or shut up;' that I couldn't just keep talking about games, but needed to do something about them."

And, as with any high-stakes position, there's always the issue of burn out. "My funny answer is that I ran out of adjectives," Mason said about leaving *Game Informer*. "The truthful answer is that it was always hard for me to review games... probably around the last E3 I was thinking about how fun it would be to work on something with a deadline further out than three weeks." The time constraints of journalism also figured into Charla's decision to move on. "I had a kid, and *Next Gen* was not conducive to normal working hours," he said.

But be warned; the move to development is not always a good one from a time management perspective. Sewart recalls working "crazy hours shipping the two games we were doing, hours that most hard-working game journalists would cringe at." The pressures of development pushed Sewart back to freelance journalism after just one year as a developer. "I was living with my then-wife-to-be and talking about starting a family, I just couldn't see myself doing that *and* putting in months of 80-hour weeks," he said.

Which brings up another question; can journalists-turned-developers eventually turn into journalists again? Signs point to no. "At some point, I'll write again for a public audience," Cole said. "However, pure journalism is probably a career I can't return too. I have too much fun in the industry." Mason agreed that while she'd "love to write now and again, but I'm six months into this design job and I know I totally did the right thing."

Still, coming at game journalism from development is not unheard of. Gamasutra editor Simon Carless worked at a variety of developers before landing at his current position. "I realized that I'd really always had more fun and felt more capable as a writer about games," he said. "I felt like I was just better suited, more capable, and would be happier writing about games, not making them. So I did that."

A 'Lancer's Life

Originally published on GameDaily, June 27, 2007

AUTHOR'S NOTE

If anything, the life of a game journalism freelancer has gotten even less stable in the years since this was written. The number of game-focused outlets willing and able to pay for work and the amount they're willing to pay have both generally continued to shrink as the tooth-and-nail fight for reader attention and ad dollars has gotten more and more desperate. On the bright side, at least American freelancers can get subsidized government health insurance now.

When it comes right down to it, video game journalists have a pretty awesome job. After all, we get paid to play and write about video games. We get to meet and talk to the luminaries behind those games and find out what makes them tick. We have a front row seat for the inside developments in one of the most dynamic and thrilling businesses out there today. What could be better than that?

Well, how about doing all that from home, in you pajamas, with a schedule that's set by you and you alone?

That's the life of the freelancer, journalism's journeyman. While other writers tether their time and effort to a single publication, a freelancer has no allegiance to any one outlet. Their time and effort is up for grabs to anyone willing to pay them for their ideas. Being a freelancer means never having to fight traffic, never having to wake up for that early morning office meeting, and never having to call anyone your boss.

Not that it's all wine and roses. Freelancers forgo the comforts of a steady paycheck and employee benefits for a life of uncertain stability. A freelancer's work schedule and pay scale are in constant ebb and flow, and the swings can be hard to bear. "It's generally a feast or famine situation," said freelancer Scott Steinberg. "You always have too much or too little— never just enough. Thankfully, it all evens out in the end."

When you're a freelancer, you're only as good as your last story pitch, and your last pitch is only as good as the assigning editor thinks it is. Even that's not enough sometimes, said freelancer Heather Chaplin, who focuses her work on mainstream outlets. "I've pitched stuff that my editor will love, and then when it goes up the ladder to the top top editor, who's probably 50 years old or something, he'll say, 'Hey we're not *Wired*, we don't do that kind of story," she said.

> "
> Fundamentally, sitting in a room and writing stuff down is my ideal career. I may be writing different stuff, but I could see myself doing this until I die.
>
> *Kieron Gillen*
> "

But the consensus among video game freelancers that I talked to is that the work is there, if you're willing to look for it. "The market's certainly growing, and it's easier to find work thanks to the explosion of blogs, video distribution sites and other online outlets," Steinberg said. "At the same time, there's also more competition than ever, so good luck finding steady gigs, let alone publications that pay a decent rate. Thousands of people want in, and the market's completely oversaturated."

So how do you break in? Well, once you've got a few clips to your name, the direct approach works as well as any. "The best approach is to simply say, 'Hi, I'm Blake and have written for XYX publications. Do you accept pitches for freelance articles?

If so, is there someone I can send my ninja-good ideas to?'" said freelancer Blake Snow.

Of course, it also helps to have a good idea to sell. "I really believe that editors are constantly looking for new ideas," Chaplin said. "If you send a great pitch that they find themselves reading before they close the email, they'll call you."

Getting a pitch accepted is often the easy part—pushing yourself to actually do the work can be the tough part. "I've been known to accidentally take a month off to play games or sit in the garden with my cats, and that really doesn't help thicken the wallet," said British freelancer Jim Rossignol. "I do love what I do, however, and my need to write and my desire to play games means I seldom lose focus for too long."

The lack of set hours or an out-of-home office means freelancers sometimes have trouble keeping their work life separate from their home life. Chaplin solves this problem by getting out of the house and doing her work at a writer's cooperative in her native Brooklyn. "If I start working at home, I do get a little nuts," she said. "I stop showering or getting out of my PJs, and the work never ends ... There's always the danger with freelancing that you end up just always working, and I don't like that."

Most freelancers, though, manage to cope with the inconsistent hours and solitary home office environment."You do feel your social skills atrophying when you've been deep in something for the best part of a week," said British freelancer Kieron Gillen. "There's a five minute warm-up period when you enter the pub when you try and remember how to communicate verbally."

Others feel the home office can be just as congenial as the one downtown. "If I want camaraderie, I pick up the phone, start a lazy IM conversation with a friend, send an email, wait until some industry event, or go have lunch with my wife and daughter," said Snow.

And that office camaraderie has its own problems, too. "I occasionally do a month or so full-time office work, and although I love the company of the people I work with it reminds me why I left," Rossignol said. "I'm incredibly self-sufficient, but also dangerously personable. If people are around I just want to chat and make water-cooler gossip. I'm so easily distracted that I get very little done in the office by comparison to how I work when left to my own devices."

So for all the problems—the uncertainty, the lack of benefits, the hard-to-maintain schedule—would freelancers give up their lifestyle for a full time position? Not the ones I talked to. "I suspect I'll stay a freelancer until another bright idea strikes me of what to do," Gillen said. "Fundamentally, sitting in a room and writing stuff down is my ideal career. I may be writing different stuff, but I could see myself doing this until I die." Steinberg agreed with the sentiment. "Frankly, if I wanted to be serially abused, overworked, and underappreciated, I'd just start dating again," he said.

Yes, despite all the problems, the unparallelled freedom of the freelance lifestyle is hard to give up. "One thing that sucks is you never have vacation time," Chaplin said. "But then again, I try to think of it that my whole life is kind of like a vacation—as long as I'm doing work I really like."

Pressing the Career Reset Button

Originally published on GameDaily, Nov. 30, 2007

It's taken years of hard work and a little bit of luck, but you've managed to secure a high-placed, well-respected position in your chosen profession. You've proven yourself as an expert in your field and your title and company name command respect wherever you go. As far as your career goes, your pretty close to the top of the ladder.

So what do you do next? One option is to jump off that ladder and start over again near the bottom rung.

That's what quite a few high-profile video game journalists

AUTHOR'S NOTE

Major new outlets pop up and fade away with frightening regularity in modern game journalism. All three "new" initiatives mentioned in this piece—GameTap, Crispy Gamer, and What They Play—have been defunct for years, despite major investor backing at the outset. More recently, *Rolling Stone* gave up on its major gaming vertical, Glixel, after just a couple of years.

Outside of a few seemingly perennial stalwarts (IGN, GameSpot, and *Game Informer* among them), it's hard to say for sure if any specific gaming outlet will still be around in even a few years time. A game journalist has to get used to a churn-filled life, hopping from ship to sinking ship if they want to keep working. Given that, the decisions here to give up stable positions for the uncertainty of something new seem even harder to fathom.

are doing these days—throwing away the comfort and prestige of their positions for the relative uncertainty of a new outlet. These game journalism veterans aren't making the usual jump to PR or game development, but starting over as the establishing names behind brand new editorial sites. The job is essentially the same, but the new business card is a little less wow-inducing.

"I had been at IGN since day one [and] I felt I had done all I could do from a creative standpoint," says Doug Perry, who recently ended his 11-year tenure at the online network for a new executive editor position at GameTap. "It wasn't burnout per se, but perhaps I had simply exhausted all that a human could do in that position. ... I wasn't actively looking to leave, but each year I searched internally for good reasons to come to work and be happy with that work. This year, I came up short. That's a problem. If I can't find reasons to come to work, to be excited, to tap some creative source, what's the point?"

> *Here we are with a team that's well-known and respected, but because we don't have 20 billion readers, we're just not as big of a priority as I was used to while at IGN.*
>
> **Doug Perry**

The desire for new experiences and challenges can be a strong factor in deciding to jump ship. "[I like] the idea of starting again from scratch," said John Keefer, who recently gave up an editorial director position at GameSpy to help develop a new, still-confidential gaming publication (This would turn out to be the relatively short-lived Crispy Gamer -ed.). "[I'm] taking what I learned in almost eight years and applying what we did right and what we did wrong to make another successful venture. ... It took a lot for me to even consider leaving, but in the end, I think this will be the right move for me at this point in my career."

Others credit a change in perspective as the impetus for a big move. "Part of it was being a dad," said John Davison, former Senior VP and Editorial Director at Ziff Davis. He left that senior position to start What They Play, a startup website devoted to navigating parents through the world of games and other media. "I was looking at things a little differently, as you do when you become a parent."

"For a start, I noticed that my own playing habits changed, because I was very mindful of what my kids would want to play, or see," he continued. "Both my wife and I felt it was very important to not have the kids be exposed to anything that wasn't appropriate. ... I started to notice that there were a lot of people in the industry feeling similarly, both on the media side, and also on the publishing/development side too."

For some, leaving an established site means leaving behind a lot of red tape. "I missed writing and the ability to turn on a dime to get things done," Keefer said. "Such is the nature of bigger companies. More hoops to jump through and more people to convince that ideas are sound. ... The bigger the company got, the less we were able to get done quickly. ... I have a clear picture of what I want to accomplish and a team dedicated to helping make it happen. That in itself is exciting."

Starting a new venture is also a chance to throw out the old rulebook. "There's no legacy. Starting completely fresh is a very cleansing experience," Davison said. "When you have a brand like *EGM* that has been around for nearly 20 years, there are a lot of things about it that are held dear by both the team, and the audience. The more entrenched some things are, the more difficult it can be to try and turn it completely on its head."

And starting over can also benefit your personal life. "I like my wife and want to stay with her," Perry said. "Each year at IGN

I put in more work, and my wife tracked me coming home an hour later each year. I eventually came home [at] 7:30 every night, sometimes 8 or 9 p.m., because I never felt like I got enough accomplished there."

That doesn't mean there aren't challenges to starting fresh. Establishing a new gaming site in today's crowded market is harder than ever. "There are definitely a lot more players than there were eight years ago," Keefer said. "GameSpy managed to survive the Internet bust and come out stronger, and many of the new competitors learned as well. Blog sites have added another layer of competition. The key is to find out what is right and wrong in the industry and try to correct it and not make the mistakes of the big boys."

Not being associated with one of those "big boys" can be an adjustment. "GameTap's editorial is so brand new and we launched with so little fanfare that it's taken us a while to get into people's radars," Perry said. "Here we are with a team that's well-known and respected, but because we don't have 20 billion readers, we're just not as big of a priority as I was used to while at IGN. I'm not mad about it. It's just a reality check."

But starting over doesn't mean throwing your established reputation completely out the window. "It is a bit easier starting over this time because people on the publisher and developer side know me now," Keefer said. "I can at least get them to talk to me and return my calls and invite me to events. When GameSpy started, I had no name, no reputation and had to build all that from scratch. The only thing I had going for me was strong journalistic principles and the vow to keep a promise."

So do these enterprising journalists think they'll be at their new positions years down the road? No one seems sure. "In the end, I suspect I will always be working, but I will have a ton of fun along the way," Keefer said. "While I like to dream about eight years from now, the reality is that success is a day-to-day exercise."

Some think it's pointless to even speculate about the future. "I barely look past the next two years, which, even then, are a little blurry," Perry said. "I certainly plan on being with GameTap for the foreseeable future; I don't know how long: three, five, 10 years—as long as they'll have me, really. In the end, one must constantly learn new things. And in my case, well, you know, one must try something really new every 11 years or so."

Meet the Game Press: Geoff Keighley

Originally published on GameDaily, Jan. 24, 2008

If you ever want to feel like you're not doing enough with your life, just take a look at Geoff Keighley's resume. Besides writing about games regularly for *Entertainment Weekly, Business 2.0* and *Gamefly,* Keighley also finds time to host Spike TV's weekly gaming show, *Game Head* and GameTrailers' online roundtable discussion series, *Bonus Round.* Not only that, but Keighley recently signed a "broad talent and development deal" with MTV Networks, the owners of Spike TV, to produce more on-air specials. And he hasn't even hit his 29th birthday yet!

The development deal isn't the only recent change for Keighley; his Spike TV show is being renamed *GameTrailers TV (GTTV)* after the popular game video site MTV picked up in 2005. Keighley calls the move "a rebranding as opposed to a revamp," and the new show, premiering Friday night at 1 a.m., will feature the same mix of interviews, reviews, exclusive trailers, and more that made *Game Head* a highlight. I talked to Keighley about his career, his network, and his recent appearance on Fox News. Some selected highlights from our conversation:

ON *GTTV*'S NOT-QUITE-PRIME-TIME 1 A.M. TIME SLOT

"People always say to me 'It sucks the show's on that late.' I get that, but I also think gamers are playing games at night and people are Tivoing stuff and watching online on GameTrailers and Xbox Live. To me it's not only about when it's on TV now, but a holistic approach across many platforms.

"Yes, it'd be great to have video game programming on prime time in Spike but I also think we have to grow the category and show the ratings will support it. My end game with all of this is to get to a point where all these networks want to do more video game programming, so it's not just Spike and G4 saying that we're going to do video game shows, it's getting all the major cable networks and all the networks to say that video game programming is a really important category. My hat's off to Spike for supporting it the way they are. Yes it's late night on a Friday but at least they're doing a show and they're letting me do the show I want to do."

ON THE BALANCE BETWEEN BOOSTERISM AND JOURNALISM

"That's something we think about a lot. You look at the launch specials that we've done, and they're all for major, blockbuster, AAA games. It's not like we did a launch special for *Lair* or something like that. They're very carefully selected—*Madden* and *Halo* were two of the highest rated games last year—it's not a question of if they're good or bad, it's how great are they.

The way we do these things is we put them together in a way that looks at the culture—like the *Madden* special was interviewing the players, or with *Halo*, we went around the country and met with a band like Corporeal, who are a bunch of high school kids that played the *Halo* theme at their high school talent show.

It's great to have gameplay footage and talk to the guys at Bungie, but to me, the way that you grow the category is by looking at the amazing human interest stories around these games and celebrating the culture. So it's a thing where my mom will tune in and be interested in the human interest stories around a thing like *Halo* even though she'll never pick up an energy sword and spike someone in multiplayer.

ON THE *SPIKE TV VIDEO GAME AWARDS*

"The *Video Game Awards* have been through an evolution of their own over all these years. I've become more involved with them over the past couple of years. ... I've been on the advisory panel so I think the great thing to say over the past couple of years is that the right games have won—no one's going to argue that *BioShock* shouldn't have won game of the year, right?

"The challenge is how do you make it a bigger, more mainstream show? There's attempts at comedy, there's attempts at bringing in celebrities. I think the thing that really worked for Spike last year ... we've been pushing them on the idea of world exclusives in the show. That's really what gamers care about, and we've found on *Game Head* that the world exclusive is really what matters.

"We're incredibly proud that we premiered *Call of Duty 4* for the first time last year on the show. Last year we delivered some major world exclusives inside the VGAs—eight or nine world exclusive trailers—and we got the best ratings yet for the VGAs.

Going forward, my focus is make sure we have huge world exclusive moments inside the show and the right games winning.

> *I feel people want to watch stuff and not read stuff.*
>
> **Geoff Keighley**

"I think it's cool also to have the Foo Fighters performing on an awards show about games. I don't think that hits the credibility because they're in *Rock Band* and ... if you can have the Foo Fighters appear on the show and then, right after that have the *Little Big Planet* premiere, you can appeal to a very wide audience. ... Every year it's going to get better and better."

ON THE DIFFERENCES BETWEEN WRITING FOR PRINT AND WRITING FOR TV

"I love print journalism and I love writing about games. I think it's more of a solitary experience to just write, as opposed to television which is much more collaborative—there are many more people involved, it's really a team that puts these things together. ... You can definitely be much more in-depth and longer-form in print, at least right now. At the same time, I also realize there's this huge revolution going on with video. These games look so fantastic in high definition. Look at the rise of web video—it's all the rage now.

"You remember the "Behind the Game" series that was on GameSpot—10 or 15,000 word articles? I haven't done those in a while and that's partly because I feel people want to watch stuff and not read stuff. My hope would be to look at what I did with "Behind the Games" and bring some of that to television and the web as far as in-depth documentaries and behind-the-scenes shows on games, so stay tuned on that. I love writing still and I hope I can continue to do that. It's a nice balance between TV and writing and I feel you need to do both these days to speak to the widest possible audience.

"I don't think print journalism about games is ever going away. I think it has to be that much better—it has to be really in-depth, well-researched, well-written or people aren't going to read it. A Kotaku is never going away—people are still gonna read blogs for quick updates on news and whatnot about games, but there are certain things that are more appropriate for video. I think they're going to coexist, but games are only going to start looking better and better in higher resolutions and I think gamers are going to want to experience those."

ON HIS RECENT APPEARANCE ON FOX NEWS [49] TO DISCUSS THE *MASS EFFECT* "CONTROVERSY"

"We debated whether I should do that or not. In retrospect I'm glad I went on to at least try to set the record straight. I sort of felt a little bit like I was on an Onion News Network skit or something like that. It was a little off the wall, but at least I was there to ... represent the industry in a mainstream sense.

"It's sad that that's the only way Fox News will really cover games, controversy like that. I said to them afterwards, 'I'd love to come back on and talk about a game like *Spore* or other big games coming out this year.' We'll see if they invite me back, I hope so. But it's tough, and all this TV programming about games, I hope some of it is going to change the perception of the industry among the mainstream and grow this category, because I want to see more great coverage of games."

Love in the Time of Game Journalism

Originally published on GameDaily, Feb. 17, 2008

"You have to love what you do." It's a good rule to live by when choosing a profession, and for game journalists, it's usually not a hard tenet to follow. After all, who wouldn't love a job that pays them to play and write about games all day?

AUTHOR'S NOTE

This might seem like a gimmicky Valentine's Day pitch for a column, but I think the resulting piece showed a variety of interesting ways journalists manage a passion for games with romantic passion. Not mentioned in this story: the handful of game journalists I know who were (and often still are) involved with developers and/or PR people in the industry. Talk about taking your work home with you!

No, for most game journalists, finding a job to love is no problem. Finding a person to love? Well, that's a different story.

"I feel like when I bring up my gaming [in a dating situation] I get a little smirk or that look someone gives you when they just smile and are polite but inside they are laughing at you hysterically," said GGL's Robert Summa."Most of the time it seems girls don't really care if you're in the videogame field, but why should they? Now if I were dating a guy, wow, I'd never be lonely!"

Don't be so sure, Robert. "I always bring up my profession when dating … and the guy's reaction tells me a lot about whether or not he'd be a good match," said freelancer Leigh Alexander. "Someone who thinks of games as juvenile or non-feminine clearly doesn't share cultural touchstones with me, and so I'm not that interested in them. … However, I find it super hot if guys are real game whizzes, and bonus points if they're better than me."

For some game journalists, a common interest in gaming can end up being the key to true love. "On our first date, my future wife had opened her wallet to show me some pictures and as the pockets fell open, I spotted a GameStop discount card," said GameCritics' Brad Gallaway. "I asked her if that was from a former boyfriend and she was slightly offended, saying that it was her own and well-used, to boot. It was at that point I knew she was a serious gamer, and I was in love."

For others, that ideal match doesn't have to be a gamer, just someone who understands their devotion to gaming. "I'm a damn lucky guy," says 1UP Editorial Director Dan "Shoe" Hsu. "My girlfriend is extremely supportive of my career, understanding that, sometimes, deadline takes precedence over dinner, [and] a review game might mean no going out to the movies that weekend. [She's] always reminding me how proud she is of me."

Not all journalists can demand such unflagging respect for their profession, though. Freelancer Tim Stevens said his wife's level of support tends to depend on the game. "If it's a fun multiplayer console game she's happy to help. If it's an MMO and I'm locked in my office for days at a time click-click-clicking away ... not so much."

Getting that respect for your job can be much easier if you're willing to show that you respect your partner at least as much as your profession. As Gamasutra's Tom Kim puts it, "You can always pause the game and take a moment to aid your spouse or significant other. The game can wait. It is more important to make sure that you make your significant other aware that they are the primary focus in your life." Ideally, the love of your life should be able to echo the words of Lindsey Snow, wife of freelancer Blake Snow: "I can honestly say that since we have been married, I have never felt second to video games. Never."

Of course, it's easier for your partner to understand your obsession if he or she shares it. Most game journalists I talked to had partners that were casual gamers, enjoying the occasional platformer, puzzle game, or RPG. But there were some exceptions. "My last girlfriend was very involved in games, and was quite up on my profession," said Gamasutra's Brandon Sheffield. "She ... could beat me about 40% of the time at *Capcom vs SNK 2*, and 90% of the time at *Halo 2*. ... It was pretty much the best arrangement you could ask for as far as approval of one's profession."

But the situation can go to the other extreme as well. "[My wife] Trish is very supportive of what I do, but she really dislikes video games, which makes her support all the more wonderful," said Kotaku's Brian Crecente. "I tried early on in our relationship to see if she'd like a game. She enjoyed *SimCity* for about a day, but loathed the original *Sims* so much because of the constant crying of her Sim. She didn't even take a liking to *Brain Age* or the Wii."

Recently, though, Crecente has noticed his wife's non-gaming stance wavering a bit. "I was playing *Super Mario Galaxy* with our son riding shotgun on the second remote and she actually sat down to watch us play. She later confessed that she thought the game was really cute and now spends time occasionally watching us play. ... I can't believe my Wife-o-meter is finally registering some movement."

Even if your significant other isn't a gamer, they can still be helpful foil for your writing. "It is actually quite nice to have someone who isn't directly involved in the industry to act as a sounding board," said Gamaustra's Kim. "If she responds positively to my story pitches, then I know I have something."

> *Someone who thinks of games as juvenile or non-feminine clearly doesn't share cultural touchstones with me, and so I'm not that interested in them.*
>
> **Leigh Alexander**
> **Freelancer**

Josh Korr, formerly a game columnist for the *St. Petersburg Times,* agreed. "[My fiancee] is not as immersed in gaming as I am, but neither is the average *St. Petersburg Times* reader, so I feel like her response to a game is a good gauge of how a non-serious gamer might respond. ... After watching inert aliens and humans talk back and forth for 10 minutes in *Mass Effect,* she asked, 'Is this fun for you?'"

Of course, if your partner is a gamer, it's always nice to have someone to offer a more informed dissenting opinion. "It's often refreshing to get the perspective of someone who hasn't been-there, done-everything," Gallaway said. "One thing that occurs quite often is that we'll both play the same game and have wildly different takes on it primarily due to our different experience levels. Something that may be a clone of five other games I've tried will be fresh and interesting for her if it's in the genre she hasn't seen much of."

And if you're really lucky, that differing opinion will come from someone who not only shares your hobby, but your profession as well. "Having a significant other who's also a game writer, it's hard not to take his opinion into consideration," said freelancer Bonnie Ruberg, fiancee of Joystiq's Scott Jon Seigel. "Sometimes, of course, we'll play the same game, and I'll say, 'Wow, that was really unoriginal and confusingly presented,' or whatever, and he'll say something like, 'No way, I totally enjoyed that game since it had a lot of classic elements.' Of course, I'm going to write what I think, but there's always that Scott voice in the back of my head."

Meet the Game Press: Ben 'Yahtzee' Croshaw

Originally Published on GameSpot, March 21, 2008

Usually, it takes years of work and hundreds of bylines for most game reviewers to reach the point where they even start to get noticed by the average gamer. British-born, Australia-residing author, humorist, and game designer Ben "Yahtzee" Croshaw got there virtually overnight. Since launching on Internet magazine The Escapist last August, his Zero Punctuation series of animated video reviews has gained a massive following for its rapid-fire delivery and razor-sharp send-ups of such games as *Medal of Honor: Airborne, Halo 3, Guitar Hero III,* and, most recently, *Turok.* He also runs his own blog, Fully Ramblomatic.

Last month, Croshaw's web celebrity was given a bit more official recognition at the 2008 Game Developers Conference, where he was commissioned to do both a series of comedic shorts for the Game Developers Choice Awards and a typically motor-mouthed recap of *BioShock* for 2K Boston head Ken Levine's keynote.

AUTHOR'S NOTE

It's hard to think of a creator that has had a bigger influence on the last ten years of game-focused videos than Croshaw. From the rapid-fire delivery to the pithy, acerbic humor to the withering world-weariness, you can see elements of Zero Punctuation in most of today's Twitch and YouTube stars.

Despite the up-and-down-and-up fate of The Escapist itself, Croshaw has continued to put his weekly Zero Punctuation reviews on the site for the past ten years, diligently sticking with the formula and persona he created and perfected. Outside of Penny Arcade, it's hard to think of any singular voice in gaming that has remained as popular for quite as long.

I chatted with Croshaw via email about how he got started, his rise to fame, and what he thinks of the state of game journalism today.

PressSpotting: How did you come up with the idea of Zero Punctuation? How did The Escapist discover you?

Ben Croshaw: I'd been watching a lot of YouTube videos at the time and the idea occurred to make a video using no actual video-making equipment, with just still images and narration. The fast-talking thing came out kind of by accident. I'd recorded the voice in what I thought was a normal way, but when everyone commented on how fast it was, I deliberately kept that going in future reviews.

The Escapist discovered me on YouTube, as everyone else discovered me, and were the first of many organizations to offer me a contract. I went with them because they were the first and I had no idea I'd be so sought-after, but on reflection, I lucked out. The Escapist are good people.

PS: Are you surprised by how big Zero Punctuation has gotten so quickly? What do you think is the key to the appeal?

BC: I think the appeal lies in firstly that they're funny, and secondly because, as well as being funny, I genuinely try to make valid points. When you're trying to get a point across, humor is always a good midwife, as most political cartoonists would tell you.

PS: Whose reviews do you enjoy? What do you look for in a review?

BC: Growing up, I read a lot of game reviews in magazines, especially the British magazine *PC Zone,* and I found I always preferred reading the negative reviews because they tended to be funnier. So I enjoy reviews that do the same thing I do, I guess—humour and negativity. One of my favourite writers from *PC Zone,* Charlie Brooker, now has his own TV show which I've been watching diligently (and has since gone on to create the Channel 4/Netflix hit *Black Mirror* -ed.), and he's probably my biggest influence. As for Internet reviewers, my personal favourite is Noah Antwiler of Spoony Experiment. I challenge you to not enjoy his video review of *The Thing.*

PS: Your reviews tend to put a lot of focus on the annoying and/or just-plain-bad bits of games. Do you think the games press in general goes too easy on games? Are they just writing for a different audience than you are?

BC: I do think there is a tendency for most gaming press to go easy, especially on big-name titles, because I think there's a feeling that ensuring the success of really popular games helps the industry as a whole. I seem to remember growing up that whenever a console was dying out, the associated magazines would always start awarding the few remaining games with bigger and bigger scores... My own position is that we're living in the early days of a new art form, and that the cruellest possible thing you can do to an artist is tell them their work is perfect when it isn't.

PS: Being of England and Australia yourself, do you notice any differences between the American and foreign games press?

BC: There's definitely more of an emphasis on humor in English and Australian gaming media. *PC Zone* was generally big on this.

> *I do think there is a tendency for most gaming press to go easy, especially on big-name titles, because I think there's a feeling that ensuring the success of really popular games helps the industry as a whole.*
>
> Ben "Yahtzee" Croshaw

PS: Do you think developing your own games makes you a stronger reviewer?

BC: I think so. As a designer myself, I have very clear ideas on what makes a game fun, and the ideal balance of story and gameplay. I tend to review gameplay design more than any other aspect, with original storytelling coming in second. I'm rarely one to be impressed by cool physics or amazing graphics (*Crysis* review notwithstanding) when the game is not essentially fun to play.

PS: What are your thoughts on the state of humor in the video game media, specifically in other game review videos found online?

BC: The trouble with the video game media is that it's mostly on the Internet, which has no quality control. Gaming humor on the Internet usually means gaming webcomics. And Penny Arcade is the only good gaming webcomic. Everything else is a rip-off of PA or just plain rubbish. Ctrl-Alt-Del is the Rubbish King, sitting proudly on a throne of rotting meat. As for other game review videos, I've already mentioned that Noah Antwiler is good, but I've been unimpressed by the other really popular ones. I watched one Angry Video Game Nerd once and that was enough for me, thank you. This is starting to sound really arrogant, isn't it?

PS: You've done a lot of written reviews on your personal site. Do you prefer straight writing or the video format, and why?

BC: They're actually very much alike, because Zero Punctuation has to start out as a straight written script before I can start animating it. A lot of my written reviews could probably pass for Zero Punctuation if I read it out loud and made funny pictures come up. So I guess I prefer straight writing to making videos, if only because it's less work.

PS: Is online video going to kill plain, written game journalism?

BC: Well, it's easier, more convenient and free, so it'll almost certainly kill print game journalism, if it hasn't already. As for online written game journalism, I have no idea. Maybe if everyone forgets how to read, which considering kids these days, is a possibility I wouldn't totally discount.

Meet the Game Press: Stephen Totilo

Originally published on GameSpot, May 9, 2008

In a previous life, Stephen Totilo helped create *Hogan Knows Best.*

Seriously.

It may seem odd to think about it now, but before he became MTV News' first full-time video game reporter, Totilo was one of the people behind the idea

for the pro-wrestler-based reality show. After his departure from the project nearly three years ago, the VH1 series was a modest hit, running from 2005 to 2007.

Despite the allure of pro-wrestler-based reality TV, Totilo wasn't destined to let his Columbia journalism degree go to waste. He parlayed brief positions at *Newsweek* and *Brill's Content* into freelance game reporting gigs for GameSpy, IGN, and *The New York Times.* Now, Totilo heads up a team that covers games on MTV's cable networks, MTVNews.com, and MTV's Multiplayer blog. PressSpotting talked with Totilo about his experience writing about games and what it means to be a game journalist today. Here are some excerpts from our lengthy conversation:

ON VIDEO GAME COVERAGE IN THE MAINSTREAM PRESS

"I really hope that other outlets see what MTV News has done and take inspiration from that and also recognize that [video games] are something that should be taken seriously. I think we're seeing other mainstream outlets moving beyond just the scare stories, and it's certainly about time that happened.

"But it's just so hard for people to parachute in to talk about video games. You really have to be playing them regularly, you have to know what really matters. What I'd like to see is other news divisions out there that cover games to step up and have somebody covering games full time, not just somebody they bring in from the outside... If you're looking at any outlet that covers entertainment news already, I think they need to get with the times and accept and understand that video games are a huge part of people's entertainment diet."

ON THE PROPER ROLE FOR A GAME JOURNALIST

"A lot of people do look at games journalism and say, 'Oh what's the point, it's just for frustrated, failed creators who can't create a movie or book or a game so they're just writing about or blogging about it.' Gaming journalism *could* be just that, but if it is just gonna be that, then why bother?

"If Luke Smith was right and gaming journalists, by and large, are just middlemen that can be replaced by company bloggers, then yeah, any game journalist that can be replaced should just quit right now, because there is no point. But I think there is a point if you take the reporting you're doing seriously and say, 'Hey, we as outsiders to this whole gaming industry have the ability and the license to probe and ask questions to figure out what's really going on and to get to the bottom of things and change the conversation from the marketing-driven factors of gaming.'"

ON THE RISE OF "SERIOUS" REPORTING ON GAMES

"What I'm hopeful for is that more gamers demonstrate that they're into reporting. I get a little dismayed when I see a great story ... that then doesn't get the pickup that I think it deserves. Because it's entertainment journalism, what's come first in gaming journalism has been the entertainment aspect of it, more than the journalism aspect of it. Things like Top 10 lists ... are extremely entertaining—you can't help but gawk at it to see what's going on, those things really draw people in. So if you write a thing that's 1,000 words with no numbers next to any of the paragraphs, that's instead a full-reported piece, it's a harder sell. You hope to be able to build up your readership by doing things that people are going to find compelling and interesting."

> *I'd just love to see a sign that more game journalists are happy and capable and comfortable being outsiders, and that they could afford to do that both financially and motivationally.*
>
> *Stephen Totilo*

ON THE GAMES PRESS' OBSESSION WITH THE CONSOLE WARS

"A lot of people tend to focus on the horse race between the consoles. People love following that. The way that a lot of the gaming media is consumed is sort of how sports media is consumed. People kind of have their favorite teams and love to kind of argue about their favorite teams. A lot of people only have one console, so they want to know if their consoles fortunes are up or down today, compared to the others. It's easy to kind of fall into that sports cheering or tribal mode of following video games. ... If you follow sports, you know ultimately it doesn't really matter in your life who wins and who loses, so you accept a certain level of frivolity with it. You can't help but get caught up in the which team is better and who's winning and taking some pride in that.

"There's so much of that in the nature of being a gamer that turns you into a sports fan, that it makes it sort of tempting to cover games as if they are sports and to not look at it much more deeply than that. It's something you have to resist. You have to have the bravery as a news institution to not be freaked out if some of the hard news or feature news that you're doing is not immediately setting the world afire. I've learned first hand that if you keep doing that kind of thing you definitely build up a reputation for yourself and for your outlet, and that there are people who are looking for that kind of stuff."

ON GAME REPORTERS LEAVING FOR DEVELOPMENT

"I'm dismayed by the number of gaming reporters who go into game development. There are challenges there in terms of pay—game journalism doesn't pay all that well, so there are certain temptations to find a better-paying job—and journalism is not that easy, because every day you find a blank computer screen or an empty notebook.

"As a journalist, you're always a little bit on the outside. You always know, deep down in your gut that I don't *need* to be here, that this thing will all be fine without me. So how do I make myself useful? What do I do so that I can look in the mirror and say, 'OK, I'm not just lucky to be able to play at this stuff all day? What can I do that could be enriching to people and maybe keep some things in check or bring some things up that people didn't already know?'

"When I see people leave game journalism and go into game development, it might be like those people feeling that being an outsider isn't for them, that they might be happier being an insider. If that's truly what's best for that person, that's fine, I'd just love to see a sign that more game journalists are happy and capable and comfortable being outsiders, and that they could afford to do that both financially and motivationally."

Meet the Game Press: Dan 'Shoe' Hsu

Originally published on Crispy Gamer, Sept. 11, 2008

After starting at major game journalism publisher Ziff Davis in 1996, Dan "Shoe" Hsu rose through the ranks to serve for six years as editor-in-chief of *Electronic Gaming Monthly* before being promoted to editorial director of Ziff Davis' Game Group in 2007. So it was a bit of a shock when, in April this year, Hsu announced that he would be ending his career at Ziff Davis, with no immediate plans other than "taking some much needed time off."

Or maybe it wasn't so shocking. Even as a member of the game journalism elite, "Shoe" was one of the game press' fiercest critics, frequently using his editorial space in *EGM* to deride what he sees as an overly cozy relationship between game journalists and game publishers. It's a tradition of criticism he's continued on his Sore Thumbs blog, where he's written a series of posts revealing insider tales of some of the more sordid wheeling and dealing that goes on behind the scenes in the game press.

Despite this openness, Hsu has been reluctant to discuss the specifics of his abrupt departure from a top position in the game journalism scene—until now. In his first in-depth interview since leaving Ziff Davis, Hsu talked with Crispy

Gamer about the reasons he left, the myriad problems with the current state of game journalism and more.

Crispy Gamer: Are you ready to elaborate any further on the reasons you left Ziff Davis?

Dan Hsu: I'd say I probably have about a dozen reasons why I left. The easiest, most immediate—and safest—answer: I've been with that company for 11 out of my 12 years in the business, and it was just time for a change of pace. I needed a break, and I needed new challenges.

I guess you can also say the business itself burned me out. Working on a print magazine is hard, hard work. And a typical work scenario could look like this: I bust my ass trying to score a triple-A exclusive, I go and see the game, do interviews, spend hours writing up and polishing a story, work with the art team to design the cover and layout. Finally, I'm all beaming and proud of what we've done, and bam, people scan the contents and deliver that scoop to everywhere for free [on the Internet].

It's not about freedom of information. *EGM* is a business, and it depends on people buying the issue—not only for those cover-price dollars at newsstand, but for circulation for ad revenue. We try to do stuff the Internet does not have, but the Internet goes ahead and ruins it. It's a no-win situation, and our business has suffered for it. And then I had frustrations competing with *Game Informer*'s business model. Those guys are smart. With their GameStop connection, we just had a lot of trouble staying competitive in the circulation department.

Crispy Gamer: Can print survive in this kind of environment? Even neglecting the piracy/copyright issues, can a game magazine compete with the speed of the Internet?

Hsu: I don't think most magazines can compete, no. The Internet offers too much too quickly, and for free. I used to think I could stay competitive at *EGM* with exclusives and unique features, but realistically, anything a magazine can do, the web can do as well.

I think you'd have to have a business model like *Game Informer's* to survive, where someone is getting those magazines out to consumers at a high rate for zero perceived cost. Or perhaps you have to make the magazine a higher perceived value and make people pay more for it. We played with that idea somewhat: better paper stock; better cover stock; a lot more pages—all stuff that would make the magazine a lot pricier to produce, but we'd charge readers more for buying it. But that's a very high-risk maneuver that we couldn't afford to try at Ziff.

Maybe we should've just gone the *Maxim* route and put lots of half-naked babes all over *EGM*.

Crispy Gamer: Any more of those dozen reasons for leaving that you can talk about?

Hsu: Another reason why I left is because my new role as editorial director was a little redundant with some of the other people that were there already. Simon Cox became my boss as vice president of content, but he's a very hands-on guy, and he has a lot of ideas on how he wants to do things around there.

I started to feel a bit like a middleman or an assistant in some ways, because Simon really didn't need me—he was the head of the editorial department and he has enough experience from there. I'm sure he'd say otherwise, but really, the company didn't need both of us there running editorial. They could've used my salary for other things, like free bagels or something.

> "*Maybe we should've just gone the Maxim route and put lots of half-naked babes all over EGM.*"
>
> *Dan "Shoe" Hsu*

Crispy Gamer: What would you say is the single biggest problem in game journalism today?

Hsu: Hmm. It could be the relationship the press has with the people and companies it's covering. Everyone likes to play so nice that they forget what they're supposed to be doing in the first place. So some writers are afraid to ask the tough questions, or to criticize what should be criticized, because they're afraid of backlash from the companies from a support standpoint, from an advertising standpoint, or worse, from their own editors who don't want to piss anyone off. This may not be a blatant problem, but it's there, unspoken, hanging over everything in the industry.

Even big outlets like *EGM* feel that pressure. It's been hinted to me several times that some developers and publishers don't want to work with us because we're too tough or critical. They'd rather work with others where they feel more in "control" over the message that would be getting out. I guess that's yet another reason I needed to get out and look for a change. This shit is just too frustrating, and I'm getting a little angry just thinking about all that BS in the business we had to put up with.

Crispy Gamer: Is this the kind of problem that's inherent to all entertainment journalism, or do you feel game journalism is especially susceptible to this kind of influence?

Hsu: I haven't worked outside of games journalism, so I don't know, but I have gotten some feedback that this type of pressure happens in other niche industries, as well. But I also feel part of the problem is we're all so young as a business and industry. Movie guys, for example, have been doing this for way longer than we have, and I'd guess the average-age writer or critic there is older than on the games side.

So I would guess it's very different in other genres. I feel a lot of games journalism is still very young, both as a business and in terms of actual ages of the people working in it. Inexperience and youth are probably factors here.

Crispy Gamer: Do you see these problems getting better as game journalism (and journalists) get older?

Hsu: I think so. I think the journalism side will mature as it gets bigger and more influential. And the way the companies interact with the press will evolve with that.

Crispy Gamer: What's the biggest change you've seen in game journalism during your tenure?

Hsu: Maybe just how big it's become. I remember that when I started out, I'd be at some events where there were fewer than 10 of us in attendance, all from major enthusiast magazines. Now, even small events are picking up huge crowds, ranging from smaller fansites to the mainstream press. It's cool to see how widespread the interest is, and that the game companies are willing to support even the small guys.

Crispy Gamer: You did some work for G4 at this year's E3. How does working for TV compare to working for print?

Hsu: Oh, that was a refreshing change of pace for me, but it was way more frantic. A lot goes into preparing each show, even each individual segment. It was amazing to see how many people work there, though. I don't even think they all know each other! Print's the easiest. You can take your time and research a story; you can have down days or even down weeks. You don't have that same pressure to get that story up, trying to beat the next guy by five minutes.

The Most Important Game Critics at E3

Originally published on Crispy Gamer, May 21, 2009

In a little over a week, thousands of journalists and game critics will be among the tens of thousands of industry members descending on the Los Angeles Convention Center for the Electronic Entertainment Expo. But 29 of these critics enjoy a special position in the throng. They're the judges in the E3 Game Critics Awards (GCAs), and they're among the most important tastemakers and kingmakers on the show floor.

While the GCAs aren't directly affiliated with E3 itself, they've become the de facto independent standard for evaluating the show's hottest playable games since their start in 1998. Winning a GCA sets a game apart from the hundreds of games that come out each year, and helps drive the kind of hype and pre-release coverage that can lead to greater interest and sales when the final game eventually comes out. Indeed, winners of the GCA's 16 categories are often among the best-selling games of the year, and marketers use the "Game Critics Award Winner" badge on game advertisements and boxes as a mark of quality.

So perhaps it's no surprise that the GCA judges themselves get some special attention at the show itself. "The judges have the best access that there is," said VentureBeat's Dean Takahashi, who represented the *San Jose Mercury News* as a GCA judge for five years through 2007. "They can get into any of the behind closed doors sessions. [Before I was a judge] I got into rooms where they'd say, 'Sorry, we're only showing this to a few people.' But if you had the badge saying you're an E3 judge, they'd say, 'Oh, there's something we want to show you!'"

That special access for judges even extends to the weeks before the show, when many publishers offer judges-only access to the games that will be on display at E3 itself. For the publishers, it's a way to make sure their games get due consideration in the judging. For the lucky critics, the early access can help streamline coverage of the show itself. "Seeing the games early was incredibly helpful," said Stephen Totilo, Deputy Editor at Kotaku, who represented MTV Multiplayer as a GCA judge in 2007 and 2008. "Even the smaller E3s are a cacophony of noise squeezed into too-short meeting times. Having more time in calmer environments with any games was hugely helpful."

But some expressed discomfort about the special access judges receive. "Now we have situations where some press are allowed to see some games, while some aren't because they're not judges," said Bitmob's Dan "Shoe" Hsu, who represented *Electronic Gaming Monthly* as a GCA judge before leaving the magazine in early 2008. "How come, all of a sudden, a game's ready to be seen by the press, but only if you're a part of this special organization? That seems strange to me, and even though I like having the access, I don't think I should be treated any differently just because I have a vote in something."

The award organizers, for their part, try to remain neutral regarding who has access to what games. "The Game Critics Awards doesn't dictate what publishers show or to whom," said Rob Smith, Editor-in-chief of *PlayStation: The Official Magazine* and co-chairman of the Game Critics Awards. "Publications should be receiving preview access to E3 games based on their reach and editorial importance, not because of their membership in the Game Critics Awards."

> *I got into rooms where they'd say, 'Sorry, we're only showing this to a few people.' But if you had the badge saying you're an E3 judge, they'd say, 'Oh, there's something we want to show you!*
>
> **Dean Takahashi**
> **VentureBeat**

Indeed, some publishers open their pre-show junkets not just to judges but other prominent members of the press at their discretion. Others, like Microsoft, don't offer pre-show access at all, possibly for fear that news will leak out and limit the impact of announcements at the show itself.

But that's cold comfort to some former judges that no longer enjoy the perks that come with the position. "As a veteran freelance journalist in this industry, I was surprised at how many doors closed when it came to pre-E3 events once Geoff Keighley cut me from the judges list this year," said freelancer John Gaudiosi, who represented *The Washington Post* and *The Hollywood Reporter* for the GCAs through 2008. "I always thought the purpose of pre-E3 events was to help reporters, especially freelancers, get access to games and developers before the big show in an effort to more accurately cover the event. I know that's what I always used these previews and judges events for and they've been priceless."

(Smith said that Gaudiosi's removal from this year's GCA judges list involved a dispute with Reuters, which refused to let Gaudiosi represent them as their judge. "We sympathize with his situation, but any decision to be allowed access to pre-E3 events is explicitly that of the [game] publishers," he said. "If publishers wanted him to see their games for editorial consideration, they could have invited him.")

The judges for each year's GCAs are chosen exclusively by Smith and co-chairman Geoff Keighley, host of GameTrailersTV and executive in charge of video game publisher relations for Spike TV. Smith said the pair tries to get a single critic from each of "the major North American video game print, online, and TV outlets," a decision he says is the "most objective way to ensure that the panel accurately reflects the current makeup of the leading games media outlets."

This year's list of participating outlets[50] reads like a who's who of major mainstream and specialist outlets covering games. It's a list that's become more exclusive in recent years, though, from a high of 38 judges in 2006 to a low 29 judges this year. Much of the change is due to contraction in the video game journalism market itself. Outlets like *Electronic Gaming Monthly* and *Computer Gaming World* no longer field GCA judges because, well, they no longer exist. Some mainstream outlets like CNN/Money, *Time* and *The Washington Post* don't field judges anymore because they no longer cover games in a significant critical capacity (though, encouragingly, *The Wall Street Journal* has been added to the judge's list this year).

For the judges themselves, though, the rules for judge selection can lead to some strange situations when journalists move from outlet to outlet. Totilo and Kotaku Editor-in-chief Brian Crecente were both judges in 2008, but only one of them gets to vote now that they both work at Kotaku (Totilo says he "already miss[es] being a judge," and that "any less time I have with upcoming games and developers makes me a bit sad."). Takahashi said he went to a pre-show judges event in 2008 assuming he'd be able to get in, only to find out that he was no longer welcome after leaving the *San Jose Mercury News* for start-up VentureBeat (Takahashi said he's "disappointed I'm not on the [judge's] list, and I'll suffer for it, but I can't say anything was done unfair to me.")

There are rumblings that other organizations may be interested in setting up competing E3 awards, with voting open to a much wider audience of E3 attendees. But there is something to be said for keeping the voting in the hands of a few hand-picked critics. "Ever watch the Oscars and get upset that the movie you like didn't win best picture? The assumption often is that not enough of the Oscars judges have taken the time to watch enough eligible movies to make the best pick," Totilo said. "So they go with the movies they know. That's human nature for any judging endeavor. But the way the GCAs have been sets up helps minimize the risk that the 'wrong' games will win awards. That's done by letting the judges look at games in a wider window than the E3-week timeframe."

The Unlikeliest E3 Journalists

Originally published on Crispy Gamer, June 19, 2009

Matt Clark is a 29-year-old union staff representative and gamer from Dayton, Ohio. Like most gamers, he's always dreamed of being able to go to E3. Unlike most gamers, he actually got to live out his dream this year.

Clark was one of a handful of gamers that won the chance to help cover E3 as part of contests held by major media outlets. He earned his chance to help cover the show for 1UP.com with a tongue-in-cheek blog post that made merciless fun of his fellow entrants. At the show, Matt filed dozens of blog posts on everything from his favorite games to goofy, man-on-the-street interviews about a fake game.

Clark said he'd been following E3 closely for over a decade and considered the show "a gaming mecca." Even after years of mental preparation, though, he said he still wasn't totally prepared for his pilgrimage. "I guess I didn't anticipate the enormity of it," he said after the show. "I mean, it's just so much to take in. I felt like I had a serious ADD spaz-out the first half of the first day. Don't get me wrong, I knew it was going to be huge ... I guess I just never imagined how hard it would be to try and see everything."

Of course, seeing everything is a bit easier when you know how to use the nearly magical powers of your press pass. "It probably wasn't until the end of the second day that I realized my badge may get me past *some* lines," Clark said. "I was waiting to see *Dragon Age Origins,* and some EA guy comes up and says, 'Uh, hey....you don't have to wait in this line. We'll get you in right now.' I thought... what the fuck?"

> *I definitely have a lot more respect for game journalists after attending E3. There is so much to write about in so little time.*
>
> **Josiah Munsey**
> **Kotaku contest winner**

Clark wasn't the only contest winner to be overwhelmed by the size and spectacle of the show. "It was ... more over the top than I imagined," said Josiah Munsey, who won the chance to help cover E3 for Kotaku. "Specifically Activision's setup. All the projection screens playing at the same time and their pulsing sound was an overload."

Paradoxically, Munsey said E3's over-the-top sound and fury made him appreciate the more understated games on the show floor. "Suddenly, it becomes overly apparent that next-gen graphics are not enough to make a good game," he said. "[When] dozens of huge projections are throwing amazing graphics in your face and you have to start deciding which ones actually look fun to play." Munsey used his temporary position at Kotaku to call attention to some of those unique, fun-to-play gems, with posts on *Pixeljunk Shooter, Critter Crunch* and *Snapshot.*

Being at E3 isn't just about checking out games, though... it's also about checking out people. "The best part of the show to me was seeing [King of Kong's] Steve Weibe getting to a killscreen in real life," said Kenneth Pereira, who earned his trip to E3 courtesy of GamePro (and who filed a single preview in return). "I don't think I'll ever see that again." Munsey was also a bit starstruck at the show, and said one of the best parts of the trip was "meeting random people, like Steve Wiebe, [Twin Galaxies head referee] Walter Day, and the creator of *Critter Crunch,* Nathan Vella."

Aside from the "celebrities," just being among so many devoted gamers also made an impression on some of the contest winners. "I guess I didn't expect the sheer amount of people who were willing to just *talk about games,*" Clark said. "I know it's a trade show... but it's these people's profession. I can't count how many badass conversations I had with random people after the day was over... who seemed genuinely interested in what I thought."

Besides changing his thoughts on those in the game industry, the show also changed Clark's thoughts on game journalists. "I think most of us have grown up believing that these jobs involved playing video games all day and just fucking around," he said. "If E3 is any indication, there is a shit-ton more to this."

Munsey agreed: "I definitely have a lot more respect for game journalists after attending E3. There is so much to write about in so little time," he said. Pereira said he was surprised some journalists "just write all day and don't even spend much time on the show floor." Sorry to burst your bubble there, Kenneth...

So, with these newfound revelations about what the life of a game journalist is really like, are any of the contest winners considering a new career in the field? "Definitely," said Munsey. "I enjoy meeting the passionate people in the industry and learning about the newest advancements in new games." Pereira, for his part, thinks he belongs on the other side of the interviews. "After talking to developers, I would rather consider a career in the development side of a game," he said. "Working on a video game would be my next dream after going to E3."

For Clark, though, there's still some trepidation about the realities of following your dream. "I guess I've kind of had this sense of dread that [this year] will be the only time I get to go [to E3]," he said. "I'm 29, married, I have two kids, and I live in Ohio. At this point, I can't really *afford* to start over [as a game journalist]. Still, if I could get a few freelance pieces in, I would be a happy camper. ... If I can give it a shot, I say what the Hell? I don't have anything to lose."

Game Journalism in the Age of Trump

Originally published in The Game Beat, Nov. 18, 2016

If your fellow game journalists have seemed a bit distracted lately, I think I know why. It has nothing to do with video games. Or maybe it has something to do with video games, at least obliquely.

I'm talking about the election of Donald Trump as President of the United States of America, an event so shocking and unexpected that it's still weird for me to type it out ten days later.

Even before election night, for me personally, following the twists and turns of the campaign, and working to affect the results of that election, was more than a bit distracting (anyone who follows me on Twitter knows just how distracting). Since election night, though, it's hard not to be totally consumed just reading about the many norm-breaking and precedent-shattering (to say the least) twists and surprises to be found in the dawn of Trump's America.

Who wants to write about something as frivolous as video games when so much of import is going on in "the real world" outside? GameCritics' Brad Gallaway probably summed up the feeling

---

AUTHOR'S NOTE

This piece is about Donald Trump, but also it's not. Even during calmer political times, anyone covering games for a living has to come to terms with the fact that the job is pretty frivolous in a lot of ways. We provide important information sometimes, but often we're just providing entertainment (or even information that helps contextualize and enhance others' entertainment).

There's nothing inherently wrong with that, and there is inherent value in escapism, as many point out in this piece. But when the news outside of video games gets more serious, it can heighten the contrast between that "hard news" and the fluff that make up most of the video game press. Then again, maybe it's the serious times when people need a little harmless escapism most of all.

of many game journalists and critics in the election's wake: "my heart isn't in it right now."

Game journalists, like journalists as a whole, have a distinctly left-leaning political bent (though there are quite a few outspoken exceptions). As such, many of those journalists are taking Trump's final ascendancy particularly hard.

I've talked to game journalists from marginalized groups who feel legitimately unsafe now that Trump has been elected. I've read posts from journalists who are questioning the value of the media in general when even basic facts about Trump seem to have trouble breaking through to the voting public. I've seen journalists who usually stay publicly focused on games start to tweet and write publicly about their political opinions, presumably as a way to vent (in an environment where game critics writing about politics at all can be a somewhat controversial idea).

The naming of Steve Bannon as a senior advisor to Trump has been quite troubling for many game journalists, thanks to his association with Breitbart and that site's role in pushing the Gamergate controversy to the forefront years ago. Some journalists who were the targets of particularly virulent threats and harassment (partially driven by Breitbart's coverage) feel a somewhat understandable sense of shame and dread at what Bannon's new role means for them and the country.

There has been no shortage of think pieces trying to link the Gamergate movement to the alt-right's ultimate electoral triumph. I think this Katherine Cross Twitter thread[51] likening Gamergate to a "canary in the coal mine" for Trump's rise is one of the best takes of how much to make (or not make) of the explicit links between the two phenomena. *The Washington Post*'s Alyssa Rosenberg also has the right idea.[52] Ditto[53] for critic Nick Cappozzoli.

The election distraction also comes at a time when those in the gaming press can't really afford to be distracted. November is the peak season for the flood of holiday game releases, and this year comes with hardware like the PS4 Pro, NES Classic Edition, and Oculus Touch controllers to throw on top of an already crowded pile. For some, all that product has provided an opportunity to avoid troubling news by allowing them to put their heads down and work. Others, like Kotaku's Jason Schreier have just been "a bit frazzled" and late with normal deadlines in the wake of the news. For still others, it's all proved utterly overwhelming.

Some writers at gaming outlets sought to explicitly comfort their audiences (and themselves) in the direct aftermath of the election results. Kotaku's list of "Five Anime Pets That Almost Make Things Better, But Not Really" was written explicitly to "momentarily distract you from this national tragedy." Polygon put together a list of "comfort food" shows for depressed liberals to binge watch as they took a mental health day, stressing that "it's OK to not be OK."

More directly, Trump's election actually intersected with the world of video games in quite a few post-election pieces. Kotaku put together an interesting look at the feelings of game developers that have integrated Trump into their work. The newly launched Glixel managed to weave Trump into an appreciation of *Metal Gear Solid 2*, explicitly examining the game "in the context of a country reeling from an election which seemed to wield and dodge truth at every turn."

Then there are those who've used Trump's election as a jumping off point to reexamine the value of games and criticism as a whole. Waypoint's Austin Walker was one of the first, the day after the election, with an excellent piece on "Why We Play"[54]

> *I believe, firmly, that the way to encourage inclusivity, compassion, and equality is by shining a light on the ways that the world is already diverse and on the people who struggle in order to make it better. Whether you're reading this as a game maker, a journalist, or a player and fan, we can all contribute in that cause.*
>
> *Those of us here at Waypoint cover games in this way not only because we love and understand them, but also because we believe that games are both a reflection of and a participator in human culture. Playing is as old as people are, and games offer us ways to laugh, think, collaborate, escape, and even to give ourselves to despondency and failure, when appropriate...*
>
> *But these were, as I said, implicit statements. Today that is not enough. So let me be direct: Our aim at Waypoint is to cover games with criticality and humanity. It is to give as much attention to the people, passion, and politics of gaming as we have been giving to the products. It is to explore how and why we play, not only because trying to answer those questions will lead us to tell great stories, but because we fundamentally believe that this will offer insight into the wider "state of play," into the culture that games emerge from and that people play in.*

Jeff Grubb's subtler examination of the value of escapism in troubled times[55] is also worth a read:

> *You have no control. You are a cluster of systems cohabitating a space with the systems of other people and the physical world. The boundless number of variables that determine your second-to-second existence is incomprehensible... And that's why we play games.*

Polygon's Susanna Polo also tweeted a beautiful multi-part defense of escapism[56] last week, and moreover, a defense of analyzing escapism:

> *I believe fundamentally in escapism. I believe in its ability to soothe and distract and support. I also believe in its ability to inspire, to predict, to expand the possible. And I believe firmly in the work artists (and critics) do to expand the borders [of] what is thought to be "possible" from what is currently true.*
>
> *And I'm going to keep talking about that? Escapism has never just been about escaping our current reality, but building the next one.*

Polygon's Arthur Gies may have the most succinct summary of the need to balance escapist entertainment with political rage, though: "Anger is valuable. but it can't sustain you indefinitely. It's OK to find things you like and take a break with them."

If video games were important to experience and write about last month, they're still important to experience and write about today. As the world of politics forces itself on our attention even more in this post-election period, games and writing about games can provide both an escape from the depressing state of the world and an important way to contextualize current events.

That's always been the role of art, and of criticism. That much, at least, is not going to change in Trump's America.

Fuck You, Pay Me

Originally published in The Game Beat, April 21, 2017

Three weeks ago, I don't think I had ever heard of Brash Games. Today, I feel like I've heard way too much about them.

If you have somehow avoided the recent controversy over this British game review site, OpenCritic has a ridiculously comprehensive 12-page report [57] you can read on their various journalistic misdeeds. In short, Brash Games changes author-submitted review scores, routinely strips authors of their bylines, and quite obviously throws up submissions without even looking at them (read through this archived *Pac-Man 256* review [58] for some undeniable evidence of this). What's more, it seems they've been has been ridiculously ham-handed in trying to cover up these antics, leading to their removal from OpenCritic's listings.

Brash is also one of many game review sites out there that doesn't pay its writers, merely offering them a chance to get their names out there in exchange for their hard work (thus making the byline removal mentioned above even more significant). This fact has led to a secondary discussion in game journalism circles regarding whether or not a critic or journalist should ever write for free, especially if that means writing for someone else.

Jim Sterling represents the "never work for free" side pretty well, channeling Harlan Ellison's famous "Pay the Writer" manifesto near the end of a recent video savaging Brash Games: [59]

> *For a long time... it was seen as quite normal to work for "exposure" in games media, but the times they are a-changing, and the tolerance for this bullshit is at an all time low, especially when blogs are no longer the only and best way to get a foot in the door.*
>
> *So let me say this right now to anybody who wants to write game reviews, editorials, whatever. If you're working for a site that's not paying you, leave it. Right now. Immediately!*
>
> *If a site can't afford to pay you, it doesn't have the credibility to give you the "exposure" you're being promised. In fact, you'd be better off starting your own YouTube channel or your own blog and going it alone for all the help companies like Brash will fucking provide.*
>
> *Build your brand. Your own name. Use whatever outlet you have and make it work for you, not the other way around. Do not ever bust your ass trying to make a name for a website, because they sure as shit won't make a name for you.*
>
> *Hell, that last part is true even if you are being paid. You could be laid off any second, and you'll only have the brand you built for yourself, not the brand you built for the company, to trade on. You want to be a success in games media. Get in, get known, get the fuck out.*

In a way, this is easy for someone like Sterling to say—he's been able to parlay successful paid stints at Destructoid and The Escapist into a well-funded Patreon career, building a strong personal brand all the while. Yet before that, Sterling was also struggling to make a name for himself on Morphine Nation, a site he founded "that's been going for about three years but still can't get more than 200 unique hits a day, despite it having comics about Skeletor on it," as he put it in 2007.

As Sterling points out, though, writing "free" content for an outlet you control is pretty different from donating that content to a site controlled by somebody else. Can the latter kind of free work ever be worthwhile?

I'd like to argue that it can. Back in my college days, when I was taking my first steps into the game journalism business, I split my professional time writing for my college paper (*The Diamondback,* which paid a whopping $30 per review, at the top end), my own game journalism critique site (The Video Game Ombudsman, which paid me next-to-nothing for most of its existence), and occasional volunteer reviews for sites like GameCritics (plus a few one-off freebie pieces for many sites that have been lost to the annals of time).

While I didn't get any money from GameCritics, I did get what I consider valuable experience working with editors who cared about my writing, and interacting with a built-in, blessedly troll-free community of forum regulars who would read and comment on my work.

GameCritics had the cachet to provide free review copies of games, too, which meant a bit more back when I was a poor college student (and when review copies for $60 physical releases were a bit harder to come by than today's indie-saturated landscape). My association with GameCritics also got me into my first E3, in 2004, though at that time I probably could have semi-faked my way in through other means.

The key point here, though, is that writing for GameCritics was about more than the "exposure," which was limited in any case. It was a way to join a community of like-minded individuals, both writers and readers, who took game criticism seriously, and whom I respected long before I applied to be a volunteer critic.

Many of the writers I worked with at GameCritics have gone on to successful, fully paid careers with other outlets (hi Scott and Gene and Brad), and been useful contacts as my own career barreled forward. The published clips I could point to at GameCritics were also useful when I was trying to get work at sites that could pay me.

In short, aside from the lack of pay, GameCritics was and is about as different from Brash Games as you can get.

> *While I didn't get any money from GameCritics, I did get what I consider valuable experience working with editors who cared about my writing, and interacting with a built-in, blessedly troll-free community of forum regulars who would read and comment on my work.*

So I guess my advice is that it can be worthwhile to write for free when you're getting your start, but only if you can find your own version of what GameCritics was for me. The web isn't as conducive to harboring these kinds of unique, non-corporate sub-communities these days, but they do still exist. If you can find a small site that you feel is doing something unique and worthwhile, and if you feel like you'd get something out of being a part of that (either personally or professionally) don't let the lack of money stop you from even considering it.

But also be careful not to get stuck there, if you want to make this anything more than a hobby. After a couple of years, once I had enough clips under my belt to start attracting regular paid work, I vowed I'd never again write for free for someone else's outlet. At some point, you have to start moving forward to avoid moving backwards.

Maybe times have changed, and the best way to a career in game journalism now is becoming a cult of personality YouTuber who doesn't answer to anybody. But just because a site can't give you money doesn't mean it can't give you *anything* in exchange for your work. Nick Chester (formerly of Destructoid) put it well on Twitter: "Knowing when you're getting taking [sic] advantage of versus knowing when you're getting/being valued is important."

As with love, you should be willing to give your writing freely, but extremely careful with who you give it to for free. (Also, getting paid for it makes you a whore. These are the jokes, folks.)

Trapped in the Pre-release Bubble

Originally published in The Game Beat, April 20, 2018

Starting today, a good deal of the gaming world will start playing through Sony's new *God of War* reboot on the PS4. By diving in on launch day, these players will get to discover the game alongside millions of other players, taking part in what's sure to be overwhelming social media discourse surrounding every plot twist, artistic choice, and mechanical gameplay decision.

There is one group of gamers that will be somewhat removed from the collective discovery and discussion surrounding *God of War* this week, though. I'm talking about the reviewers (myself included) who rushed through the game in relative seclusion weeks ago, so they could write embargoed reviews that went up last week.

Getting to play big new releases before everyone else is one of the biggest perks a game critic gets. It's a perk that's often necessary for us to be able to inform our audience in time to make launch day purchase decisions. After a while, a critic gets used to playing many if not most of the biggest games ahead of the rest of the world, existing in a sort of time-shifted parallel universe where brand new games can already seem old and played out.

This isn't a natural way to experience games, or necessarily one that gives an accurate idea of how most players will enjoy them. As critics, we often miss an important part of the "regular" gaming experience when we play games in our own little pre-release bubbles.

This is explicitly true for titles with a heavy online component. When I first tested *Super Mario Maker* for review, it was in a limited pre-launch test environment with a few dozen other game journalists. I played and made some clever levels during that time, but it was barely a taste of the brilliant universe of millions of player creations (and responses) that would explode in the post-launch period.

> *We don't just play games to experience them, but to share that experience with a community that's playing alongside us.*

Similarly, my first, pre-launch experience with *Dark Souls* was hampered by the lack of an online community to leave in-game hints or invade my solitary dungeon crawl. And pre-release online deathmatches with fellow journalists and developers give a necessarily skewed view of what the competition (and server stability) will be like once a big release goes live.

Even with offline games, though, I feel early critics get a different experience from those playing after launch. Gaming is an extremely social activity, and that applies even to single-player games, where sharing parallel, contemporary play experiences with others can be a huge part of the appeal. Before writing their first review, an early critic doesn't get to share in the meme-worthy screenshots and videos, surprising glitches, never-intended gameplay strategies, and community-driven inside jokes that inevitably get discovered and spread through the Internet shortly after a game launches.

There's a reason most gamers don't just save money by playing all their games on a five-year lag, as XKCD cleverly points out.[60]

That's because the collective player culture surrounding a game often matters to the experience just as much as the software itself. That shared culture doesn't really exist before a game comes out (pre-release hype culture notwithstanding), and it often evaporates or changes significantly soon after that crucial launch period.

We don't just play games to experience them, but to share that experience with a community that's playing alongside us. For many players, being able to talk about the hot new game with others is at least as enjoyable as actually playing the hot new game itself. The people who feel this most acutely tend to be the kind of people who work towards careers where they get paid to talk about hot new games.

But for early critics, our first experience with most new games is instead an isolated one. Even when we first get to discuss a game in that launch day review, we have to be intensely worried about giving any details that could be considered spoilers for those launch day players (I'm often shocked by what innocuous gameplay or plot details some readers would consider to be spoilers). By the time we join in the wider-ranging discussion post-launch, that first review is already set in stone and our first, lonely playthrough is calcified in our memories.

All that said, critics can derive some value from playing in a bubble. I feel like I was one of the only people who got to play *The Witness* in its purest form, pre-launch, before every one of the game's dot-and-line puzzles could be solved quickly with a spoilerific online walkthrough. Sure, an average player can ignore the siren song of those easy answers and struggle through the "intended" way. But after the launch, players always have the option of cheating their way out of an extremely tricky puzzle, something that was decidedly not an option during my pre-release playthrough.

(Quick aside: Most players will never experience the exquisite agony of getting helplessly stuck in a game while faced with an impending review deadline. Normal players always have the option of consulting a strategy guide or simply giving up for a while if they get frustrated with a difficult section. Not so for your humble critics!)

Of course, early reviewers aren't completely isolated from other players. We can always lean on our fellow critics for help, for sympathy, for a sanity check on our own analyses, or just for a release valve on the thoughts we just can't hold in until the public embargo is up. There are almost always Facebook and Slack chats, email threads, and intra-office conversations among early critics that can provide a taste of the wider discussion that will surround a game after launch.

I've done this kind of pre-release kibitzing myself, but I always feel a little weird about it. Given the delicate nature of personal taste, and how malleable our reactions can be to social pressures, I worry about being exposed to other thoughts and feelings about a game before writing my own "unbiased" review. The value of playing in a vacuum, critically, is that it gives an important opportunity to figure out what you think about a game, and not just what you think about what *other people* think about a game.

(Interesting case study: the snowballing post-launch fan outcry over the ending to *Mass Effect 3*, which received more muted criticism from more isolated early critics. Were those critics just out of touch? Were the players swept up in a social frenzy of ire?)

In a lot of ways, playing a game before release is like going back to a time before the Internet revolutionized how we communicate. Instead of sharing our love of a game with the entire world at large, we're stuck playing alone in a sort of secluded basement, sharing with a small "local" community of fellow players and trading thoughts and tips in a virtual schoolyard. It can be a fun and valuable throwback, but early critics should be aware that, in many ways, they're getting an entirely different gaming experience from their audience.

THE
PRACTICAL
SIDE

Even the simplest piece of gaming journalism is the result of countless decisions, big and small, that help determine what the final result looks like. This section examines how some of those decisions get made, and how the results of those decisions impact what you read.

This section will give you a behind-the-scenes peek at how journalists deal with sources and shadowy rumors, mainstream editors who might not "get" video games as a medium, and even how we secure early review copies from companies that are more reluctant than ever to provide them. We also address with the time pressures involved with reviewing games, and get quite a few journalists to admit that, no, they didn't necessarily finish that game before reviewing it.

Half-Life 2 Debacle Shows the Perils of Pack Journalism

Originally published on Joystick101.org, June 19, 2003

AUTHOR'S NOTE

I wish I could say the situations described in this article were less recognizable after 15 years of progress in the industry. Unfortunately, too many outlets seem content to write summary stories based on the reporting of others, checking with the original sources later (if ever).

Sometimes the story is so big that it can't wait. Much of the time, though, a little bit of extra confirmation would go a long way.

On June 8, *The Puget Sound Business Journal* was the first to make note of a big "story" seemingly hiding in plain sight at the end of an innocuous article[61] about Microsoft's rising and falling Xbox fortunes. Xbox Product Manager David Hufford told the *Business Journal* that Microsoft was getting "mixed messages" from Valve about a port of the highly anticipated *Half-Life 2* for the Xbox. "As of now, *Half-Life 2* is not going to be on the Xbox," Hufford said in the quote.

It wasn't long before video game websites had picked up the scent and were linking to the story with abandon. Evil Avatar was one of the first to post it, positing mid-Sunday that Valve might be trying to get more money from Microsoft by waffling on their implied commitment. By Sunday night, Slashdot had picked it up with links back to Evil Avatar and the *PSBJ* story. By Monday morning the feeding frenzy was on, with sites from Gamerfeed to GameIndustry.biz to GameSpot and Blue's News all reporting that *Half-Life 2* would not be coming to Microsoft's console.

The full force of the video game journalism conglomerate was now on the trail of this important story, broadcasting it to an eager audience. There was only one problem...

The story wasn't true.

By Monday afternoon, sources from Valve and Vivendi Universal, the game's publisher, were coming out of the woodwork to re-confirm that *Half-Life 2* would be coming to the Xbox. GameSpyDaily was one of the first to quote Valve's Doug Lombardi as saying that "*Half-Life 2* is planned for the PC and Xbox." GameSpot posted confirmation of an Xbox version from Universal's Amy Farris just eight hours after their original story on had run. The aforementioned websites, along with many others, were quick to post follow-up stories acknowledging that Hufford's comments seemed to have no weight.

There are quite a few disturbing things about how this story shook out. The first is that *PSBJ* reporter Jeff Meisner obviously didn't realize the impact Hufford's statement would have on the business futures of both Valve and Microsoft, not to mention the futures of countless Xbox owners. Instead, Meisner buried the quote at the very end of the article and didn't bother to check Hufford's assertion with any other sources. While this is sloppy journalism, Meisner can perhaps be forgiven because he writes for a local business publication and not a specialist video game website.

The herd mentality of those specialist websites, however, is less defensible. Yes, the situation was cleared up so quickly that many readers probably missed the inaccurate original reporting. But this debacle is indicative of the larger trend of lazy link-and-quote reporting that passes for "news" on most video game sites. Rather than calling up sources and finding the news on their own, most website editors seem content to have the news spoon-fed to them from public relations managers and conventional, mainstream news sources. Kudos to GameSpot and GameSpy for actually doing the legwork to confirm the story, but these two outlets shouldn't be the rare counterexamples in a media circus that links to information first and checks it never.

Accuracy aside, link-and-quote game journalism is also limiting for the range of gaming stories out there. The link-and-quote process succeeds in that it quickly gets many important stories to gamers who might not otherwise see them. But when every site posts the same big press releases and links to the same big articles as everyone else, it becomes impossible to find the smaller, more in-depth stories that bring new information or new angles to light.

It also becomes easier for a small bit of misinformation, like that in the *PSBJ* article, to become a full-fledged juggernaut that can be hard to stop. Even the follow-up articles posted by many websites simply linked to the GameSpy or GameSpot refutations using a simple, "This site quoted this person as

> *The full force of the video game journalism conglomerate was now on the trail of this important story, broadcasting it to an eager audience. There was only one problem...*
>
> *The story wasn't true.*

saying this thing," template. This kind of journalism is lazy, sloppy and unfair to gamers who should demand more accurate, original reporting from their news outlets.

In a June 10 story, GameSpyDaily talked with David Hufford, who asserted that he "never said *Half-Life 2* wouldn't be available for Xbox," and that he had deferred the question to Valve in the original interview. Interestingly, the original PSBJ article has now been edited to say that *Half-Life 2* will be coming to the Xbox.

Evil Avatar has posted a nice summary of the drama with the apt observation that "the world may never know" whether Hufford or the *PSBJ* were in the wrong. But what is clear is that online video game journalists as a whole need to follow up on leads and check the sources behind important stories rather than settling for echoing the reporting of others. When the actions of many big-name, national media outlets wouldn't even pass muster in a college journalism course, you know something is very wrong.

Is There Something About Mario?

Originally published in The Video Game Ombudsman, July 1, 2003

AUTHOR'S NOTE

In recent years I've taken to calling the type of story discussed here a "How $_{62}$ awesome? So awesome!" story. That's as captured in a Penny Arcade comic where someone asks a developer how awesome their game is going to be, and the game-maker predictably replies, "So awesome!"

If the best headline you can come up with amounts to a simple, content-free marketing message that the publisher would put in an advertisement, it's probably best to skip the story entirely. The line isn't always clear cut—maybe the quote reveals actual unreported details about the game as well—but usually it's possible to separate what's news and what's bare marketing.

These kinds of stories are a lot rarer at the biggest publications as I write this in 2018, but there are still a few old-school blogs that can't help passing along verbatim publisher quotes about just how awesome their next game will be.

You may have heard that the next Mario game will be the best thing since sliced bread. Actually, you've definitely heard it if you've seen any of the articles that quote Japanese magazine *Nintendo Dream* in saying that the next Mario game was not shown at E3, "for fear that other developers would copy ideas from the game," according to Gamesindustry.biz. Madgamers adds that *Nintendo Dream* reported the game might be shown in England by the end of August and could be released in Japan by the end of the year, which begs the question... should the media wait to see the game before simply hyping any supposed innovations it may contain?

Of course, any bit of information that comes out of the generally secretive Nintendo usually qualifies as big-time news. The Mario series is one of the most highly regarded in gaming, so people want to know as much about it as possible. Those who were wondering why the next Mario game wasn't shown at E3 deserve an explanation as to where Nintendo is on the project, and *Nintendo Dream*'s reporting helps provide that context.

On the other hand, there is no doubt that the video game media is being used to an extent here. Nintendo knows that anything they say about the new Mario game will be reported all over the internet and in video game magazines. Saying the new game is too innovative to show to the public is a "nice way to gain a bit of free publicity post-E3," as GamesIndustry.biz put it. It's equally plausible that Nintendo is simply covering for a game that was too early in development to show this year. But that spin wouldn't get "Mario" and "innovative" written into the same sentence in game publications far and wide.

> In truth, it's a tough balancing act between giving the readers the information they need to know and becoming a tool for a game publisher's PR department.

It's not like this is the first time Nintendo has used this line, either. Spong points out that Nintendo at one point claimed that *Super Mario Sunshine* and *Pokemon Mini*—two products that were relatively ill-received—were "too innovative" to show the public. All this "free publicity" could backfire on Nintendo by raising expectations for what could well be an unimpressive game (of course, Miyamato always seems to get the benefit of the doubt, which is a topic for another time).

So what's the solution? In truth, it's a tough balancing act between giving the readers the information they need to know and becoming a tool for a game publisher's PR department. News organizations simply have to use their best judgement to determine whether reporting the company line on a game, sight unseen, is worth the risk.

In this case, I would say it's probably not worth reporting the quote verbatim. The game media as a whole will be able to decide for itself on how innovative the new *Mario* game is soon enough. Many video game websites have been ignoring this story so far, probably for this very reason. Regardless of whether the game turns out to be as innovative as Nintendo says, these sites deserve praise for erring on the side of caution.

Battle of the Reliable Sources

Originally published on The Video Game Ombudsman, Sept. 3, 2003

You probably heard rumblings from a variety of sources about a possible deal between Sony and Nvidia for the PS3 graphics chipset. Chris Morris first broke the story[63] on Aug. 27 (later updated Sept. 2) in his regular CNN/Money column. He based his article on the commentary of industry analyst Erach Desai,

AUTHOR'S NOTE

This story shook out years before Sony finally confirmed that Sony would work with Nvidia for the graphics chips on the PS3. Regardless, looking back at how two different reporters generated two very different look-ahead stories on the subject, based on two very different types of sources, is fascinating to me.

who said that Nvidia "are in discussions with Sony for the PS3."

You might not have heard about the report calling the reported link between Nvidia and Sony "ridiculous." Rob Fahey at GamesIndustry.biz broke that one[64] on Sept. 1, quoting a "senior source" at Sony as saying that teaming up with Nvidia, "would simply make no sense either technologically or commercially."

So what do you believe: The commentary with the named analyst, or the news article with the unnamed source? I talked with the authors of the competing articles to try and make some sense of this controversy.

WHEN COMMENTARY BECOMES FACT

First off, it should be made clear that Morris intended his article to be taken as commentary, not as a hard news story. "All of my columns... are labeled as commentary at the top of the page - above the headline," Morris told me. "That affords me the luxury of interjecting opinion, speculation and analysis into the stories. When it's a straight news story (say, the launch of a new console), we put it in a news template and just go with a standard byline."

But just because it was a commentary piece doesn't mean Morris didn't do his homework. "Mr. Desai has been on record with those [positions] for some time and I called him to make sure they still reflected his thoughts on the matter. Sony and Nvidia were also asked for comment and responded as they saw fit."

> So what do you believe: The commentary with the named analyst, or the news article with the unnamed source?

The commentary heading didn't seem to prevent many sites from reporting the story as if it were fact, without even seeking outside confirmation. Fahey said this sort of lazy journalism is simply unacceptable. "It's a bit sad to see dedicated, professional games sites spreading this kind of story without asking any of the obvious questions," Fahey said. "Obviously it's fair enough to expect sites to run the story as it emerges— that's the difference between web news reporting and print news reporting—but nobody seems to have asked any tough questions about it, even a few days down the line."

Unfortunately, Fahey doesn't think this is a trend that is likely to change anytime soon. "It's not the first time and it's certainly not the last time that the online media covering the games industry will jump on a story like this and print sensationalist nonsense without really thinking about what they're saying."

The problem, Fahey said, is that many video game "journalists" are not informed or critical enough of the industry they cover.

"Anyone familiar with both Sony and Nvidia would have raised questions about this story as soon as it emerged, but apparently some elements of the games media... just chose to report the story in a totally credulous way."

NAMING YOUR SOURCES

Setting aside such concerns, some might say that Fahey's refutation doesn't hold as much weight because he doesn't name the "senior source" at Sony who provided the basis for the story. There's no way for the reader or other members of the press to confirm what the source is saying, or that the source even exists!

Fahey said that while GamesIndustry.biz usually won't base a story on an unnamed source, he decided to make an exception this time. "In this particular case, our source was simply talking a lot of sense, and while I'd have loved to have named him, his comments still carry weight regardless," Fahey said. "It's always unfortunate when ongoing business negotiations or other concerns prevent very informed people from putting their names to their comments, but that's just how the industry works and I think we all appreciate that."

Fahey went on to say that the sources he used for his article go beyond the unnamed one that ended up being quoted. "Although I only quote one source, I've also spoken to a number of Stateside analysts about the story," Fahey said. "Writing a story that rebuts something which has been reported elsewhere is something that has to be even more carefully researched than an original news story, in my experience, purely because you're stepping on a lot of toes when you publish it. If you set a foot wrong, the people who you're leaving red-faced will come in and tear your story to pieces."

As for Morris, he said he doesn't have any reason to believe that GI.biz didn't have a "senior source" to back their story. However, he did say that he had no way of knowing whether their source was a "decision maker" or not. "The guessing game about the next generation of consoles has been going on pretty much since the last batch came out," Morris said. "It will continue until the exact specs of the 2005/2006 machines are revealed."

DON'T LOOK BACK IN ANGER

In the end, Morris said he stands behind everything in his story. "The column never said Nvidia's tie with the PS3 was a sure thing. It speculated, based on reliable sources, that the companies are talking and that a partnership might make sense for a series of reasons. I'd write it again today the exact same way."

Fahey, on the other hand, said in retrospect that he could have handled his refutation a little better. "I could probably have been a lot more professional and less tabloid-style with the story - but it was the weekend after a very long, tiring trade show, so I guess I can be excused having a bit of fun with it. It's not every day that I get to write "MONSTER RAVING LOONY NVIDIA RUMOURS CONDEMNED AS DAMNED LIES!" style headlines, whereas some of the other guys out there seem to be making a living off it."

Rob Fahey vs. Microsoft

Originally published on The Video Game Ombudsman, June 28, 2004

In a story[65] published June 21, Rob Fahey at GamesIndustry. biz cited "sources close to Microsoft's senior Xbox executives" as saying the company's next system would not be backward compatible with the original Xbox. The story got picked up by a number of sites around the 'net.

Breaking from tradition, the usually quiet-on-rumors Microsoft responded to the story directly,[66] blasting the report as irresponsible speculation.

I conducted an email interview with Mr. Fahey to find out more about how the story was reported and to gauge his thoughts on the controversy surrounding it.

Video Game Ombudsman: So, first off, who's your source?

Rob Fahey: Nice try! Seriously, I'd love to be able to reveal who my sources on this were—it would end the discussion about it straight away, frankly. However, I have made a promise to a source and I obviously cannot go back on that—even if that anonymity is causing me a headache right now.

VGO: OK, OK, you can't blame me for trying. But how did you get in contact with this "extremely senior member" of the Xbox team? When did you talk to him? What exactly did he say (if you can reveal that)?

RF: Actually, he got in contact with us directly and we had a fairly lengthy discussion about Microsoft's general plans for "Xbox 2." One of the things which emerged from that discussion was the whole attitude to backward compatibility within Microsoft, which while it wasn't surprising, exactly, was certainly worth following up. I confirmed the story past a number of developers who are in the loop on Microsoft Xenon development plans for confirmation, so while we are certainly one primary source, the story has been corroborated past several different people.

VGO: Do you feel that video game journalism is too dependent on "official announcements?" Where should insider journalism (such as your story) fit into the mix?

RF: There's a fine balance to be struck; obviously reporting official announcements is important, and it's vital that journalists be able to take those official statements and put them into a proper context for their readers. However, it's also very important that publications do proper "insider" journalism—the games media equivalent of traditional "on the beat" stories, I guess—or they risk becoming nothing more than mouthpieces for the big companies in the industry.

The one thing that we need to be very careful about is ensuring that insider journalism—like speculative reporting or opinion-based commentary—is clearly delineated from reporting on official announcements. That isn't to say that insider reports are necessarily less reliable than official statements; just that the reader should be clear on which is which, so that they can draw their own conclusions.

VGO: What sort of ground rules do you use when a conflict arises between what inside sources are saying and the official company line?

RF: This happens less often than you might think, actually. In general, you don't get a company saying one thing, and an insider there telling you the opposite; what's much more likely is that you'll get a company making no statement, and an insider source giving you information that the company won't comment on. That's what has happened here; in these circumstances, our basic rules are to run the story past as many people who might be able to confirm it as possible, and then go to press with an article which reflects the degree of confirmation we've been able to garner for it.

Obviously that isn't a very strict rule, and a lot depends on how reliable and senior the original source for the story was.

> *It's also very important that publications do proper "insider" journalism—the games media equivalent of traditional "on the beat" stories, I guess—or they risk becoming nothing more than mouthpieces for the big companies in the industry.*
>
> **Rob Fahey**
> **GamesIndustry.biz**

VGO: Did you worry about breaking a story like this without confirmation from another source or without official comment from Microsoft? Why or why not?

RF: I would not have run this story without checking it past other sources first. However, their confirmation wasn't important—what was important was the direct information from our senior source about Microsoft's thinking on backward compatibility and its importance, not the simple technical confirmation from developers.

As for an official comment from Microsoft—I actually have a macro in Word for "Microsoft does not comment on rumours and speculation." (I'm not kidding!) That's their standard response, and I have never seen them deviate from it to actually furnish useful information about a story such as this, so we chose to run without their comment.

VGO: Microsoft usually gives a quiet "no comment" to stories like these, but yours got a quick, vociferous response after the fact. Why do you think this is? Do you think the fact that their response didn't directly deny anything in your story is significant?

RF: I think it's very significant. As far as I can gather, Microsoft is annoyed because a lot of information about Xbox 2 is leaking, and sees us as one of the publications responsible for finding and publicizing those leaks. Which is probably a fair assessment.

As for the name-calling (Microsoft called GI's report "irresponsible" and said "the credibility of any publication willing to compromise fact in favour of a catchy headline must be questioned." -ed.) well, a journalist a lot older and wiser than I am once told me that if you don't have someone refusing to take your calls, trying to sue you or just calling you names in public, you aren't doing your job right. I'll take Microsoft's attack on my credibility as being a compliment, then!

VGO: Are you worried about any potential legal or other retribution from Microsoft for your story?

RF: No. I hope that we can continue to enjoy a good working relationship with Microsoft going forward, and I'd be disappointed if this spat damaged that relationship in the long term. Legally, though, I know exactly where we stand and I'm not aware of any action Microsoft could take over our reporting.

VGO: What is it like to report on a story where you're part of the story? Do you think you were able to remain impartial?

RF: We certainly tried very hard to do so. However, it's something I'd rather not have to do very often. I think it's a failing for a publication when they stop reporting the news, and become part of the news, and it's a situation I'd like to avoid wherever possible.

VGO: Final question: if you had to give a percentage figure for how sure you were of Xbox 2's lack of backward compatibility, where would you put it?

RF: I am 100% certain that, right now, the plans for the Xbox 2 don't include backward compatibility. I'm also 99% sure that the console won't have this feature when it launches, because I'm aware of the technical and legal difficulties surrounding its implementation, and because I know that Microsoft doesn't think it's important. Like we said in our response to their statement last week—we absolutely stand by the story.

The 1% doubt about their eventual plans comes from the simple fact that they're a company that is very quick to react, and if a lot of consumer opinion now suggests that backward compatibility *is* important, they may well reconsider. That's a very remote outside chance, however; as I said, I'm 100% sure that their current plans don't include the feature. I'm only a reporter, not a prophet.

When the Latest News Isn't

Originally published on The Video Game Ombudsman, Sept. 9, 2004

A few weeks ago, the story broke that Nintendo had been granted a patent for an add-on device with "communication and storage capability via a modem and hard disk drive."

Some in the enthusiast press community (and some in the non-video-game press)

AUTHOR'S NOTE

I still see too many stories like this, where a number of gaming news sites will run with a story that could be proven false with basic fact-checking (often a simple Google search). That said, I think a greater proportion of the big news sites these days will go through the legwork and track down the original source, especially for a story that seems too good to be true.

quickly filed speculative reports on the device as an XBox Live-style GameCube peripheral. One source featured the highly misleading headline, "Nintendo Patents XBox Live." Another source enigmatically guessed that the device might function as a Personal Video Recorder. It was race time at the rumor track.

To my knowledge, GameSpot's Tor Thorsen was the first author on this story to track down the actual patent, rather than relying on the summary provided by the U.S. Patent and Trademark Office site. What he found[67] revealed the "newly-approved" patent was just a 1999 filing for the now-defunct Nintendo 64 Disk Drive. Hardly breaking news.

I talked with Thorsen via e-mail about the fact-checking that went into his story and how the video game press as a whole handled the situation.

The Video Game Ombudsman: How were you first tipped off about this story?

Tor Thorsen: If told you, then I'd have to kill you. (Just kidding—see below.)

VGO: When you get a tip like this, what sort of fact checking does it go through? Does this process apply to all articles, or only some? Take me through the process.

TT: Initially we were tipped off about the patent. I looked it up at the US Patent & Trademark Office (USPTO) and found out it was legit. I looked at the description, and checked the "granted" date. I also sent off emails to Nintendo's reps (who can be very slow about getting back). Then I wrote an initial draft of the story, which heavily played up how strange it was that, the week before, NOA reps were talking up game-only devices and blasting the PSX. According to that patent, they were making something that sounded a lot like a cross between the PSX (TV integration) and Xbox Live (online & game-content downloading capabilities). That version got sent to copy edit while I did a second round of fact-checking.

VGO: Was there anything about the story that made it seem particularly suspicious to you when you first heard about it?

TT: The whole situation seemed bizarre—either Nintendo's whole PR effort for the last year was BS, or they had done a "Crazy Ivan" about-face. It just seemed off. My spider sense was tingling, but there was the official government USPTO listing right in front of my face. Then I got hold of the scan, and I realized it was the 64DD.

VGO: What part of the patent scan first indicated to you that the patent was for the 64DD and not a new system or peripheral?

TT: The diagram and the other dates—neither of which was including in the listing on the USPTO website.

VGO: Are you surprised that articles that preceded yours (and some since) did not notice the connection to the 64DD? Do you think these sources actually read through the entire patent?

TT: Online game news is a two-headed beast. You want to be first to put it up, but you also need to get the facts right. I think a lot of sites let the former override the latter. I come from a more traditional journalism background, so I've had fact-checking drilled into my head since I worked at my college paper.

That said, the online USPTO listing did not have the diagram or the initial date on it. The one thing that set my alarm bells ringing was the original date on the page, which said "Filed: April 4, 2003." That meant that either Nintendo's PR people had been putting on a very false front by pooh-poohing "convergence" (or whatever the marketing droids are calling it this week) for over a year, or something was amiss.

> *Online game news is a two-headed beast. You want to be first to put it up, but you also need to get the facts right. I think a lot of sites let the former override the latter.*
>
> **Tor Thorsen**
> **News Editor, GameSpot**

Reading the original listing from the USPTO site—an official document from the U.S. government—you can see how it would be really easy to think it was a brand-new patent.

VGO: If you hadn't figured out the true nature of the patent, how long do you think it would have continued to be reported incorrectly? How far do you think the speculation would have gone?

TT: Not long. Shortly after my story went up, Nintendo called to explain it to me. They called other people too, but, ironically, only one of our competitors bothered correcting it immediately. The others let it run until the next day, and many smaller-level sites were parroting it as fact days later. Nintendo was smart to do damage control, though—a lot of publishers don't understand that rumors will persist only for as long as they let them and stay silent, fueling speculation.

VGO: What do you recommend to other video game news writers to avoid oversights like the one your article corrected?

TT: Something like 75 to 80 percent of news stories are based on press releases, so no fact checking is really necessary (though, due to the vague wording, clarifications often are). It's easy to get sloppy when you're getting spoonfed stuff all the time and you've got about a half-hour to write the thing, proof it, code it, publish it, and make it not sound like crap.

That said, a lot of people have been in this game a lot longer than me, so I wouldn't presume to tell them how to do their jobs. My advice to myself is simple: Check your facts and trust your instincts. If something feels wrong, that's probably because it is.

Playing Like the Audience

Originally published on The Video Game Ombudsman, June 28, 2005

An odd thought occurred to me as I was playing through my review copy of *Kirby: Canvas Curse* for Happy Puppy. The thought had to do with whether or not the experience I was getting playing the game was truly comparable to the experience my audience would have if and when they played it.

This wasn't purely an idle musing on the superbly subjective nature of interactive gameplay (well, it didn't start out that way, anyway). I thought of this because I happened to be playing through the game using a *Mario Kart DS* stylus given to me by a Nintendo representative at E3 (who says all swag is useless?).

Anyone who has used this stylus will immediately know why I chose it over the tiny, flexible, cramp-inducing piece of grey plastic that comes with the system—the increased size and weight of the *Mario Kart* stylus makes playing the DS infinitely more enjoyable. But I couldn't help but wonder as I played whether that additional comfort was doing a disservice to my readers.

I'll make a small assumption here and say that most people who will be reading my review did not attend E3 and will not have access to this special stylus, or any stylus besides the

> **AUTHOR'S NOTE**
>
> The kinds of questions in this story are newly relevant now that console and VR hardware makers are routinely splitting their platforms into "high-end" and "low-end" versions, which play the same software at vastly different levels of quality. Should you review that new game on the PS4 Pro or the original PS4? The Xbox One X or the original Xbox One? The HTC Vive or the Vive Pro?
>
> Ideally, I think comparing and contrasting the different hardware's performance is best. If that's not possible, though, disclosing what you used in your review setup should be the minimum.

one that came with their system. So my question is: should I have used the superior *Mario Kart* stylus, or used the standard stylus that most of my readers would be using (or a mix of both)? If you think I should have used the *Mario Kart* stylus, should I have told my readers about it?

This may seem like a trivial example, but there are plenty of other situations I can think of where the same basic question applies. Do you use the fancy joystick or the default mouse/keyboard controls for a flight simulator? Do you test a *Dance Dance Revolution* game with a high-quality metal dance pad or the cheap plastic version packaged with the game? Do I play that new console game on the 52" plasma display or the 13" black and white TV (or even the 7" flip-top LCD screen)? Even things like a broadband connection or an optical mouse can impact the gameplay.

> But I couldn't help but wonder as I played whether that additional comfort was doing a disservice to my readers.

Regardless of the choice, how much information do readers need about the reviewer's setup to judge the review? On the one hand, readers ought to know if the review they're reading is colored by extravagant extras or substandard equipment, even if it doesn't relate directly to the actual game itself. On the other hand, no two people will play the game in exactly the same conditions in any case.

Do we have to set up our reviews like a scientific test, setting the lighting, seating and humidity conditions to present a truly controlled play experience? I know a few computer game magazines list the technical specs of the system they use to review hardware-intensive games (or used to, at least), so there's a start.

In this case I did use the "good" *Mario Kart* stylus throughout and didn't reveal this fact to my readers, so you know where I stand on this particular example. But on other issues of which hardware setup should be considered the "default" I'm not sure exactly where I stand. Where do you draw the line between too much information and too much deviation from the norm?

Jane's New News

Originally published on The Video Game Ombudsman, July 12, 2005

GameGirlAdvance's Jane Pinckard was recently hired as a news editor at 1UP, and she has some very interesting ideas[68] about where their news section is headed. In short, Jane wants for there to be "a personality that anchors the news section." This means writing that has "humor, style, and a point of view."

In short, she wants it to be a blog.

It certainly reads like one. Check out this tidbit from a story[69] about a recent poll showing Japanese gamers aren't very excited about the Xbox360:

> *As much as we might complain about lack of innovative game titles in the West, Japan has it even worse. Some of the quirkiest, most fascinating games ever made come from Japanese game studios, but they wither under the unending domination of Dragon Quest. A new console launch is not going to change that trend any time soon. Too bad.*

This mix of analysis and opinion isn't entirely new for 1UP, which has always favored quick, punchy news stories over the kind of fact-filled, dry reporting found at places like GameSpot. Jane puts up a rather defensive, um, defense of her style by arguing that objectivity in journalism is dead or dying:

> *There is no such thing as writing without a point of view. Okay? it's not possible. Either you don't CARE, in which case, why are you writing? Or you have a point of view. Even if you're undecided. So why not just be straight-up about it? It's far more insidious, in my view, to pretend to be objective. I know this flies in the face of standard journalistic practice. But in my view, and with all due respect, that's why standard journalism is feeling so old and tired now. Why shouldn't writers take stands? Express opinions? Is it going to confuse readers?*

Jane is right, to a point. True objectivity is never possible in humans. Our experiences and opinions always have a way of coloring our actions and our writing, no matter how hard we try.

But I don't think that news writers shouldn't try to be objective. The point of a news section, to me, is to try to present as much information and as many sides of a story as possible and then let the reader decide what they agree or disagree with. This doesn't mean you have to be dry or that you can't provide informative analysis, but it does mean that you should leave your own personal views on the matter for the opinion page. Jamming a heavy-handed opinion into a fact-based news story might not confuse a reader, but it won't necessarily appeal to them either.

I've long maintained that there is a place for both news and opinions in mainstream gaming outlets, just not mixed together in the same article. Blogs (this one included) have had great success cherry-picking factual reporting from other sources and mixing it with their own opinion into a concoction that has become a media revolution. I can see why big-time news operations would want to emulate this, but I really hope they don't.

People rely on these news outlets to give them the basic information *before* they go to the bloggers and the satirists that make them look at it in new ways. If the base of hard news reporting goes away, all that's left is a hodge-podge of fact and opinion that doesn't do full justice to either.

Besides, if news sections get into the opinions business, what will be left for bloggers like me to be snarky about?

It Never Hurts to Ask

Originally published on The Video Game Ombudsman, Aug. 1, 2005

Thanks to Ombudsman reader Justin McElroy for pointing me to a Computer and Video Games article (since removed) about some alleged Nintendo Revolution videos uncovered by a French gaming website. It's a pretty standard, substance-free rumor-mongering article, with an added twist that seems to imply psychic ability on the part of the author:

> ### AUTHOR'S NOTE
>
> I can't count the number of times I've reached out for comment on a questionable story, expecting a perfunctory no comment as a response, and instead ended up getting a nugget of information that differentiated my reporting from everything else out there. These instances might be proportionally rare, but the positive outcomes more than make up for the time wasted chasing "no comments" around. Just remember, you can't know if you don't ask.

> " *We can't confirm or deny whether they're true either way, and of course if we asked them, Nintendo would issue its standard, 'we don't comment on rumour and speculation.'* "

This C&VG author is most likely right. At least nine times out of ten, big companies like Nintendo do just issue a standard no comment when asked about rumors like these. But there are at least a few times when they will break that shell of silence, and those rare cases can move a story forward in important ways.

Yes, it's very unlikely that Nintendo would confirm the footage was real. Even if it was real, they would likely issue a "no comment" until they could officially unveil the footage themselves, albeit with much less fanfare than if the footage hadn't leaked out. A "no comment" doesn't reveal much information, but it at least shows that you, as the journalist, tried.

What's slightly more likely, and more interesting, is that Nintendo might deny that the footage was real. Nintendo has done this in the past, for example, denying rumors of a potential sale to Microsoft or reports of technical problems causing a delay in the GameCube's launch. Imagine if the reporters in these stories had failed to ask, simply assuming that Nintendo wouldn't comment on the rumors. Readers would be left without some truly vital context, wondering about the veracity of the rumors without the knowledge that Nintendo was actively trying to swat them down.

Even better, when a company does actively deny something, it's a great chance to catch them in a lie later on. Take, for example, this story,[70] in which Nintendo denied it would lower the price of the GameCube just three days before taking just that action. Or this story[71] where Nintendo denied Sega would be making games for the Game Boy Advance roughly a year before the release of *Sonic Advance* (maybe they just changed their mind in the interim?). These little nuggets of self-contradiction are gold for any journalist, and poison for any PR department (this is why companies give so many "no comments" in the first place).

Of course, if I contacted C&VG about this, they'd probably just tell me that they didn't have time to contact Nintendo before posting this little airy nothing of a story, and that they just made up an excuse to avoid looking lazy. Hey, if they can make up likely answers, then so can I.

Where Does the Time Go?

Originally published on The Video Game Ombudsman, Aug. 11, 2006

AUTHOR'S NOTE

In the 12 years since I wrote this piece, I feel the pressures of playing a wide and deep enough slate of games to stay conversant on the medium has become harder and harder to satisfy.

Part of this is likely just due to my getting older, and having more responsibilities and less energy to devote to the next 40+ hour mega-game. But part of it is also due the sheer flood of games that are released these days, to the point that even playing the important ones sufficiently would require multiple full-time-jobs'-worth of time.

The time crunch of modern game journalism is a topic I return to in "Game Critics Face their Own 'Crunch Time'" elsewhere in this book, but this piece may have been my first inkling that it would become a big problem.

The threads of Chuck Klosterman's recent musings on the "Lester Bangs of Game Journalism"[72] are surprisingly still unraveling. The always-excellent Jim Rossignol jumps off from a bit of Clive Thompson's response to Klosterman[73] to speculate on the question of depth and breadth of experience among game reviewers.[74]

> *The longer games take to play, or books to read, or films to watch, the smaller our range of comparable experiences becomes. I can't usefully review flight sims. It's impossible. I don't have the palette of previous experiences do so with any authority, or even much creativity. Of course I've played a number of the big sims, but I'm acutely aware that my capacity to be funny or observant about the genre is always hamstrung with uncertainty.*

How can a reviewer be sure he's significantly experienced with the wide array of games available? Ben Kuchera at Opposable Thumbs has a simple suggestion: play more games![75]

> *The author notes he wouldn't be able to review a flight sim well; I say he simply hasn't played enough of them. I have a homework assignment for him: go buy* IL-2 Sturmovik, *the last* Microsoft Flight Simulator *game, and play both for one weekend. Just one weekend. Get to know what makes a good flight sim, and also bring your knowledge of other games to it. ... If you have a working knowledge of good game design and theory, and spend a good day or so on both of those games you should then be able to review any flight sim. Will you be able to make jokes and references to obscure to flight sims you missed in the past? Probably not, but that kind of thing only appeals to hardcore flight junkies to begin with. You will be able to say if you had fun playing the game, and talk about the flaws that jumped out at you.*

The essential conflict is clear: one has to play enough games to have a basis of comparison for anything that comes along, but one must also play the games long enough to really understand them. Personally, I often worry that I have too little experience with sports games to review them effectively. Similarly, my friend Jeremy always complains that most fighting game reviews are simply useless to the serious fighting game fan because the reviewer doesn't have the time or experience to get into the higher-level theory of the game.

But the balance between breadth and depth isn't the only conflict—the balance between playing and writing must also be considered. Every hour spent playing a game, after all, is an hour that can be spent writing the review for it. Simply eating into time spent Doing Nothing doesn't help because, as

Rossignol notes, a good critic should ideally be spending that time becoming "literate, politically informed and knowledgeable of music, art and broader culture."

If a reviewer is so obsessed with a game (or games in general) that they play to the exclusion of all else, they may end up rushing out a review just under the deadline. Conversely, if a reviewer plays a game for 30 minutes, they'll have plenty of time to pore over its every flaw and write the perfect scathing evisceration. Without discipline, a better game might paradoxically get a worse-written review than a worse game.

The solution, of course, is to learn how to write well and write quickly at the same time—an ability good journalists and good game reviewers both need. Luckily, the more you write, the easier it is to write well quickly (or, in my case, the more anal you get about endlessly poring over every word you write), so for most writers this problem works itself out. What is harder to learn, though, is how to "have enough respect for the subject to make it feel like it's worth [your] time to play as much as [you] can to stay relevant," as Kuchera puts it. If you don't have that, maybe you're better off not even trying...

Straight to the Source

Originally published on GameDaily, Feb. 15, 2007

"SAYS WHO?"

It's not just a petty response to a schoolyard taunt — it's the heart of good, solid journalism. Raw information is only part of the story — who's providing the information is often just as important. A reader might think they just want to know the facts, but a discerning reader also wants to know how you know the facts so they can know what they think about the facts being facts or just things you think you know. Unfortunately, finding out the original source of a news story on major gaming sites is often as hard as parsing that last sentence.

AUTHOR'S NOTE

Over a decade later, I still run into too many situations where clicking through to the "original source" for some gaming news story instead goes to a summary of that story written by someone else. The capricious nature of what becomes popular on aggregators like Reddit and Google News makes it a bit of a crapshoot whether the real source of new information is getting the proper credit via links.

By the way, remember "via" links? In the early days of blogging, writers used these routinely to indicate where they first saw the link to the (separately linked) source material. You don't see that much these days, and sometime I wonder why it fell out of favor.

The news business is not just about getting the right information, but about getting it first. So it can be pretty galling for a news site to have to cite a competitor as the source for a story. The speed of the internet makes the problem worse — nobody wants to be chastised for posting an "old" link to information from two whole days ago. The glut of sites devoted to the relatively narrow niche of gaming exacerbates the problem further—with so many sites and so little original news, it's common to see essentially the same information appear in dozens of places in slightly different forms.

Not that this is a problem in and of itself. As long as reporters do their best to reference and link back to the original source for their information, a curious reader can confirm for themselves whether the secondary reporting is accurate. Most sites have trouble living up to this ideal in reality, however. "Among the major sites, proper credit is probably given something like 90 percent of the time," GameLife's Chris Kohler says, "but that other 10 percent is a hell of a lot of stories."

1UP News Editor Luke Smith knows what it's like to be burned by part of that 10 percent, and he isn't very fond of the experience. On his personal blog, he launched a salvo[76] against competitor IGN for failing to provide proper credit on a story he broke about the Stamper brothers leaving Rare.

Smith told me he understood why a site might not want to link to a competitor, but that he thought hiding the original source showed insecurity. "It's trying to erect a facade that 'X information is only available here,'" Smith said, "And for the most part, it's not. Why would you want readers who believe that 'X site is the only place for Y information'? It seems like they aren't using the full power of the Internet, then."

IGN, for its part, later updated their story with the proper source. IGN editorial director Tal Blevins told Video Game Media Watch that it was "always our intention as reporters to cite relevant sources." Other bloggers and news writers I talked to said without exception that their outlets had similar linking policies to ensure that credit was given where it was due.

But even with a policy in place, providing a link back to the source is not always simple as it sounds. When essentially similar information is being reported on numerous sites, figuring out which version to link to can be tricky, for instance.

Gamasutra's Simon Carless says his writers "make a serious attempt to work out who actually broke the story... if it's original reporting. More to the point, we go back to the original press release or statement if that exists so as to work from primary evidence." Failing to perform this due diligence can lead to problems, as Carless pointed out in a GameSetWatch post[77] about a questionably-sourced Joystiq post that turned into a public gaffe.

> *Raw information is only part of the story — who's providing the information is often just as important.*

Even when the correct credit is given, the person who originated a story is not always the one who ends up getting the benefit from it. Carless notes that web users would often rather read a two-paragraph summary of a ten-page interview than the interview itself. "There's often little incentive to click through to that external site, yet the external site conducted the interview or originally reported the fact," he said. GameLife's Kohler summed up the frustration involved with this misplaced crediting. "When people [use] my stuff, but they link to Joystiq's coverage of it or whatever, well, that pisses me off," he said.

Indeed, the peculiar nature of news aggregators and the questionable linking policies of smaller, less scrupulous sites means a bad copy can often become more popular than the original story it's based on. 1UP's Smith pointed out a recent example where his story on Xbox 360 matchmaking got little attention from news aggregator Digg. A quote-filled summary of that same piece on GameStyle, on the other hand, was heavily promoted by over 800 Diggers. "This is why there's no such thing as 'videogame journalism'," Smith said.

The quick spread of facts revealed in interviews and press releases is one thing, but the rampant cross-linking on the internet can also allow a rumor to get around the world before the truth has a chance to buy a pair of pants, much less put them on. And the decision to run a rumor being reported elsewhere on the 'net is not an exact science.

"Sometimes, there's enough smoke around a rumor to safely guess there's a fire." said Joystiq's Christopher Grant (who I work with as a blogger for the site). "Often, we'll play the role of debunker when a rumor is too stupid to go on living. Case in point: the rumor that Sony was planning on removing Blu-ray drives from the PlayStation 3—if so, every PS3 game shipped to date wouldn't work on future PS3s!"

Sometimes, the best way to report on a rumor is to actually do some legwork to determine the truth behind it. Kotaku's Brian Crecente said he always tries to get a response from the company involved in a rumor if he thinks one might be available. "A blog, a true blog, is essentially opinion, so I can understand not calling someone, but as larger sites like Kotaku transition from blog to something that mixes original content with hard news and reporting, then more calls need to be made."

This gets into the best way to set your news site apart in a sea of seemingly random links and endlessly repeated information—

original reporting and content. "I think it's important to present content which people do have to read in depth to understand," Carless said, "because that will differentiate you and attract people to your site." Of course, this doesn't necessarily mean you have to uncover secret information in every story—a new angle on an old story can be just as good. "We all, I believe, get the same press releases. The difference is how we analyze those press releases and write the story," Crecente said.

Of course, that original content isn't worth much if it isn't noticed and linked to by the other sites that make up the largely incestuous world of online gaming news. But in the end, those who refuse to link to outside sources are probably hurting themselves more than anyone else. "The creation of a walled garden of information is ultimately an attempt to deny the reality that there are a host of outlets out there where your readers could go," Smith said. "As an editor, you shouldn't be afraid about your readers reading somewhere else. You should be confident that the product you're putting together will bring them back."

Is Anyone Listening?

Originally published on GameDaily, June 7, 2007

Every critic believes, on some level, that their opinion is the "right" one. In the critic's mind, the world would be a better place if games they loved sold well and games they hated sat unloved on store shelves.

In the real world, that's very often not the case. In the real world, even massive critical consensus on a title often has little to no impact on a game's popularity or cultural impact. For evidence, look no farther than games like *Psychonauts, Ico,* and *Beyond Good and Evil* that sat unloved on store shelves despite consistently glowing reviews. On the other side of the coin, consider mediocre cash-ins like *Enter the Matrix* and *Spider-Man 3* that shot to the top of the sales charts despite critical drubbings.

It's enough to lead review writers to the brink of an existential crisis. Is anyone even listening to our advice? Does what we write have any effect on the market at large? What good are reviews, anyway?

"Game reviews are only useful in reinforcing a pre-existing decision to buy," says Slashdot Games Editor Michael Zenke,

AUTHOR'S NOTE

On the one hand, the vast explosion of review sources since I wrote this piece has likely lessened the impact of any single review. Even the critical consensus, as represented by the almighty Metacritic score, usually has trouble moving the needle in the face of a game's deafening marketing hype (or equally deafening marketing silence).

On the other hand, there are dozens of YouTubers and Twitch streamers with enough of a following to launch an unknown game to success with a single 15 minute gameplay video. In a world where hundreds of games are coming out each week, that's the kind of real power the average game magazine reviewer could only dream of.

voicing a cynical but somewhat commonplace view among game journalists. "They're useful to the publisher as a means of confirming a gamer's interest in a game. As far as swaying opinions, I don't really think so. My experience is that for a lot of the folks we'd call 'enthusiasts' or 'hardcore', their decision is made long before the review appears."

Indeed, those in the know often base their purchasing decisions on the mounds of information that comes out before stores even start taking pre-orders. Between screenshots, video trailers, TV and print advertising, hands on previews, downloadable demos, and public beta tests, there's often nothing left for a review to really reveal these days. "You likely aren't giving gamers any really unique information beyond the final verdict," said freelancer Troy Goodfellow of early reviews, "and, if you blow the review in a rush to get the 'FIRST' tag, you lose credibility with readers."

Even those who don't pay attention to the pre-release information often make that all-important decision to buy as soon as they hear a game's name. "*Madden* will always sell millions of units each year because of its established brand and its penetration into the consciousness of the general public," said Gamer 2.0 Managing Editor Anthony Perez. "*Halo* will always sell, as will *Grand Theft Auto, Zelda, Mario,* et cetera. At this stage, marketing and advertising have a much larger effect on mainstream consumer spending than any game reviews."

When readers do deign to consult a review, it's often in the most cursory manner possible. "Most people just want to know the score and maybe the plus and minus bullet points," said freelancer Tim Stevens. "Of those 10 percent who do care about the text of a given review, 90 percent of them probably spend no more than a minute skimming, only reading a few paragraphs closely."

So should all game reviews be condensed into bullet points? No, Stevens say, because "that remaining one percent who read everything top to bottom is certainly a sizable market worth catering to."

> *Is anyone even listening to our advice? Does what we write have any effect on the market at large? What good are reviews, anyway?*

Believe it or not, such comprehensive review readers do exist. "As a kid who only had the funds to pick up a game or two a month, my purchasing decisions were based mostly on reviews," recalls *Game Informer* Executive Editor Andy Reiner. "I followed every video game magazine, found the reviewers that had interests that were comparable to mine, and entrusted my funds to their opinions."

But how common is that careful attention to bylines among people who don't grow up to be game journalists themselves? "There are damned few reviewers whose opinion carry much weight," said *Tips & Tricks* Editor-in-chief Bill Kunkel. "When a review is used to hype a game, the author of the review is rarely mentioned, just the magazine or site." Goodfellow agreed that "readers tend to see these reviews as the product of a publication, not a specific writer."

Are there any reviewers out there whose opinions can break through the noise and actually cause a blip in the charts?

Maybe a couple. "Certainly the Penny Arcade guys hold a good deal of influence," said (Harrisburg, Pa.) *Patriot-News* columnist Chris Mautner. "I'm sure there are a number of players who will pick up *Odin Sphere* based on their recommendations."

For the most part though, there isn't a game critic that has the name recognition and influence of a Walt Mossberg or a Roger Ebert. Perhaps that's a bit much to ask for, though. "Roger Ebert is, in many ways, a unique figure in cultural criticism," Goodfellow said. "He is a knowledgeable critic, an excellent writer and, most importantly, a TV personality. No other TV critic has the gravitas of his body of work and no other print reviewer has his television profile. ... [X-Play hosts Adam] Sessler and [Morgan] Webb are as close as we are going to get for a while."

Maybe reviews do matter, but we just have to change our idea of who counts as a reviewer. "It used to be the only game reviewers that mattered were the reviewers at *Computer Gaming World* or other game magazines," said *San Jose Mercury News* columnist and blogger Dean Takahashi. "Now everything is turned upside down. Websites that do reviews, blogs, mainstream news sites, and enthusiast fan sites are now producing reviews. It's hard to figure out who is the most influential."

Indeed, the open community of the web has allowed people to get their gaming opinions through communities of like-minded friends rather than the distant strangers that pen most official reviews. "Reviews always matter, it's just that it isn't always the formal reviews that matter most," Kunkel said. "I suspect that more gamers opt to buy or not buy a specific game due to informal reviews on forums as they do based on a game review in *Rolling Stone* or *Entertainment Weekly* or even *EGM*."

So why even bother, then? While it might be true that "good criticism offers ... a conversation between the reader and the critic" as Mautner eloquently put it, a forum thread or IM conversation with someone who bought the game will beat that critic/reader conversation any day.

Still, there are some who believe in the power and promise of the traditional review. "It's not that people are ignoring reviews when they go into buying games," *Game Informer*'s Reiner said. "I really believe that they don't know that the reviews are out there. Video game critics are still very much tucked off to the side. ... As our medium continues to grow, I wouldn't be surprised if we start seeing game critics gain respect like Roger Ebert did."

Pulp Friction

Originally published on GameDaily, Aug. 2, 2007

AUTHOR'S NOTE

If anything, the death of print gaming magazines presaged in this article only sped up in the years since I wrote it (you can thank the ubiquity of smartphones for helping that process along). Of the myriad US gaming magazines published in 2007, only *Game Informer, Official Xbox Magazine,* and *PC Gamer* still exist in print form. Two of those three only exist thanks to the largesse of a major retailer or platform-holder.

All that said, the prediction regarding game magazines becoming a lucrative niche is starting to come true. Indie, crowdfunded, print-on-demand efforts like *Nintendo Force, Pure Nintendo, RETRO Magazine,* and *A Profound Waste of Time* found a way to reach the small audiences that still want the nostalgic appeal of longer features printed with large art on glossy paper. Print may be dead, but it's also enjoying a bit of an afterlife.

For more on the 2012 death of *Nintendo Power,* which truly marked the end of an era in game magazines, check out this remembrance on Ars Technica.

When I insinuated that print gaming journalism was dying in a column a couple of months ago,[78] not everyone was happy with my conclusions. Apparently, there are some people out there who are still committed to squeezing gaming articles onto the severely limited space provided by sheets of dead trees, then distributing it through a slow, costly newsstand- and bulk-rate-mail network. Who knew?

In all seriousness, though, the writing has been on the wall for print journalism in general and print gaming magazines in particular for a while now. Subscriptions for print publications are stagnant or falling across the board, and advertisers are increasingly moving their money from print to online outlets. Gamers—who tend to be more tech-savvy than the general public—are increasingly going online to get the news and reviews weeks or months before a magazine can compete. Given these problems, can print still be relevant to the gaming conversation?

"The relevance of journalism has very little to do with the delivery method," said John Davison, senior vice president and editorial director for Ziff Davis' 1UP Network. "Print has both strengths and weaknesses, just as online does, just as TV, or online video, or radio, or podcasts. The key is stuffing the right stuff through the right tube."

While the bulk of gaming discussion is moving online, Davison said, magazines are still helping drive what the discussion is about. "Communities express themselves online, but often the lead for the 'narrative' comes from elsewhere. Often it comes from print, because editors on a monthly print product have the time and the space to develop and research an idea."

That may be true, but the battle for attention in the gaming space seems to be tilting decisively towards online sources. For evidence, just compare *Game Informer*'s million or so in monthly circulation to GameSpot's 4.7 million unique monthly visitors. How can print be relevant when it's so much less visible?

"It's senseless to condemn magazines for having smaller audiences than websites," says Dan Morris, publisher of Future's *Official Xbox Magazine*. "To suggest a metaphor: the web is our daily bread...we all need to eat every day. Luckily for everyone in this metaphor, daily bread is free. But at least once a month, you really do want to splurge and treat yourself to a nice steakhouse dinner. Magazines need to be enticing steakhouses. They need to be Ruth's Chris to the web's McDonald's."

Indeed, being freed from the burden of posting up-to-the-minute news allows a magazine to cater to the higher-end consumer of gaming news. "Instead of trying to compete on timeliness, we went for accuracy, better-informed views, and hopefully more context," said Steve Bauman, who worked at *Computer Games* magazine for 12 years before it was shut down earlier this year. "The way it should work is that print is more readable than online. A multi-page web article is a chore to slog through; in print, it's relatively easy."

Bauman also sees print features as an ideal way to highlight games that are important and fresh. "Not everything is news, and not every game deserves coverage," he said. "Because websites cover everything in such detail, nothing really stands out. Nothing lasts. Nothing lingers."

But in practically the same breath, Bauman expressed skepticism that readers were really interested in these magazine-specialty features. "While [readers] may devour some lengthy previews of certain specific games, my own anecdotal impression... is that no one really cares about or reads features," he said. "Oh, they may say they want them, over and over again, but they won't buy a magazine for an amazing feature."

Morris argues that there are obviously some readers who want this content, and they're voting with their wallets. "Clearly print is delivering something of unique value," he said. "The best evidence for this is the fact that millions of people continue to pay money for subscriptions and newsstand copies of games magazines, despite there being so much freely available content online."

It's true, gaming websites haven't yet managed to kill off the gaming magazine, despite a deep (read: total) pricing premium on online content. But there have been victims—this year alone has seen the shuttering of *Computer Games*, the *Official PlayStation Magazine* and, most recently *Tips & Tricks*. Is there enough interest to sustain all the magazines currently on the market?

> *My own anecdotal impression... is that no one really cares about or reads features. Oh, they may say they want them, over and over again, but they won't buy a magazine for an amazing feature.'*
>
> **Steve Bauman**
> **Editor, Computer Games**

"There are maybe too many magazines trying to be the high-end steakhouse currently," Davison said. "I think that a print reader is a more agnostic customer, with a different set of tolerances and expectations. We will see a shakeout over the next two years."

Part of the problem with the magazine business, Davison says, has nothing to do with the content or the readers and everything to do with the business itself. "The business of print is a real pain in the ass," he said. "The distribution infrastructure is prehistoric, and the processes for reporting sales data are inconsistent, and painfully slow. Printing, and distributing magazines is expensive, and the business model has a number of ridiculous qualities."

And despite the increased focus on features and in-depth content, Davison says magazines are sometimes hurt by their lack of timeliness. "Just looking at the most recent issues of all the print pubs this month, at a really rough guess I'd say you're looking at more than half of the games reviewed being pretty late," he said. "Research shows that you have about four seconds to snag a newsstand customer when he's scanning the shelves. If he thinks, 'I know that already' when he sees your cover, you're fucked."

But, again, this disadvantage can be a blessing in disguise for magazines. "We can all get opinions online the day a game ships, but print needs to be following up later and tackling criticism with the benefit of time, and some more ponderous consideration," Davison said. "If a review is late, we can take advantage of that, and look at how the community received the game as well as the qualitative stuff about the experience. We're in a transitional phase right now, but I've got to think that this is where we're all headed."

And where print is headed may be even more nichey and upscale than it is currently. Morris sees the possibility of premium magazines with "circulations below 100,000 and subscription prices north of $40," making an appearance on the market.

Davison, for his part, sees print sustaining itself on its reputation. "People see something in print, and believe it a little bit more," he said. "This may be a generational thing that will disappear over time, but it's also connected to the vanity of print. On the games publisher side, there's still a very compelling reason to get a game featured in print, and an especially compelling reason to try and get a cover."

What's the Score?

Originally published on GameDaily, August 9, 2007

There are two main parts to most game reviews. One part consists of hundreds of carefully-considered words, precisely arranged to paint a complete picture of the gameplay experience. This outline of a game's good and bad points often delves deep into a reviewer's thought process and explains,

AUTHOR'S NOTE

A few prominent outlets, including Eurogamer, Kotaku, and Polygon have decided to do away with review scores in recent years. For the most part, though, the one-number-summary still has outsized importance in the way reviews are written and read across the game journalism landscape. The issues highlighted in this article are still exceptionally relevant today, as highlighted by this 2015 Ars Technica piece.[79]

sometimes in excruciating detail, everything an informed consumer and game fan needs to know before making a purchasing decision.

The other part is usually a single number.

Try to guess which part is better at catching a reader's attention.

"People are always asking me what I would rate a game, expecting me to blurt out a number and thus convey my opinion of a game," says Joystiq blogger Ludwig Kietzmann. "Though I suppose brief attention spans and the expectation of quick answers are mostly to blame, I find that the inclusion of review scores in articles often overshadows all the words before or after it. The review becomes the score; it becomes a number."

Indeed, the whole concept of condensing a work as complex as a video game into a single number can be a bit ridiculous. Yet a shorthand score has become a de facto part of the large majority of modern game reviews, mainly because the readers demand it.

"At the tail end of *Computer Gaming World*'s run, we tried removing review scores, because we really felt that people were focusing too much on the numbers and not enough on the reviews themselves," said *Games For Windows* Reviews Editor Ryan Scott. "Our audience was largely disappointed when we did this, to put it mildly. I think that, at this point, if you publish a game review in an enthusiast publication sans score, you're gonna get smacked by your readers for essentially taking something away."

> *Indeed, the whole concept of condensing a work as complex as a video game into a single number can be a bit ridiculous. Yet a shorthand score has become a de facto part of the large majority of modern game reviews, mainly because the readers demand it.*

For better or worse, readers have just been trained to look for that summary judgement. "We hid our ratings in hopes that readers would take a greater appreciation of the text," said GameCritics owner and founder Chi Kong Lui. "But the reality is, unless games are more thought-provoking and conceptually challenging, gamers won't look to game reviews to better understand the game experience. They will think as consumers and expect reviews to be something you find in *Consumer Reports* as oppose to something in the arts section of the *New York Times*."

So if getting rid of scores isn't really a viable option, maybe getting rid of some of the scoring options can help. "Thumbs up/thumbs down leaves zero room for ambiguity," says freelancer Greg Sewart. "The reader doesn't have to figure out the real-life value of a particular number score that way. The only real purpose of a game review is to tell the reader whether you think they should buy it or shouldn't buy it. ... Is the game worth the MSRP? Yes or no?"

While some journalists see value in a finely-graded scale, most reviewers I talked to agreed with freelancer Kieron Gillen's assessment. "Marking is an art, not a science," he said. "The more 'definitive' a marking scheme gets, the more it's pretending to be in some way objective, and lives in denial about the squishy human stuff glooping around inside our heads. I often talk about doing a mark-scheme out of 72,384 or something to just really push the fact marks are ridiculous—yet fun—to the forefront."

Even then, though, the question would become whether a midpoint score of 36,192 out of 72,384 is really an "average" game. "The whole 'average score' thing is such a huge can of worms," *Games For Windows*' Scott said. "The 70 percent/C-average mentality is drilled into our heads at a young age. It's a weird sort of Pavlovian conditioning—'anything below 70 is terrible!'—that doesn't make any sense when you actually sit down and examine the logic behind it. Yet many writers and publications slavishly defend it."

"I feel a 7/10 average doesn't make good use of a 10-point scale," said *Electronic Gaming Monthly* Editor-in-chief Dan "Shoe" Hsu. "So you can have three scores for 'good'...and seven scores for 'bad'? That seems so unbalanced to me. At that point, what's the difference between a score of a two or a six? It's all 'fail' when it dips below a seven."

And when a game does fall below the average, there's more hanging in the balance than a simple individual buying decision. A PR rep's job can hang on an aggregate review score, as detailed in a recent Gamasutra article.[80] "The score would never live up to the expectation," former Rockstar PR rep Todd Zuniga said in the article. "If it scored a 99, the expectation was for every other review to be 100."

Sewart thinks blaming PR people for low scores is ludicrous. "The score is (or should) be based solely on the quality of the game, which the PR reps have absolutely nothing to do with," he said. "To use average scores to judge marketing effectiveness is the same as saying they're trying to figure out whether the 'payola' worked or not."

More than just PR jobs, though, review scores can have a profound effect at the retail level. "Aggregate scores are being used to determine re-orders at retail, to greenlight sequels, and as payment bonuses," says former *Computer Games* editor Steve Bauman. "It's a depressing trend. A collection of arbitrary numbers, when added together in a rather arbitrary way, becomes an even more arbitrary and meaningless number. While they provide a good general indicator of quality (or a lack thereof), they're an overly blunt instrument."

So how can we make readers focus less on the scores and more on the text? A few journalists suggested that making the actual writing better would help, but others doubt how effective that would really be. "No one reads text," Bauman said, "so if a reader can't be bothered to care about the 'why' of a score, there's little a writer or publication can do."

One interesting solution might be doing away with numbers and simply adding more words. "You can say a lot about a game with a single word," Kietzmann says. "Epic. Miserable. Bubblegum. Moving. Stick a nice, bold word at the end of the review that captures how you felt about the game."

Or, if you prefer, just stop worrying about it so much. "If readers want to base their decisions off a random number, then so be it," Sewart said. Or, as former *Tips & Tricks* Editor-in-chief Bill Kunkel more bluntly puts it, "Anyone who buys/rents ... any game based solely on somebody's star or number-based rating rather than the review itself is pretty much a tool anyway."

Swimming Against the Mainstream

Originally published on GameDaily, Aug. 16, 2007

In March, 2000, the presidential campaign was just beginning to coalesce around Al Gore and George W. Bush. Vladimir Putin has just been elected president of Russia. The NASDAQ composite index reached yet another all-time high amid fears of a dot-com bubble burst.

Looking at all this major news, *Newsweek* decided to devote a cover to the Japanese launch of the PlayStation 2.

"It was our ninth best-selling cover that year, behind the 'final four' on the first *Survivor*," says N'gai Croal, *Newsweek*'s video game reporter, who worked on the cover story with Stephen Levy. The cover came after an awakening for Croal and his editors about the importance of this burgeoning medium. "[In 1999] my editors signed off on me going on a two-and-a-half week trip around the industry, from Bungie to Ion Storm to Microsoft. At the end of that, I said, 'I've seen the future, and we need to cover this more.'"

AUTHOR'S NOTE

Today, you're a bit more likely to see quality reporting on the artistic and cultural importance of video games in major mainstream outlets like *The New York Times*, *The New Yorker*, and *The Guardian* (the rise of esports as a bona fide phenomenon certainly hasn't hurt this trend). But the frequency of that reporting still pales in comparison to the column-inches given to movies, music, and TV in those same pages.

Part of that is still likely due to the star power and PR maturity of those other media, which helps draw readers and writers. But a larger part, I think, is that the editors in charge of these august publications still overwhelmingly come from a generation that didn't grow up with video games, and struggles to understand what's becoming a dominant form of entertainment for a younger generation. To a large extent, fixing this problem is (still) just going to be a matter of waiting for a new class of younger editors to rise through the ranks.

Convincing a mainstream outlet they need to cover games is not always such an easy sell, though. "For me, it was a constant struggle at CNN," says Chris Morris, who wrote CNN/Money's Game Over column until this March. "It took years of lobbying—and even when the Game Over column proved successful, there was still a contingent of management that didn't want it to run ... I wrote for CNN/Money, so a good bit of the resistance came from the mindset that games weren't 'serious enough' for the audience."

> *Games can't really match the sexy, celebrity-fueled image of music and movies in the competition for entertainment coverage space.*

Yes, despite increasing penetration into the public consciousness and industry revenues that rival annual box office receipts, video games still have trouble attracting one important audience—mainstream editors. "My editors don't know videogames, so they can't tell me how to cover it," says Croal. "They kind of get it, in the abstract. But they don't play games, so for them, it's invisible. They're interested in games to the extent that my blog is our most successful blog, by an order of magnitude. That's it."

But that's beginning to change, at least at some of the younger, hipper outlets. "My editors play games, and beyond that, my company makes games," says Stephen Totilo, who covers games for MTV. "Not just web games, but they do things like buy Harmonix, so people here buy into the relevance of games in a big way."

Indeed, compared to other mainstream outlets, MTV seemed eager to jump into the games space. "In my case, it was actually a major media outlet seeking out a games reporter, which struck me as unusual but refreshing," Totilo said. "They brought me in for an interview and told me they knew that celebrity-based gaming coverage wouldn't cut it. I was, quite frankly, shocked. It helps that my boss and his boss both have game systems and play stuff."

Others had to use a different angle to break into the mainstream. "I found sympathetic editors on the Marketplace page of the *Wall Street Journal,* where our coverage gave people insight into weird subcultures of strange animals doing funny things like winning Ferraris in game tournaments," said Dean Takahashi, who currently writes about games for the *San Jose Mercury News*. "I think the 'celebrities' in the game space are the folks that are viewed as weird, like the people who play *WoW* all night long or the pro gamers. They're curiosities that can be laughed at."

And that's part of the problem. Games can't really match the sexy, celebrity-fueled image of music and movies in the competition for entertainment coverage space. "Game developers are not celebrities, and we're very much in a celebrity moment," Croal said. "Until Jade Raymond is on the cover of *US Weekly* and David Jaffe is on TMZ, celebs will keep trumping games." It's both a blessing and a curse, Croal said. "The irony is that we have way more access to developers and publishers than reporters have to actors, musicians and movie execs—but we can't get the space because games aren't sexy."

Getting editors and readers to care about something besides celebrities is just one challenge of writing for a mainstream audience. Getting them to just understand games is another. "We all get used to the vocabulary," Morris said. "But say 'd-pad' to your parent or grandparent and they'll look at you like Victor, the RCA dog. ... I always considered it my challenge to write for a mainstream audience, but in a style that gamers will appreciate and not feel like they're being spoken down to."

The key, mainstream writers agree, is to find angles that will appeal to gamers but also to a wider audience. "I've written pieces that were about how developers decide what to do with virtual dead bodies after you shoot enemies," Totilo said. "That kind of story doesn't depend on people knowing what games I'm referring to. It's just interesting ... I hope!"

Good angles or no, video game coverage in the mainstream might just be a victim of bad timing. "I think many newspapers embraced gaming coverage to go after young readers," Takahashi said. "I fear that they may conclude that they've lost that battle. Therefore the gaming coverage will never measure up to online coverage. So it may be cut back."

With the entire print journalism industry in decline, game coverage is often one of the first things to go. "The declining interest in games in [Newsweek] has to do with evaporating ad pages as advertisers move more to online," said Croal, who now writes the bulk of his coverage for Newsweek's Level Up blog. "Look at a recent issue of Time or Newsweek. The mags are getting thinner and thinner. In that kind of environment, covering games in print is a luxury they can't afford."

So will game coverage ever become another universal pillar of coverage at mainstream arts desks? It depends on who you ask. "I don't think video games will ever be covered as broadly as movies, because I don't think they'll ever quite attain as universal an appeal," Totilo said. "Even as a greater percentage of the population is made up of gamers, individual games will continue to require more time, money and effort to engage in than a movie you can drive to the theater to see or download off the internet."

For others, it's not about whether games will remain popular, but whether newspapers and magazines will. "I think that as older editors die off and young game-savvy editors take over, the coverage will shift, following the same demographic trends," Takahashi said. "The question is whether mainstream media will last that long."

In the end, no matter what the format is, people will always want to know about the latest games. "With the future of journalism moving online, video game coverage is well-positioned to thrive and survive," Croal said. "As for the nature and quality of that coverage? To be determined."

Rumor Reporter

Originally published on GameDaily, Nov. 8, 2007

Being a news reporter in the video game industry is a constant balancing act. On the one hand, if you just report on the official announcements and public information released by the game companies, you're little more than a stenographer—a PR person by proxy. On the other hand, if you rely on unofficial, rumored information, you run the risk of misinforming your readers and getting burned if and when the information is proven false.

Then again, if you wait for the official word, you could be left with old information that other outlets reported much earlier, when it was "just a rumor." Then again (again), the game companies you rely on for comment and cooperation might not be too happy if you ruin their finely-honed information dispersal schedule.

The key question for any reporter, then, becomes this: When should you publish a rumor and when should you sit on it?

Or maybe a better first question for reporters is where to get those rumors in the first place. "Regarding leads and sources ... following the journalistic model is the key," says GameSpot Senior News Editor Tor Thorsen. "Cultivate relationships with PR reps and developers at events by being genuine, friendly, and polite."

Thorsen says staying respectful is essential to getting sources to open up. "Sure, after-hours carousing can—and often should—get a little rowdy. But the enthusiasm aroused by games mixed with the free-flowing booze at press events has led to some pretty ugly scenes of reporters cornering developers and PR reps. I can think of one instance with a pretty prominent writer ... actually berating a developer about his game at high volume to his face." That's not a good way to cultivate a source, to say the least.

"Regarding rumors, we cultivate sources pretty much every way you'd imagine,' says *Electronic Gaming Monthly* Senior Editor Crispin Boyer. "Folks we meet while doing reporting for features, news, or cover stories; PR people who sometimes slip up and say too much; industry folks who leave and move to another company but are willing to dish details about their previous employer; or just friends of the staff who work at developers. ... We also hear a lot of stuff at industry events. Alcohol plus idle chatter equals good stuff for our rumor section."

OK, so now that you've got the rumor, the question again becomes what to do with it.

"We created Rumor Control so we could address less-than-solid items getting wide play without lumping them with regular news, which is an alarmingly everyday occurrence amongst most blogs out there," Thorsen said. Indeed, one of the best ways to avoid letting your readers get taken in by rumors is by separating them out in a separate rumor section.

If you can't do that, you have to take extra care to let the reader know that what they're reading isn't coming from official sources. "When I do post a rumor I make sure to phrase the post title in the form of a question as a visual hint, and make it clear in the post text that the information should be taken with some salt," says Slashdot Games editor Michael Zenke. "When it is 'low hanging fruit,' I do try to confirm rumors ... but generally I've found people appreciate being alerted to persistent, if unfounded, ideas."

While solid confirmation for most rumors can be hard to come by, asking for an official comment from the affected company is just good policy. "I think the proper journalistic approach is (duh) to follow proper journalistic practices," Thorsen said. "Make your inquiries, see what you get back. If you don't get a response in a timely manner, note you had not received comment in your piece, move on, and update it later. When you pull the 'No response had been received as of press time,' trigger depends of course, on the urgency and/or merit of the story."

> *The enthusiasm aroused by games mixed with the free-flowing booze at press events has led to some pretty ugly scenes of reporters cornering developers and PR reps.*
>
> *Tor Thorsen*
> *News Editor, GameSpot*

That doesn't mean it's always easy doing things the proper way. "For me personally, waiting for publisher comment is the most annoying thing in the world," Thorsen said. "When you finally get a response and present all the evidence on the table in a solid news story with context, the kids set upon you like jackals in the forums. 'SO SLOW GameSpot! I heard this TWO HOURS AGO! LOL! LMAO!' Some reward for doing things by the book."

Official comments are all well and good, but what about those juicy stories that you can only get by promising a trusted source that he or she won't be named? "Anonymity, I think, is vital," says Thorsen. "I'll give it to anyone who I trust is not bullshitting me. I mean look at reporters for major newspapers—they go to jail before they reveal their sources, if they know they're valid. Why should we be any different?"

EGM's Boyer agrees. "Usually any of these sources are pretty trustworthy, and we're willing to grant them anonymity for juicy rumors," he said. "Readers know what they're getting into because we publish this stuff in a special rumor section … Sometimes rumors come from industry folks who may leak info before they're supposed to—as dictated by, say, an embargo or certain marketing milestone—so we protect their identity by putting the info in our rumors section rather than as a news item."

Others don't necessarily agree. "Most rumors are pretty inconsequential," says Steve Bauman, former editor of *Computer Games Magazine*. "We're talking about games here, not national security issues. Printing a rumor of a sequel should elicit, 'Well, duh' reactions... hell, it'd be bigger news if someone announced that they weren't doing a sequel."

That doesn't mean you can just print anything that sounds plausible, though. Being able to trust your source is of prime importance."If it's an Xbox 360 rumor from billgates@yahoo.com, maybe you shouldn't run it," Bauman said. "If it's from someone you can verify would know this kind of information, by all means run with it. But briefly consider that if it isn't true, it's your own credibility you're putting on the line."

In the end, when in doubt, it's probably better to sit on a rumor that might be false than to run one that might be true. "When it comes to reporting on rumors, I tend to err on the side of caution," Zenke said. "If it sounds even slightly fishy, I'll keep it off of the site. If it's something so obvious that anyone could have seen it coming, I'll keep that off the site too since I assume an official announcement along those lines will be made shortly. Deciding what falls into that middle ground is hard, sometimes, but I try to make my best effort."

RIP, *Games for Windows* Magazine

Originally published on GameSpot, April 10, 2008

I wasn't even alive when *Computer Gaming World* launched in 1981, but I was around this week when the print version of the magazine, which was renamed *Games for Windows* in 2006, was repurposed for inclusion in Ziff Davis' online gaming portal,

1UP. I talked with 1UP Vice President for Content Simon Cox about *GFW*'s move online, the state of print gaming journalism in general, and the difficulties facing Ziff Davis. Some excerpts from our conversation:

ON THE REASONS BEHIND THE MOVE AWAY FROM PRINT

"I can tell you that *GFW* closing is a direct result of dollars and eyeballs moving from print to online way more quickly in the PC space than they are, from our reckoning, in the console space. Part of it is, [on the PC] you can surf the web and play a game without leaving your seat. These guys are obviously more connected online, they tend to be more into the community aspects online. ... I think it's sort of a natural fit to have PC content where PC gamers are hanging out, which is more online.

"The circulation of the mag had been challenged over the last year, certainly. I'm not going to go into details but I would say that the newsstand had dropped, and it was a tougher environment for the newsstand. That was part of the problem too—you have less advertising, less success on the newsstand and that really all adds up to one thing: people are obviously getting this information somewhere else. It's not that they don't want it, they're getting it somewhere else, and our feeling was they were getting it online. ...

"This is a sad day here, no doubt about that. A 27-year-old magazine has gone away and it's sad and people are definitely pissed off here about it, but we're also kind of going, 'You know what, we kind of saw it coming, it makes sense, and it's where the business needs to go.' It was really hard for me to watch these guys work their asses off month after month that fewer and fewer people were reading and fewer and fewer advertisers were advertising in. It was very tough to watch that."

ON THE FUTURE OF ZIFF DAVIS' *ELECTRONIC GAMING MONTHLY*

"*EGM* remains viable. We have advertiser support, and the newsstand was not as bad as with *GFW*. Newsstand has slipped a little bit, but it's nowhere near the downturn we saw with *GFW* in the past year. Will *EGM* be around forever? No. When will it kind of cease to be? When there's not enough advertising or enough people reading it. ...

"Particularly with information-based magazine publishing. If you're in the business of publishing a magazine that gives timely information to readers, the internet is going to kill you at some point one day. It's just a question of when, and with *GFW* that day was today, and with *EGM* that day will be some time in the future, but not for a good while."

[**EDITOR'S NOTE:** *EGM* would shut down its print edition in January of 2009, about nine months after this piece was first published. The magazine would briefly limp back to life a few years later under different ownership, and now exists as a purely digital brand.]

> *A 27-year old magazine has gone away and it's sad and people are definitely pissed off here about it, but we're also kind of going, 'You know what, we kind of saw it coming, it makes sense, and it's where the business needs to go.'*
>
> *Simon Cox*
> *Vice President for Content, 1UP*

ON THE POSSIBILITY OF PC GAMING COVERAGE COMING TO *EGM*

"That's something we're kicking around. We need to talk to the audience, figure out if they want it, does it make sense. When you think about one of the factors that has made today what today is—the idea of PC eyeballs moving online and advertising revenue as well—obviously it's sort of a limited market, I would suggest, for too much PC coverage in *EGM*. Does that mean we couldn't cover some PC games, or list 'PC' as an alternate format in some of the features and previews that we do in *EGM*? No. We could, and we need to talk about that internally and talk about what makes sense for *EGM*."

ON THE DIFFERENCE BETWEEN WRITING FOR MAGAZINES AND THE WEB

"When I look at the top ten features on our site over the past six months, almost all of them were from *Games for Windows*. ... The idea that these features don't do well [online] is actually kind of wrong. Sites like Digg really help with that. If somebody finds something they find interesting it'll do well on Digg and people will spend the time to read it. I don't think longform is inappropriate for the web, I think it just has to be done in the right way and with the right subject matter and presented in the right way, but we believe we can do that and these guys are great at it."

ON CLOSING A MAGAZINE AMIDST A BANKRUPTCY FILING

"The timing is terrible. Make no mistake about it, internally here we've been wringing our hands about the timing of this announcement because of the Chapter 11 filing. We're just saying, 'You know what, people are going to put these two things together, there's not much we can do about it' ... and I can understand why they'd do that, but the truth is they don't have anything to do with each other.

GFW's financial issues with advertising revenue and with the newsstand are completely separate from the [bankruptcy] filing. The filing is about restructuring the debt and basically turning over the company to the people who own that debt over time. The courts are going to be taking care of that ... *GFW* is not a factor at all in that. This would have happened with or without a filing."

ON ZIFF DAVIS' PLAN GOING FORWARD

"I've been through some magazine closures—you know that this company has been through a lot—and we're going through that transition and it's been very very hard, no doubt about that. But this closure, it's wasn't one of those deals where everybody's lost their jobs. We're taking this team, Jeff [Green] and Shawn [Elliott] and Sean [Malloy] and Ryan [Scott], and we're putting them all online, which is very, very different than magazine closures we've had in the past. ... This is the first time we've done that in our history, and I think that speaks to the whole plan, and there is a plan, which is that we need to grow online, which is what we're doing. ...

"Going forward, you can only sustain so much of [an unprofitable magazine] until you say, 'Look what's the outlook for the magazine,' and the outlook was bad and you have to make that decision and it's the right decision. The vision going forward is we know we need to be a bigger player online, and we're not going to do that if we keep resources on a magazine that not enough people are reading and not enough advertisers are advertising in."

Are You Done With That Game?

Originally published on GameSpot, July 14, 2008

In a perfect world, every game reviewer would be able to play every game to completion before crafting a thorough and well-researched critique of the gameplay and narrative. Of course, in a perfect world every game would be perfect, so there would be no need for reviewers at all.

AUTHOR'S NOTE

Over the years, I've really taken Gillen's quote here to heart: "When you reach a point where you know there's nothing that a game can do to change your buying recommendation, I'd argue it's fair to mark it from there." That about sums it up for me... you can skip to the next piece if that satisfies you, too.

Unfortunately, we don't live in a perfect world, and practically every professional reviewer admits to falling short of the ideal, play-it-to-the-finish standard at one time or another. The reasons behind these lapses range from the practical to the personal.

"When you reach a point where you know there's nothing that a game can do to change your buying recommendation, I'd argue it's fair to mark it from there," says freelancer Kieron Gillen. "If a game has been awful for 10 hours—hell, even less—there's no way you can recommend it. It is a bad game." Gillen also argues that the opposite is true: "If a game has been excellently entertaining for, say, 20 hours...I'd say you could recommend it strongly. If you can say, 'If the game stopped at this point, I'd still give it a rave review,' you can be justified in doing exactly that."

Of course, not everyone agrees with that take on things. "Years ago, *Halo 2* hooked me with smooth controls, intense battles, an excellent multiplayer system, and all that good stuff, but the horrible ending soured every experience that came before," said freelancer Brian Rowe. "Had I only played 99.9 percent of the way through *Halo 2*, my opinion would have been vastly different. Just because a game begins on a high note does not mean that the developers can maintain that pace through to the end."

Although standards vary for different outlets, most American specialist magazines and websites insist that their reviews be based on a full playthrough of a game. "There's a real need for us to strive to give readers a definitive take," says *Wired*'s Chris Baker. "A game is a work of art and a piece of software, and it demands to be addressed in depth on both of those levels in our criticism."

That said, Baker admits that this sort of comprehensive coverage is not always possible. "*Wired* magazine has a three-month lead time, so getting access to final code is incredibly difficult... Given the nature of games, and given issues of timeliness and access, I think that there has to be room for other sorts of coverage that don't aspire to be an exhaustive critique."

New reviewers learn quickly to make the most out of situations in which the game is long and the deadline is short. "When you're handed a game rated at 40-plus hours, and you only have two days to get the job done, you do the best that you can and leave it at that," says Rowe. "It's not the optimal situation, but reviewing games is a business. It doesn't matter if your writing skills make Hemingway look like a talentless hack. If you can't get a review published in a timely fashion, the readers are going to move elsewhere. Gamers have money to spend and they don't want to wait until next week to find out how to spend it."

> *When you reach a point where you know there's nothing that a game can do to change your buying recommendation, I'd argue it's fair to mark it from there.*
>
> *Kieron Gillen*
> *Freelancer*

Many reviewers cite epic, sprawling role-playing games such as *The Elder Scrolls IV: Oblivion* as the bane of their tight schedules. "I'd much rather knock out three or four action games than spend the same amount of time on one RPG," said veteran GameCritics reviewer Brad Gallaway. "Since story and characterization are such an integral part of the RPG experience, they're games that usually demand being played to completion in order to be discussed with any authority... It's just not time- or cost-effective." Freelancer Raymond Padilla agrees that the pure dollars-per-hour economics makes reviewing RPGs a tough sell. "If you have a choice between [reviewing] a mainstream action game and a Japanese RPG—neither of which you're too interested in personally—you'd be an idiot to take the RPG."

Should readers be aware if and when a review is based on an incomplete playthrough? Many reviewers seem to think so. "The launch of *Grand Theft Auto IV* should be a boon to reviewers," said freelancer Chris Dahlen. "Most of the critics admitted they didn't, and couldn't, finish the game before they went to print. While some of the reviews were premature and uncritical, the whole blitz raised the reader's awareness of the fact that meeting a deadline while finishing a 40-plus-hour or 100-plus-hour game story is impossible—and anyone who tries would skim over everything that makes the game worth playing in the first place."

But others don't think that the amount of time spent by the reviewer is vital information. "I don't tell readers when I don't finish a game," Rowe said. "I know it might sound shady, but I guarantee that it's standard practice. If every reviewer started listing playtimes in reviews, readers would start flocking to whichever publication has the highest completion ratio, as opposed to the most worthwhile opinions."

Of course, this fast-and-loose attitude towards review completeness can lead to important omissions in a review. "There's been a number of times when something pops up in a game in the middle or at the end," says GameCritics' Gallaway, "and I'd say about half the time when I check other reviews to see if that same issue is mentioned, there's not a peep. I'm not pointing fingers, but the smart money would say that those reviews were written in the early 'honeymoon phase' that just about any game can provide. But, is a game good all the way through? That's the real question that a good reviewer should try to answer."

Nevertheless, some reviewers argue that there's no reason for a reviewer to finish a game when most readers aren't going to complete it either. "The last figures I saw for *Half-Life 2: Episode 1* said that only 50 percent of the people who bought it completed it," says Gillen. "And that's on a game which lasted four hours. Even for the increasingly common

6- to 10-hour games, you wouldn't expect a completion rate [that's] any higher, let alone the 80-hour RPG epics. Hell, failure to complete [a game] doesn't even mean that a player dislikes the game—they can get distracted and move onto other things, but still love their time with the game."

"The normal state of gamers is to leave a game uncompleted," Gillen continued. "A reviewer doing likewise isn't the same as a book reviewer stopping halfway through."

Going Indie

Originally published on Crispy Gamer, November 24, 2008

AUTHOR'S NOTE

The gaming world that existed when this story was first published is practically unrecognizable today. Back then, a relative handful of indie games were primarily fighting with the major publishers for attention. Today, they're mainly fighting with the literally hundreds of other indie games that come out *every week*.

Today, it's hard to find a major gaming outlet that totally ignores indie games (for various values of "indie"). At the same time, at many outlets it's hard to argue that indie games are getting coverage commensurate with their relative size, novelty, and influence in the gaming world. A handful of select, well-marketed indies seem to break through to sizable coverage every year, but dozens of other worthy titles are fighting to get a single review or interview.

As a few sources point out in this piece, getting a "mainstream" gaming audience to pay attention to "niche" indie games is always going to be an uphill battle. Still, I think a lot of members of the game press could do a better job trying to even out the balance.

Imagine that you've got the best game idea in the history of game ideas. You don't work at a major video game publisher but you do have a modicum of programming and artistic skill, so you set yourself to many long nights of work getting your vision out of your head and into an executable file. Finally, after months of toil, you're ready to share your wholly original, accessible and eminently playable creation with the world. You upload your creation to some free web space and... despair as a grand total of ten people download it in your first month. Hey, at least your mom said she liked it.

Independent games—generally, games released without the support of a major publisher—can't rely on major marketing campaigns or months of hype to generate interest. For these games, the challenge of convincing people to download a demo or buy a copy only comes after the challenge of simply making people aware of your game's existence. This is where the video game press can theoretically help, turning readers on to the best under-hyped indie gems.

So, how well is the press performing this vital function? Well, it depends on who you ask.

"A passionate games journalist who loves your work will get you more coverage than an entire PR department," says Kieron Gillen, one of four people behind indie-friendly PC site Rock Paper Shotgun, in a 2005 essay on the vagaries of marketing indie games.[81] And Gillen should know... as the essay details, his review of *Uplink* for the UK's *PC Gamer* helped pull the game out of obscurity and push it towards a modicum of success. Seven years after *Uplink*'s release, though, indie game coverage is in a very different place. "I wonder if it's in a transitional phase," he said in a recent interview. "We're still trying to work out what we want indie games to be. As in, everyone—readers, journalists, and developers."

Gillen is particularly concerned that some outlets are reluctant to cover indie games because the readers themselves haven't show much interest. "It seems that all the major websites are going through a belt-tightening phase... I'm worried that people running websites want to maximise their money into page impressions. And if spending the money on an indie review will get fewer page impressions than spending it on a feature comparing the frame-rate of a 360 and a PS3 game, they're going to spend it on the latter."

Indeed, the difficulty in getting readers to care about underhyped indie games is enough to make even committed indie boosters despair. "To be honest, I've come to the conclusion that the lack of [indie game] coverage is due to a lack of interest," said Russell Carroll, editor-in-chief of major indie games portal GameTunnel. "If you watch posts on popular game sites like Joystiq and Kotaku, there are a lot fewer comments on the posts about indie games than on the ones about just about anything else. That's really disappointing to me, and shows just how big of a marketing problem indies have."

Carroll sees a distressing level of groupthink around which games get coverage and attention. "There is definitely a lot of peer pressure, for lack of a better phrase, to like the same types of games that everyone else likes in order to be a 'gamer,'" he said. "I like to think that the press is nobly above that, but that's really not the case. ... At best, when indie games are talked about on game news sites, there is a cautious tone as if the writer isn't quite sure how the audience is going to react. Typically the writer approaches the task as though they are trying to convince you of something."

Of course, there are exceptions. Indie games like *Braid*, *Everyday Shooter* and *World of Goo*, to name but a few, have broken out of obscurity thanks largely to glowing coverage from the press. These success stories, though, can help obscure how shallow the indie coverage is on most sites. "In the last half year I've seen people give a lot of attention to a few [indie] games, but less so to the second tier," Gillen said. GameTunnel's Carroll agrees, calling out most sites' coverage for inconsistency. "Some games, like *Audiosurf*, get noticed, others, like *The Spirit Engine 2* don't. ... Lots of sites will cover indie games with a few great articles in a month and then not mention anything for months."

> *The difficulty in getting readers to care about underhyped indie games is enough to make even committed indie boosters despair.*

Then again, it's understandable that many larger sites aren't putting indie games at the top of their coverage plans. "Indie games are sometimes indie because they are actually not that... mainstream," says Simon Carless, publisher at Gamasutra and *Game Developer* magazine and chairman of the Independent Games Festival. "So it's natural that some big sites, especially sites that review games, might not be covering them as a first choice."

But this sort of reluctance to cover indie games has a huge effect on the publishers themselves. "The only way for most gamers to hear about Introversion games and to understand the premise of our games is to read reviews of them," says Introversion's Chris Delay in a recent forum post. "We've heard disturbing rumours from more than one source that major games websites are now cutting back on the number of games they review—and it's [indie] games like Multiwinia that are getting dropped because there will always be hundreds of bigger games. If this is true and is widespread (as we are starting to believe), it has grave repercussions for all indie developers who rely on press reviews as their primary form of publicity."

The good news for these publishers is that many journalists seem to have a vested interest in really pulling for the little guy.

"I think independent games are 'in vogue' right now, which can be great for indies, and that does mean that in some cases, they get covered a lot more," Carless said. "When I think about the indie game coverage which is most important ... to a certain extent they are creating a community and evangelizing to it, rather than, say, telling someone what score out of 10 that they gave a game."

Or, as Gillen put it in his 2005 message to indie developers, "We're on your side. Generally speaking. ... Everyone likes an underdog, and games journalists more than most. ... You're an indie developer. Don't be afraid to play it up or underestimate how, as the rest of the industry marches toward kerzillion dollar budgets, that makes you attractive to the press. You represent the ideal of why we want to write about games in the first place."

The Review Copy Revue

Originally published on Crispy Gamer, Sept. 10, 2009

When I was growing up and dreaming of a position as a game journalist, I envisioned three primary perks to the job: 1) Getting to play games all day, 2) Getting to see games months early at the Consumer Electronics Show (the precursor to today's Electronic Entertainment Expo) and 3) Getting to play early review copies of games before they reached store shelves.

Of course now that I'm a full time game journalist, I know the somewhat disappointing reality behind of all these perks. Yes, I get to play games during the work day, but more of my time seems to be spent writing about them, which is the part I actually get paid for. Yes I get to go to E3, but after a while the show seems less like a massive, freeform arcade and more like an endless, hellish slog filled with massive lines and boring appointments. And while I do get access to plenty of reviewable games before release, getting such access from public relations departments has sometimes been a struggle, especially when I was just starting out.

AUTHOR'S NOTE

Today, PR people have the advantage of being able to send almost any reviewable games as a downloadable code (rather than bulky physical packages). These codes still often require paying money to the distribution platform, though, meaning PR people still often have to pick and choose which outlets get access and which don't.

To compound the problem, the ease with which one can create a YouTube profile or free blog can make it unclear who's really trying to build an audience and who's just in it for the free loot. At the same time, influential streamers can often supercharge a game's sales much more readily than traditional written reviews, meaning the latter sometimes find themselves dropping down the "tier list" of influential media these days.

In an ideal world, of course, there would be enough early press copies of a game available to satisfy every legitimate journalist with an interest in writing a review. In reality though, almost every journalist I've talked to says they've gotten some form of the "we just don't have enough copies available" excuse when requesting a game for review. And the public relations people I've talked to say that's the line isn't just a cop out.

"For example, with independent developers, review units cost money and they usually have limited budgets so you unfortunately can't give everyone a copy," said Sean Kauppinen, Founder & CEO of International Digital Entertainment Agency. But even larger publishers may be constrained when it comes to providing the early copies that reviewers need to prepare that launch day review. "Keep in mind that most PR departments work towards a strict budget on each title and have to 'buy' their review copies using that budget," explained Matt Frary, a partner at Maverick PR. "That is money that could have been used for one more media tour, one more event, or one more video, so you really find yourself reviewing the list critically and measuring the return on investment (ROI) for each copy."

So which outlets and writers get those limited copies when review time comes around? Most PR professionals I talked to admitted they had a list of "Tier 1" or "VIP" outlets which were the first to receive copies of all their new games, whether they requested them or not. These lists tend to include outlets with large readerships, long histories, and outsize reputations in the industry, including newspapers like *USA Today* and *The New York Times*, magazines like *Game Informer* and websites like IGN and GameSpot.

For many, it's just logical that the biggest outlets get access to games first. But some PR professionals think you can get better results with a more targeted approach. David Tractenberg, President at Traction Public Relations, disregards an outlet's size and instead uses a first-come-first-serve model for distributing most of his promo games. "The reporters that are most interested in a title will contact us sometimes months in advance to get a copy," he said. "We always send to those people first as they want it the most and will usually write about it. Once we have satisfied those people we start sending to the people we have known the longest who have always been fair to us and take the time to review the game properly. After that we send to the larger sites and the outlets where we have established relationships."

Some PR reps prioritize access based on an outlet's specific focus. "Knowing that they are legitimate journalists working for outlets that are relevant to the product's target audience is the key factor in determining who gets review units if they are limited," said Kaupinnen. "We always review the list based on what we're promoting and who is relevant for the specific game. ... If you can't be bothered to target your reviews, you probably shouldn't be doing PR or marketing." Others pick and choose based on how much they trust the writer or outlet they're working with. "For pre-launch [evaluation copies], we work with a select number of journalists who we know well and can trust to not disclose embargoed information prematurely," said Garth Chouteau, President of Public Relations at PopCap.

All of this is fine if you're working for an established site with a unique focus, or if you have a large PR rolodex and the foresight to call ahead. But for new outlets and writers with few clips and fewer PR contacts, it can be difficult to break on to the review copy radar. Many journalists I talked reported running into brick walls with PR when they were starting out, and being forced to buy or rent their own retail copies just to run late reviews. At least one major publisher reportedly requires a new outlet to exist for six months and have an Alexa ranking of 100,000 or less (i.e. a few hundred unique visitors a day) before the outlet can receive promo copies of its games.

> *In reality though, almost every journalist I've talked to says they've gotten some form of the "we just don't have enough copies available" excuse when requesting a game for review. And the public relations people I've talked to say that's the line isn't just a cop out.*

In part, policies like these are a defense against the dozens of opportunistic "review" sites that pop up overnight just to try and scam free games out of publishers. "For a while there, I was getting several requests a week from review sites located on Geocities," said Maverick's Frary said. "'My-game-reviews-rock.geocities.net' just isn't that impressive on the coverage report, and I could get just as many hits by posting my own review online somewhere."

The problem has only gotten worse as the media environment has gotten more fractured. "It's worth noting that Twitter is going to be the real acid test," said Popcap's Chouteau. "There are countless Twitterers who are starting to position themselves as journalists by virtue of having 500 or 1,000 followers and an opinion (How quaint -ed.). We have started saying 'no' to many of those, and we'll continue to do so."

But most of the PR professionals I talked to said that refusing to send review copies to sites just because they're small isn't a winning strategy in general. "Some publishers ... still refuse to expand their list and stick only to the 'big' players in the space," Frary said. "This is really too bad and they end up missing a massive, and growing, segment of the market. ... [It's] particularly frustrating because when you look at the smaller video game sites out there as a whole, they have a huge voice that reaches a critical audience that the larger outlets sometimes miss." Or as Traction's Tractenberg put it, "Even if a site only has 150 fans, if those fans are rabid and they like the game, they will buy it which makes the review copy money well spent."

Plus, in today's media environment, you never know when a small article from a small site will turn into a big article from a suddenly hot site. "Rating a site as 'too small' is short-sighted, because you never know what story will 'blow up' for a site," said Calico Media PR rep Ted Brockwood. "Recently, one smaller site we deal with frequently published a story that got posted on Digg, and so they saw a nearly 500% boost in their total monthly traffic in just one day. If the PR people on that story had ignored the site for being 'too small' they would have missed a fantastic opportunity."

The quickest way for a journalist to lose access to review copies isn't by being small or new, though. It's being unfair or narrow-minded. "For example - if a writer has said flat out (either in a column, a preview, etc.) that they hate FPS games, then why send them one for review?" Brockwood asked rhetorically. "It only wastes their time and yours by trying to force them to review something they dislike already."

And if you do receive games, PR reps say, for goodness sakes actually play them. "We also had a site that didn't actually play the game," Tractenberg said. "They said they played one level and based their review on that. I understand having limited time to review products, but if people are going to destroy a title a developer spent four years building they could spend a few hours trying it out first."

In the end, the only thing separating a new journalist from the mountain of early review copies they envision is a bit of elbow grease put into writing and building relationships with PR. "If you're serious about kicking off a game site and are looking for PR support, you need to do the early legwork to establish yourself," Frary said. "Go buy some just-released titles and write up some great reviews, request to be added to several publisher's news distribution lists, knock out some thoughtful interviews and run some news stories. Be proactive and open up a dialogue with PR people across the industry to create unique coverage for your site. ... PR folks don't send out review builds for fun or to make friends. They send out review builds to secure coverage that will help the game succeed and sell more copies. That's it."

Let Us In to Your Crappy Conference for Jerks!

Originally published on The Game Beat, Oct. 14, 2016

I know that developers often want a time and place to discuss things by themselves, without the potential for the press to listen in to share (and possibly distort) everything they say. But the lengths some developers take to insulate some of their larger gatherings from the press can be kind of ridiculous.

Take this week's Steam Dev Days. This is the third year that Valve has hosted its no-press-allowed conference, and the very first keynote speaker led off with a riff on why the media wasn't there.

> Another thing we don't want Dev Days to be is a PR event, so it isn't one. This isn't really all about livestreams and a lot of super-high production values. Instead, this is a relatively private event where we're just here to talk to each other. Of course it's not all the way private—we haven't closed the doors and made you all sign NDAs to be here—the information we say here will make its way out into the world, and that's a good thing.
>
> But it's a pretty different event because we haven't invited the press to be here, so there aren't press people here. That means that the kinds of conversations that go on are pretty different. They're more like collaboration and work, getting things done together.
>
> At least I hope there aren't press people here... if you see one, I'm not really sure what you should do. Maybe point them out to each other and make them feel bad about their life choices (laughter and applause).

Good natured "life choices" ribbing aside, the whole "Dev Days isn't a PR event" shtick is starting to wear a little thin. For one, events like the Game Developers Conference are absolutely crawling with press, and I'm pretty sure the developers that attend don't feel that they're constantly under surveillance or anything. They can collaborate and "get things done together" just fine even if one of those nasty, nasty members of the media happens to be nearby. Apple's Worldwide Developer Conference is a similarly developer-focused affair, but Apple encourages the press to attend and cover that event and its announcement-packed keynotes.

For another thing, Dev Days does seem to be turning into a PR event, of sorts. In previous years, insider accounts of the internal Dev Days activities revealed relatively dry affairs focused on the minutiae of game development at a level that's probably not of much interest to the generalist press (though, again, GDC seems to function just fine while granting technically-minded journalists access to these kinds of sessions. But I digress).

This years Steam Dev Days event was different, packed with interesting news from the opening keynote onward. This included the first reveal of a new SteamVR controller prototype, the announcement of increased Steam support for the Sony's DualShock 4 controller, coming SteamVR support for OSX and Linux, a mention of new lighthouse trackers and "aysnchronous reprojection" for SteamVR, and hints at internal work on a new piece of Valve-produced VR software, among other things.

It's not like Valve didn't know this information was going to leak out, either—as that keynote speaker said "the information we say here will make its way out into the world, and that's a good thing." In fact, the only reason I have that quote in the first place is because someone live-streamed the entire keynote on Periscope. Anyone watching the #SteamDevDays hashtag on Twitter could also get a pretty good idea of the announcements emanating from Valve at the show, too, in real time.

That being the case, it's hard for me to understand why Valve wouldn't want to bring the press into the tent at least a little bit, to hear all of these relevant announcements directly, rather than having them mangled through secondhand sources. Even if you don't want developers to feel weird with press in the hall, at least throw us a bone with an official livestream of your keynote and a quick press release detailing any relevant announcements contained therein. Or just host an embargoed, pre-conference press call with any general interest announcements you want to make, then focus on the developers when the conference is ongoing.

Maybe Valve is trying to preserve its famously aloof image, and thinks that information that merely leaks out of a "closed" conference takes on some sort of illicit patina of "insider info." Maybe they're even right about that. But I still think the idea of keeping the press away from a major gathering of game developers—one where major announcements are going to happen—is getting kind of silly. You can pretend that developers are the only audience for your "developer conference" all you want, but that doesn't make it true.

Game Critics Face Their Own 'Crunch Time'

Originally published on The Game Beat, March 24, 2017

> *Eating a big steak dinner is great. Being forced to eat 30 steak dinners in the span of a week approaches torture.*

This is the best analogy I've heard for describing the "hardship" of reviewing an epic-length game on a tight embargo deadline (I think Ben Kuchera was the one to first mention this great saying to me, and it's definitely stuck).

I put "hardship" in quotes, of course, because even the most arduous game review assignment isn't nearly as bad as the vast majority of jobs out there. As another famous game journalism saying goes, "the worst part about this job is that you can't complain about it" (or, my personal refrain, "It beats the salt mines").

That said, putting 40, 60, even 80 hours into a single game in the space of a week can be a specific difficulty of this job. It's a problem that's pretty unique to game criticism, too. A film critic only needs a few hours to watch a work before forming their review. A TV reviewer can binge-watch the first six episodes of a new drama in an afternoon. A music reviewer can listen to a new album dozens of times in a single day to capture its nuances. The only thing that really comes close to a game critic's "burden" is a book reviewer facing a thousand-page tome, but even at a page a minute average, such a book can be consumed in about 17 hours.

Facing multiple multi-dozen hour games in a row can make things even more trying. That's a situation game reviewers usually face around the holiday season, but early 2017's back-to-back releases of *Horizon: Zero Dawn*, *The Legend of Zelda: Breath of the Wild*, and *Mass Effect: Andromeda*—not to mention the Nintendo Switch hardware itself—could push some reviewers to the breaking point (especially if they don't have the ability or desire to spread those assignments out to freelancers or other staffers).

Ars Technica's Lee Hutchinson captured the draining nature of a quick turnaround in Ars Technica's "preliminary review" of *Mass Effect: Andromeda*[82] (Full disclosure: I served as editor on this piece).

> I got the press review code for Andromeda on a Saturday, and the game unlocked that evening. "Perfect," I thought. "This will give me at least six days to play. Plenty of time to beat the game, write the review, and have it edited and scheduled to run when the embargo lifts!"
>
> I look back on my stupid optimism with chagrin... Now, as I write this, it's six exhausting days later and I'm 30% of the way through a game that's even longer and more packed with stuff to do than BioWare's previous epic, Dragon Age: Inquisition. I've got about 30 hours of game time committed so far, and, based on a quick bit of back-n-forth with BioWare General Manager Aaryn Flynn, I have probably 90 more hours to go before I really finish the game.
>
> [Later in the review]
>
> Lesson learned: you cannot properly and fully beat this game in a few dozen hours if you're doing it "right"—if you're doing it in the way that we've been trained to beat BioWare games all the way back to Baldur's Gate. You can slapdash your way through it quickly, but like I said earlier, going by the game's progress bar, I'm not even a third of the way finished.

Hutchinson isn't alone. Polygon Reviews editor Arthur Gies says he put in a 100-hour work week to get his *Mass Effect* review done ("Seriously, the *Andromeda* deadline sucked," he added. "It super sucked.") *Wired*'s Julie Muncy recounted writing "like 10,000 words in the past ~five days, which is, in the expert opinion of science, too many." This level of crunch isn't a new problem, either: former GameSpy reviews editor Sterling McGarvey tweets about "the time I slept at GameSpy HQ for four nights to wrap up *RE4* PS2."

Simply finding that kind of time in the week can get harder as reviewers get older, with more work, family, and life responsibilities getting in the way of marathon play sessions. This in turn can help contribute to the burnout that leads many longtime game journalists to leave for other jobs before they've even hit a decade in the business.

Reviewers facing tough deadlines might not compare directly to the well-documented problems game *developers* face with crunch time. But beyond reviewer discomfort, these kind of short deadlines on massive games can lead to a warped critical perspective on the games themselves. The average player, who may put a couple of hours a night into an open-world quest for months on end, will have a very different experience than a reviewer who's rushing through the game as quickly as possible to meet a deadline.

(Part of me wonders if sheer fatigue on the part of reviewers played into *Mass Effect: Andromeda*'s surprisingly negative critical reception this week. Take a look at these excerpts[83] and keep in mind that the people writing them had almost certainly played the game practically non-stop for multiple days just before writing them.)

> *Beyond reviewer discomfort, these kind of short deadlines on massive games can lead to a warped critical perspective on the games themselves.*

Still, the audience (understandably) wants to know a reviewer's thoughts on a game before or as it comes out, rather than waiting weeks or months for impressions of a more leisurely playthrough. Many outlets have resorted to the "review in progress" format to deal with this tension, giving early impressions that are updated as the reviewer comes closer to completion. It's a format that's increasingly being forced on reviewers in other contexts, as games with online components and titles where early review code is not available become more common.

In any case, most game reviewers will tell you they're relatively happy to put in the occasional crunch time on a big release because they love the job. Long hours or not, it's still thrilling to get the opportunity to take on a game completely fresh, before everyone else, and be among the first to share your opinion on that game with the world. To adapt yet another common saying, game reviewing is the kind of job where you'll gladly work 80 hours a week just to avoid working 40.

Sipping from the Fire Hose

Originally published in The Game Beat, April 14, 2017

I'm old enough to remember when Imagine Media launched the short-lived *Game Buyer* magazine with the lofty goal of being an authoritative review resource for every single title released for game consoles at the time. That was a tough but doable feat back in the late '90s, even with a small staff of dedicated critics. As the audience for game reviews started shifting from magazines to the web, sites like IGN and GameSpot did their best to replicate this ideal, offering reviews for even the tiniest and most oft-ignored games, often through freelancers.

Today, it would require a team of hundreds if not thousands of writers to review every new game that comes out. The iOS App Store sees 500 new games submitted each and every day. PC gaming clearinghouse Steam has gone from 379 games released in 2012 to over 4,200 launched in 2016. Things don't look that much better if you stick to the console space: Just three-and-a-half months into 2017, Metacritic lists over 200 PS4 games released for the year—roughly two a day. Of those, a full 55 percent don't have the requisite four reviews needed to generate a Metascore. A few don't even have a single review.

Going by Sturgeon's Law, one can probably skip a full 90 percent of this flood without missing out on anything worthwhile. The question, of course, is how you determine the 10 percent that's worth your time (or less, depending on how much time you have to give).

It's a particularly vexing problems for a critic, or an outlet that's focused on game reviews. You need to critique the big-name games that people have heard of to stay in business, but you probably don't want to limit yourself to just the blockbusters. You want to include a good mix of indie games, but you don't necessarily want to waste your time (or that of your readers) on a bad review of an unheard of game.

Do you challenge your readers with games that might be outside their comfort zone, or pander to them by focusing your attention just on games you already know are going to be popular? Do you sink a precious few hours into an unknown game on the off chance it might develop into something more than the cookie cutter clone it seems at first glance?

On the PR side, having your game ignored by the press can be as bad or worse than getting savaged by bad reviews. Even a video where Jim Sterling calls your game a crime against humanity is more valuable than nothing, in some ways.

The big games are usually able to buy their way to significant coverage through the sheer marketing force of a company or franchise name. For the rest, developers and PR reps are stuck trying to find some angle that will get critics and journalists to pick their name out of an extremely crowded hat. Look, this game has a guy who used to work on *World of Warcraft*, but quit to pursue his passion for free-to-play mobile card games! No, look at our game, it has a voice actress that was a minor character on *Buffy the Vampire Slayer*! Our game is the first Twitch-enabled VR title that lets Twitter users vote on what *Minecraft*-style blocks your character gets to place in a thrilling esports MOBA arena!

In this environment, the modern game critic has to become a curator of attention, both for themselves and for their readers. So we scan social media to see what games are getting buzz from other critics. We walk down the aisles at "indie showcase" events, glancing at screens to see what game concept can grab our attention in ten seconds flat (if it can't, there are dozens of other games to look at in that same aisle). We skim press releases and animated GIFs and trailers looking for titles that might stand out from the crowd enough to at least generate an interesting news blurb.

It's an environment that tends to lead to a certain clustering of attention among the game press as a whole. One intrigued preview or glowing review for a previously unheralded game from a major site can quickly propagate through the critical establishment, turning a no-name indie title into a critical darling. This isn't a totally new phenomenon—I remember when games like *Katamari Damacy* and *Scribblenauts* became sleeper hits at E3s past through the magic of word-of-mouth among critics. Today, that organic awareness happens with a ridiculous *Goat Simulator* GIF on Twitter, or some 16-year-old YouTuber screaming his head off about *Five Nights at Freddy's*.

Maybe the idea of reviews itself is outdated in this kind of environment. Instead of offering a single authoritative take on a game at launch, maybe we should refocus on just writing about what's interesting in gaming in a way that makes it clear why it's interesting. Where the "final review" used to be the end point for most mass market coverage of a game, maybe now a light touch review should be just the beginning of a continuing conversation about what's worth paying attention to in the ever-changing gaming landscape (For more on this thesis, read "The Future Of Kotaku's Video Game Coverage Is The Present,"[84] which has proven a bit prescient some two years later).

Maybe the idea of an "expert" critical establishment sifting through this flood of games is outdated in this day and age. Faced with a never-ending avalanche of games, maybe we should just give in to the wisdom of crowds and let big data determine what games are worthwhile. That certainly seems to be the opinion of Steam Developer Relations Specialist Tom Giardino, who recently told VentureBeat:

> *We don't want a world where people feel like they have to get someone at Valve to give the game a stamp of approval or a thumbs up for it to ever show up in front of customers. There are games that launch every day on Steam that nobody at Valve has played before or [is] familiar with that quickly end up on the front page of our store because they are delighting customers.*

This end run around the gatekeepers of critical consensus seems to be the core idea animating a number of upcoming changes to Steam's user curation systems. Why listen to a small group of experts when you can crowdsource gaming recommendations from dozens of friends and millions of strangers online who share your tastes, though the magic of algorithms?

This is probably the future we're faced with, where the critical establishment is a step behind the algorithms that can tell what the vast, heaving crowd of online-connected gamers are interested in. But I can't help but think that somewhere, out there among the thousands and thousands of games released every year, are some worthwhile gems that are being completely ignored by the gaming press and gamers alike, just waiting for an influential critic to call out their brilliance.

The Pressure to Stay In Line

Originally published on The Game Beat, March 31, 2017

I'd like to start off with two quotes this week. The first comes from IGN's Alanah Pearce, who admitted her trepidation before bad-mouthing *Mass Effect: Andromeda* during some lengthy video impressions[85] last month.

> *I, full disclosure, am scared of saying negative things about it, because I know how passionate people feel about this, but it feels a little more bro-ey than previous games did, and it feels more like a cover-based bro shooter than it does of* Mass Effect.

The second comes from Deadspin writer Albert Burneko, who felt the need to apologize multiple times before bad-mouthing *The Legend of Zelda: Breath of the Wild*.[86]

> *I feel a strange but real impulse—as a nostalgic lover of the* Legend of Zelda *series (and, yeah, of Nintendo itself) whose heart swells at the sounds of the Hyrule Field theme from 1998's* Ocarina of Time—*to apologize for this take . … I'm sorry! It's just not doing anything for me at all.*

These apologetic quotes both get at a truth that's rarely explicitly acknowledged in the world of game criticism: being out of step with the critical or fan consensus on a big-name game or franchise is often not an easy thing to do.

At best, having a contrary opinion about a big game these days means being subject to a huge stream of nasty comments, tweets, and e-mails about your view. Many of these will simply point out how many other outlets disagree with your opinion of the game, as if that's supposed to convince you that your opinion is *objectively wrong* or something. Worse, maybe rabid fans might try to DDOS your site, as happened to Jim Sterling after a less-than-perfect 7/10 review of Breath of the Wild this month.

I feel like the lack of tolerance for a wide range of differing opinions on a work is somewhat unique to popular video game criticism. That's probably because most video games don't see a truly wide range of varied opinions from the critical establishment. This also extends to the mass of fervent "core gamers" that usually quickly converge around one "safe" conventional wisdom on a title's quality, and which can refuse to acknowledge the validity of any other takes.

I once heard a story (I don't remember from where) that movie review aggregator Rotten Tomatoes at one point tried to apply its simplified "thumbs up/down" ratings to video games (this is true: here's a link to an Archived version of the section).[87] The site supposedly gave up rather quickly because the results for games were never very interesting. Every game's summary, it seems, came back nearly 100% or 0% "fresh" -- there was little in the way of varied gradations between "universal praise" and "universal scorn" that characterize the site's movie and TV reviews.

This story might be apocryphal, but it's also eminently believable. Just look at the ratio of "positive" to "negative" reviews on Metacritic for most games. It's very rarely anything close to balanced, even if the specific numbers on the site's 100-point scale may vary up and down a bit. When you get down to it, though, a 90/100 review and an 85/100 review both pretty much agreed on a game's overall merits. It's rarer to see an even split between 90/100 reviews and 40/100 reviews.

While there are a few polarizing exceptions (*Beyond: Two Souls* immediately comes to mind), game reviewers as a whole tend to agree much more than we disagree on what makes a game "good." Some of this is due to a lack of diversity (both in background and in taste) of the people writing the bulk of game reviews. But part of it, I think, is a kind of groupthink that can easily infect the popular discourse surrounding some of the biggest games.

After you play enough games and read enough reviews, you can generally predict what kind of aggregate reception a game is going to get from the bulk of your colleagues, even if you never talk to them about it beforehand. Reviewers also generally know what sells, and can also sense the level of hype and name recognition of a big-name game before its release. We can also probably tell you what range of scores will be considered "acceptable" to a hype-frenzied fan base before a review copy even hits our hands.

> *After you play enough games and read enough reviews, you can generally predict what kind of aggregate reception a game is going to get from the bulk of your colleagues, even if you never talk to them about it beforehand.*

After conventional wisdom has congealed post-release, it can be even harder to knowingly give an unpopular opinion. You know you'll be accused of just being contrarian as a form of clickbait, or hating on a game just because you can't stand that it's popular, or of Slatepitching a ridiculous "actually, this bad thing is good" hot take. What's worse, given all the research into how our brains are hardwired to seek the agreement of those around us, what you think of as an "honest opinion" can't help but be infected somewhat by the overwhelming critical discourse. What is beauty?! What is truth?!

This pressure probably isn't enough for a critic to give a rave to a game that's they truly think is bad, or to pan a game they unexpectedly loved. Consciously or unconsciously, though I think a lot of reviewers subtly tailor their opinions towards this expected consensus, afraid of attracting too much reader or publisher ire for being the lone dissenting voice with the "wrong" opinion on a game (how do I know it's wrong? Because everyone else disagrees, you biased idiot!)

In the end, the simplest way to fight back against this problem may be for reviewers to simply be aware of it. Once you realize the how the pressure of the critical consensus might be affecting your views, you can take steps to try to combat it in your own work. Sure, there's always the chance of overcorrecting to an overly contrarian viewpoint, or being overly analytical about what your actual opinion would be in a vacuum. Still, I think this kind of self-awareness is important to being a critic in today's hyperconnected age.

Defending the Indefensible

Originally published on The Game Beat, Aug. 25, 2017

The concept of "crunch"—the practice of working 12 to 16+ hours a day, sometimes for weeks or months at a time, in order to get a game finished on time—is probably the most universally reviled in the whole of the game industry and media. When crunch gets discussed in the video game press, as it seems to in cycles every few months, the headlines usually include words like problem, horrible, bullshit, death march, and exploiting. The conventional wisdom is as set as it can be.

So when a headline at a site as big as Polygon promises to discuss "Why I worship crunch,"[88] it's bound to turn some heads.

The excerpt from Walt Williams' upcoming book *Significant Zero* is a bit less incendiary and defensive than that headline suggests. GamesIndustry.biz talked about the same excerpt with the headline "Confessions from a crunch addict," which I think captures William's more ambivalent feelings towards his unhealthy *need* to lose himself in his work. When you get past the headline, the full piece is somewhat more nuanced take which at least makes passing reference to crunch's exploitative, destructive, and altogether unnecessary impact on developers' lives.

That said, Williams is willing to say positive things about crunch that are pretty much never said in video game circles, much less written down. The good parts of crunch are "rarely [heard] over the sound of righteous indignation," he argues. Crunch is a sign that the system is "working exactly as designed." After a good crunch, you should "be happy with the fact that your sacrifice is helping bring someone else's vision to life." Williams even pushes back directly at some of the headlines above, saying directly that "crunch isn't a pandemic or a death march."

These are the kind of outrageous, provocative, contrarian, #slatepitch-worthy arguments that would be easy to lump together as mere clickbait, if they weren't originally written as part of a deeply personal book (Amazon-bait?). As it is, plenty of people accused Polygon of simply running the excerpt as a way of just generating controversy for the sake of eyeballs. Better to be hated than to be ignored, right?

Polygon Opinion Editor Ben Kuchera, who commissioned the article, hints on Twitter that that's not how he saw the piece. "Ask yourself: Do you think the writer really enjoys the practice? Do you think the wording is meant to portray it positively?" he writes. "Much of this conversation seems based on the idea that writing about games should stop at pointing at something and saying 'good' or 'bad.'"

It's true, pretty much 100% of the discussion of crunch has pointed at the concept and shouted "bad!" at the top of its lungs. Is that a problem? In an industry where even the most horrible games and companies can get impassioned defenses, is there room for a more well-rounded debate about crunch's pros and cons from a conflicted developer? Or is covering crunch more like covering climate change or white supremacy, where even acknowledging that there are "many sides" to the debate gives too much attention and credit to discredited ideas?

In any case, on Twitter, Kuchera seems to be happy (since deleted) with the "illuminating" discussion that has popped up surrounding Williams' piece. Williams echoes that sentiment in his own tweeted follow-up thread, an edited version of which now runs atop the Polygon excerpt itself.

> *As an industry, we need to talk about crunch—how we define it, and especially how exploitative it can be. I didn't go into that, because I didn't want it to seem like I was forced to work this way. I did this to myself. Still do, to be honest. And, if I'm being just really open about it, I wasn't sure I could do that discussion justice because I have a hard time seeing it clearly.*
>
> *But, we're talking now, and that's good. My hope was that by being honest, it would encourage others to do the same. This has to be a conversation. We each have to recognize how we feed into it. This is mine. I hope it helps.*

There have definitely been plenty of gems in the wider discussion Williams' excerpt has generated. Game designer and writer Elizabeth Sampat highlighted the idea that crunch for your own project can be more valuable than crunch for someone else. Paradox's Johann Anderson suggested that a few days of "rare" crunch can be much more beneficial than the long-term variety. *Night in the Woods* developer Scott Benson shared a chilling account[89] of how crunching on that game literally almost killed him.

But "starting a conversation" isn't really a full defense of publishing incendiary opinions. Kyle O'reilly likened (since deleted) Polygon's published excerpt to publishing "an article titled 'opiods are fucking rad as hell' and then claiming that, 'If you would just read the article you would see opioids are actually bad guys.'" Former Polygon Features Editor Russ Pitts put a finer point on it (since deleted): "The only thing worse than a expressing a destructive opinion is putting a microphone in front of it for personal gain."

The main problem with the "starting a conversation" argument is that you don't see any of that conversation on Polygon itself (at least not at the moment). Williams' account may have been raw and personal and worthwhile to voice, but in and of itself it lacks the necessary context to provide a truly balanced and full look at an important issue.

Maybe that's justifiable when you're trying to push back against years of universal condemnation from industry and the press. But when an issue is as fraught as this one, it can't hurt to include a little bit more push alongside your pushback.

THE
ETHICAL
SIDE

"Actually, it's been about ethics in game journalism for a while..."

Despite a certain group recently using "ethics in game journalism" as a rallying cry (at times against me directly), I've "actually" been interested in the ethical questions surrounding the business for well over a decade now. This section mainly focuses on ways game journalists can maintain a comfortable, adversarial distance from the companies they cover. That includes ways to deflect the constant PR attempts to close that distance with free swag, lavish trips, and other detritus.

It also covers a few specific situations where abstract ethical questions became serious practical concerns for specific outlets, including times when outlet were getting "frozen out" by major publishers or using journalists as de facto PR people for games. And then there's Gerstmann-gate, that brief period in 2007 when many felt we finally got that "smoking gun" evidence of an advertiser exercising adverse influence over a game review (but where the truth might not be so simple).

Editor vs. Critic

Originally published on The Video Game Ombudsman, May 13, 2005

A recent blog post (since deleted) by freelance game reviewer Nich Maragos has turned in to a minor public relations debacle for IGN/GameSpy. The post, written early yesterday, indicates Maragos' displeasure with edits made to the text and score of his review of *Donkey Konga 2* for GameSpy. The article's editor added "an extra star and a half ... from its submitted version, along with several laudatory phrases that I didn't write and certainly don't mean," Maragos said in the post. "I hated the game. It's not a 3/5," he added.

The review has since been taken down and Maragos has updated his post with a conciliatory message, saying that the issue "was resolved pretty quickly after my initial complaint." But what was the issue exactly? And what ramifications does its resolution have on other game reviewers and editors?

"Yes, it was edited, but no, it didn't go beyond the usual editing scope," said GameSpy Editorial Director John Keefer when asked about the changes made to the review. Keefer refused to identify the editor assigned to the review, but noted that the editor "feels terrible about how this happened." The edits were made to correct what the editor saw as too much of a music focus in Maragos' original review, Keefer said. "We scored the original game four stars and this new version hasn't changed much aside from some gameplay tweaks and music selection," Keefer said.

While defending his editor's decisions, Keefer also acknowledged some problems with how GameSpy handled the situation. "This was a rare breakdown in communication," he said. "We did not talk to [Maragos] about changes before we made them, a move that goes against our standard policy." Keefer would not reveal the exact wording of the internal policy, but did say that the "common sense" policy "has been addressed with the editor and ... reinforced with the entire staff." GameSpy has "a very open relationship with freelancers and try to address their concerns whenever possible," Keefer said.

> *This was a rare breakdown in communication.*
>
> *John Keefer*
> *Editor, GameSpy*

For his part, Maragos confirmed in an email that he was no longer angry about the situation. "I felt wronged at the time, but they've done a very quick and exemplary job of addressing the problem, so I'm satisfied. It seems to have just been a communication error."

This attitude seems to have done little to silence Internet message board accusations of advertiser-influenced bias, charges that Keefer vehemently denies.

"We are *not* influenced by ad buys, tech licensing deals, the fact a beta was on FilePlanet or the fact a game may use GameSpy Arcade," Keefer said. "Conspiracy theorists may not want to hear this (or believe it), but editorial integrity demands a separation of church and state. I was in the newspaper business as an editor and writer for 15+ years before coming to the gaming press. That stuff wouldn't fly in the newspaper biz and I try to make darn sure it does not happen here."

What of the removed review? Keefer said that it may be assigned to another writer, but any replacement review would be examined to "see how well the new writer justifies his score." In any case, I think it's safe to say that GameSpy's editors will be very careful not to make any overzealous edits to that or any other review any time soon.

Tina Wood and Nintendo's G4
Marketing Machine

Originally published in The Video Game Ombudsman, May 31, 2005

AUTHOR'S NOTE

There's always been a symbiotic relationship between the gaming press and the companies we cover: they need us for access to our readers, we need them for access to their products and developers. Still, most outlets at least pay lip service to some sort of editorial independence and try to display an adversarial relationship with the companies we cover.

G4 was a large exception to this rule, and using a major network personality like Tina Wood as an unpaid presenter at a major press conference was one of the most flagrant examples of "crossing the line" I've seen in my years on the beat. Over 13 years later, I'm still a little shocked by it.

If you didn't witness the spectacle of G4's Tina Wood appearing at Nintendo's E3 press conference earlier this month, you can jump to about 22-and-a-half minutes in this video archive.[90] There, you'll see Wood get introduced by everyone's favorite cult of personality, Nintendo Chief Marketing Officer Reggie Fils-Aime. I'll let him speak for himself:

> *We thought maybe an outside perspective would help illustrate [Nintendogs], so we've given an advance copy of the U.S. version to Tina Wood, host of G[4]TV.com, the hit interactive show on G4 video game TV, and she joins us here today to put her puppy through its paces.*

I'm pretty sure I made an audible gasp when I heard this announcement (this gasp was drowned out by the Nintendo employees behind me whooping and hollering, but that's for another post). Wood proceeded to show off a dog she had made in the days before the conference and had the dog interact wirelessly with a Mario-hatted dog controlled by game creator Shigeru Miyamato.

Wood's appearance at the conference was widely mocked around the blogosphere, probably most vociferously by Brian Crecente of Kotaku, who wrote "it was sort of appropriate that the little affair wrapped up with Shigeru Miyamoto's dog fucking Tina Wood's." Wood defended the appearance on her own blog, writing, "I did not do this to kiss the rears of Nintendo. I did it for the company I work for and am passionate about and the opportunity to work with a man I absolutely admire." Wood also mentioned that she did not get paid for her appearance.

Getting paid is not the issue here, though. The real question here is whether Wood herself, and G4 in general, want to be considered independent, journalistic entities or simply a part of the video game marketing behemoth.

If it's the former, I think that letting Wood on this press conference is a mistake. Most of the gaming press was in the audience of this conference, reporting on the events instead of taking part in them. Generally, it is not the media's job to help a company make its pitch, and putting a major TV personality in that position doesn't help one's credibility. Even if Wood's participation didn't affect her opinions about Nintendo and its products, the mere appearance of a conflict to her audience should have been enough to give her pause if G4 wants to maintain a reputation of fair, balanced coverage of the video game race.

After Wood's E3 performance, I'm not sure that maintaining that sort of detached independence is G4's goal at all. I'm now more inclined to believe that G4 is content simply to be a marketing mouthpiece for whatever company will have them, and anything they or any of their talent does should be taken with a large grain of salt.

Need more evidence? Check out G4's online press release section where they trumpet programming like "Nintendo DS Day," "*Halo 2* Day" and "*GTA* TV," as well as endemic programming partnerships with GameFly and *America's Army*. Look at shows like *Video Game Vixens* and *CinemaTech*, which show off game videos and characters with little to no intelligent commentary. Look at an interview with G4 founder/CEO Charles Hirschorn in the latest *Game Informer*, in which he talks about G4 branching out to provide gaming services in addition to television programming. All of it points to an entity that wants to use its content mainly to help sell games rather than to analyze them.

This is not to say there's nothing worthwhile on G4, or that all of G4's content is merely meant to be a mouthpiece for advertisers. But moves like Wood's appearance at the Nintendo conference reinforce the impression I get that G4 as an entity is more interested in selling a lifestyle than in covering the business and art of gaming; more interested in providing entertainment than unbiased analysis; more interested in becoming *Entertainment Tonight* than *The Hollywood Reporter*.

Freebies, Junkets, and Junk

Originally published on Next Generation, Oct. 7, 2005

BMX Bikes. Video cards. Ipods. HDTVs. Pre-release copies of the hottest games and hardware. Trips across the country. Open bar parties. Football season tickets. World series tickets. Life-sized statues of game characters.

These are just some of the items that video game journalists get offered in the course of their work. Public relations managers from around the world offer up these premium freebies in an effort to get their product more mindshare and more favorable treatment by a notoriously fickle games press. That doesn't even get into the smaller detritus like tote bags, plush toys, bobbleheads, and t-shirts that practically bury attendees at trade events like E3.

Sounds like a pretty sweet gig, right? Not so fast. For many established journalists, the world of free stuff is not all it's cracked up to be.

"For someone in a critical/journalistic profession to accept gifts of value would be not only unethical but also amoral from my perspective," says Greg Kasavin, Executive Editor of GameSpot. Kasavin says all of GameSpot's writers abide by a

AUTHOR'S NOTE

In the years since this article ran, I've met a freelancer that resold free review copies in bulk to help pay the rent. I've met other journalists who got to go on a free "zero-G" parabolic flight that had little if anything to do with covering the game being promoted.

These kinds of fringe benefits don't necessarily bias a writer to any specific game or company. At the very least, though, the optics of accepting such gifts don't exactly encourage trust among the readership.

strict editorial policy that says the must refuse any "benefits that could cause the giver or others to perceive that CNET Networks is beholden to another company."

That means no gifts of more than "nominal value." No attending events that don't directly relate to game coverage. No cross-country trips to "frivolous junkets" paid for by game publishers. GameSpot reviewers have to donate their review copies to the company's game library once the article is finished. Writers can't keep review hardware for more than six months under CNET's policy.

Dan Hsu, editor-in-chief of *Electronic Gaming Monthly*, says corporate and editorial policy often gets in the way of personal desires, such as when Hsu was randomly chosen as the winner of an HDTV at Microsoft's keynote speech at the Game Developers Conference. "I didn't keep it, even though I don't personally own an HDTV and would love to have one for free. ... It could be perceived as conflict of interest, which we can't have. In the end, I gave mine up to the company to use as a future monitor to show videos in our lobby."

> *For someone in a critical/journalistic profession to accept gifts of value would be not only unethical but also amoral from my perspective.*
>
> **Greg Kasavin**
> **Executive Editor, GameSpot**

That's fine for the major established outlets, but the rules aren't nearly so strict for other writers. Freelancers usually get to make up their own rules for what they can and can't accept, and what they do with it once they receive it.

Freelancer Dan Dormer wasn't alone in receiving a custom Nintendo DS card containing a trailer for the upcoming *Legend of Zelda: Twilight Princess* at Nintendo's E3 press conference this year. He also wasn't alone in putting the cartridge up for sale on eBay shortly after the conference. Collectors quickly snapped up the trailer and other freebies from the conference at premium prices. Dormer made over $100 on his sale.

Dormer had some ethical qualms about the sale at first, but "after I saw all my friends jumping on to eBay to sell theirs I just decided to take the plunge myself. I don't think having made money off a DS cart makes me more likely to favor Nintendo in any way shape or form. Honestly, what use is there for this compressed version of the trailer that only plays on a Nintendo DS—that was my thinking."

Many smaller game review sites offer their writers free review copies of games and access to big, freebie-laden events like E3 in lieu of payment for articles. "The writers are looking to gobble up all the freebies they can since the don't get paid much and they don't get much in way of other support," says Dave Thomas, founder of the International Game Journalists Association and a freelance game writer for the *Denver Post*. Thomas said he would never look down on a journalist for selling a game or a freebie, even though he's never done it himself. "It depends on where you are in your career. Where you want to get and what you can get away with."

"Everyone has to deal with their own personal code of ethics and their publication's," says Brian Crecente, who covers video games for *The Rocky Mountain News* and gaming blog Kotaku.

Crecente gets tons of free games from developers looking for coverage, especially around the holidays, and says he "usually succeeds" at playing each one. When he's done, Crecente will give the games to friends or relatives, or offer them up in contests on his blog.

The non-game freebies aren't as big a deal for Crecente. "I figure it's more of an issue of marketing, that they want to get a little free advertising out there. I can't imagine anyone thinks a game sucks and then sees it came with a t-shirt and is all, 'Wait a second, I *do* like this game. I mean, shit, it comes with a cool t-shirt.'"

Thomas agrees that most of the free stuff out there doesn't really have much of an effect on coverage, but there are exceptions. "When you get a console prior to launch, man, that's way on the line. It sure feels like Santa came to visit."

Another exception is Sony's big E3 party. The invite-only event is a highlight of the show—this year's bash at Dodger Stadium featured three live bands, extravagant side shows, and tons of free food and drinks.

"Count the negative Sony stories prior to E3," Thomas says. "They start to dry up. No one wants to piss off Sony and have their ticket pulled. I really believe that is true!"

Such lavish affairs that don't directly involve reporting on games inhabit an ethical grey area for larger publications. *EGM*'s Hsu doesn't see such events as a conflict of interest because they provide an "opportunity to develop relationships, make contacts, and get information from industry folk in a more informal setting." GameSpot's Kasavin says his staff isn't prohibited from going to these events, but they take lower priority than the work that tends to surround them.

Journalists are very mindful of the effect that any perceived conflict of interest can have on their audience. Dormer remembers overhearing two customers at an Electronics Boutique say that a reviewer must have gotten some great "service" to give the game such a high score. "It made me a little sad to think that gamers don't really trust the opinions of reviewers. But, that's partially because we don't give them enough reason to," Dormer admitted.

But Thomas thinks that some readers actually like to live vicariously through their favorite game journalists. "If a game writer takes a free trip to Mars, or to meet models or to shoot guns or race cars or even just to stay in a nice hotel to look at new games, what do you think [as a reader]? You think, 'Man, that would be *awesome*!' By and large, our readers like the fact that we are fans. They don't think that taking freebies ruins us. And that matters a lot."

EGM EIC Accuses Competitors of Pay-to-play Shenanigans

Originally published on Video Game Media Watch, Dec. 19, 2005

AUTHOR'S NOTE

Any time a game critic publishes a controversial review, it doesn't take long for readers to level accusations that the author was "paid off" for their opinion, either by the game's publisher or its competitors. Rumors of such payoffs abound in the industry, and journalists I've talked to always have vague, hand-wavey stories about how they heard someone else was engaging in this kind of shady practice.

Hsu's editorial, discussed here, is the most public and damning such accusation I've found from a journalist in a position to know. Take note, though, that Hsu's accusations center directly on which games get cover space and coverage inches in game magazines of old. He doesn't actually accuse anyone of changing scores or tilting reviews to please advertisers (though giving advertisers pre-publication notice of the text certainly comes close).

These days, the FTC has highlighted how YouTube is the primary forum where advertisers try to trade ad purchases for positive coverage, often with little in the way of disclosure.

When editor-in-chief Dan "Shoe" Hsu led off the introductory editorial in the latest *Electronic Gaming Monthly* (#199, January 2006) with "My industry pisses me off," I knew it was going to be an interesting piece. Sure enough, in the following paragraphs Hsu paints a picture of widespread ethical misconduct that he says has infected large swathes of the video game journalism industry. Without naming any names, Hsu's editorial mentions three separate publications—two magazines and one website—that he has heard are willing to exchange advertising considerations for editorial considerations.

After finishing the short editorial, it seemed pretty clear that these serious accusations required further elaboration. So I talked to Hsu alongside NintendoNow's David Gornoski to get some more information on what he's seen and heard.

Hsu said he first became suspicious of other magazines' practices when he noticed some odd games appearing on one specific magazine's cover. "They're not high-profile games, they're not sleeper hits, they're not marketable," Hsu said. "They're games no sane editor or publisher would ever put on their covers."

Hsu says his suspicions led him to contact a public relations representative from "a major game publisher... as big as they get," who confirmed that the suspicious magazine's covers could indeed be "bought" with ad space. Hsu also heard stories of another magazine and game publisher that arranged an ads-for-covers deal "on the golf course" with no editorial involvement (Hsu said he heard the game company even has a name for the practice, "editorial marketing"). Another PR person from a small publisher told Hsu that a major gaming website told the publisher flat out "if we want coverage, we need to buy ads."

Hsu said he has experience with this type of pressure from game companies himself. "Game companies generally know they can't boss us around or try to influence our scores, but that doesn't stop some of them from trying," Hsu said. "Some companies actually feel they have the right to look over your story before it goes to print! Do you know why? Because other magazines have given them that leeway."

In our interview, Hsu refused to go public with the names of the magazines and publishers mentioned in his editorial. He did note that the outlets in his examples did not include IGN and *Game Informer*, "who were often accused by some readers." Hsu defended his silence by saying that naming the outlets would look petty. "While I want to call them out because I want the industry to shape up, I don't want to get into petty fights. I feel like we're above that." Hsu also worried that an investigative piece looking at these accusations would not be a good fit for an entertainment magazine like *EGM*.

So if Hsu isn't willing to investigate or even give specifics on his accusations, why did he do the editorial at all? "I had a selfish reason for doing that editorial," Hsu said. "I'm hoping that, with this added pressure for everyone to do the right thing... and for the press to start acting like press...that it'll make it better for *all* of us across the board... If all of my competitors would not allow game companies to read their copy before going to print ... it'd make my life a lot easier."

How will these changes come about? "The consumers have to rise up and demand better from the press," Hsu says. "I'm not sure how they can do this if they themselves are not sure who's doing the right things, and who's not... but I hope the industry watchdogs ... can help us clean things up, so we're all get the proper respect that we deserve, as an industry as a whole."

The Game Beat Gift Guide

Originally published on GameDaily, Oct. 18, 2007

The free stuff you're about to read about is real. The names have been removed to protect the innocent... and the not-so-innocent, too.

While the pay in the game journalism business usually stinks, the perks can be pretty nice. From pre-release code and game-related trinkets to lavish trips and parties, developers and publishers will go to sometimes ridiculous lengths to keep their games at the forefront of journalists' minds.

Ideally, a journalist could protect themself from undue influence by just saying no to anything and everything that's paid for by a developer or publisher they're covering. But that kind of hard line, zero-tolerance policy could actually get in the way of informing the readers in an industry where junkets and freebies are still the norm. Here are some tips for journalists who want to balance their desire for free stuff with their journalistic integrity.

AUTHOR'S NOTE

In my current job at Ars Technica, I'm pretty proud of our blanket policy not to accept travel provided by publishers we cover. On the other hand, a limited travel budget results in our missing out on coverage events for certain games and hardware that other outlets can attend thanks to publisher largesse.

I'm also pretty proud of the annual Ars Technica charity drive, where we give away mountains of free swag to readers that donate to a good cause. My family is also a big fan of this charity drive, which ensures that our house is not filled floor to ceiling with game-related toys and collectibles.

These days, I try not to be too judgemental of journalists that may not be in a position to take a hard line stance on this stuff. As I say up top in this column, though, disclosure is pretty much the least you can do if you take free stuff from publishers.

DISCLOSURE

Probably the best way to shield yourself from charges of undue bias, or allegations that you're in some company's pocket, is to be up front about anything and everything you get from any company you cover. This doesn't have to be the focus of the writing — you don't have to include an itemized receipt of what you received or anything. But the reader should have some idea of what material considerations factored into your time with the game

Just mention that the racing game preview you're writing is based partly on time with the game and partly on a hands-on time with a sports car at the Michelin Test Track, for instance. Or tell your readers that parachuting out of a transport in the war game is just like the real parachuting you did with the game's publisher. For review copies, simply add a line at the end of a review saying that the piece is based on code provided by the publisher (or put a blanket note to that effect on your publication's "About Us" page).

By coming clean right there in the text, you can let the reader decide what is or isn't important to your impartiality as a journalist. What's more, you eliminate the risk that the publisher's largesse will come out in some embarrassing blog post or message board thread that you can't control. Chances are the readers will enjoy your behind-the-scenes peek into the "superstar" life of a game journalist.

What if the perk is something you wouldn't be comfortable disclosing to readers? Well, maybe that's a good sign you shouldn't be taking it in the first place.

TRIPS/EVENTS

A simple two-part test for whether to spend time at a publisher-sponsored event (and whether or not to accept paid travel to and from that event from the publisher):

1) What's the reporting value of that trip?
2) Could you provide the same value to readers some other way?

The reporting value at these events sometimes comes down to what you make of it. Attending Sony's lavish E3 party at Dodger Stadium is OK if you use it as an opportunity to make connections with developers and big-wigs in attendance. It's less OK if you use it primarily as an opportunity to get drunk. Going to a Best Buy-sponsored concert at a posh LA club is OK if you take advantage of the only opportunity to play an early demo for *The Incredible Hulk: Ultimate Destruction* sitting in the corner of the party.

It can be a tough balancing act sometimes, because the reporting value of a trip or event is often extremely outweighed by the value of the freebie being offered to you. You have to ask yourself if the reporting value of seeing *Dead or Alive Beach Volleyball 2* early is really worth the potential ethical stain of accepting a Tecmo-sponsored trip to Hawaii? Does accepting a trip on a "Zero G" flight worth thousands of dollars really increase your appreciation of an MMORPG set in outer space?

If at all possible, pay your own way for such lavish demos or insist that the company get you access to the game some other way (sign an NDA or loaner form if you have to). If they still want you to come to the lavish junket, turn down portions of the trip that aren't directly related to the game if you can (stay in a Motel 6 down the road instead of getting put up at the Hyatt, for instance).

GAMES/HARDWARE

Being a game journalist usually means getting mountains of free games and systems. It's why a lot of people get into the business in the first place. But what to do with those games once you're done with them? My main rule here is to avoid trying to convert those games into personal or monetary gain. Don't trade finished (or, worse, unopened) games to GameStop, sell them on eBay, or regift them to friends when you're done. Remember, you're getting these games to do your job, not to make some extra cash (or social capital) on the side.

> *By coming clean right there in the text, you can let the reader decide what is or isn't important to your impartiality as a journalist.*

Building a personal "reference library" of freebie games for you or your publication is OK (you never know when you'll need to go back and install *Zoo Tycoon 2* again) but the sheer volume of games can overwhelm your living/work space if you are on a good number of lists. Loaning or giving extra games to friends is a little more questionable, but not too awful—the only problem there becomes friends squabbling over your collection.

A better solution is giving extra games to charity. Get Well Gamers will take used games and hardware and Child's Play will take sealed copies and unopened boxes. Don't want a gamer-focused charity? Your local Goodwill thrift store or

Toys for Tots drop location will probably take your old stuff. If all else fails, give it away to your readers in a contest or put the lot on eBay and assign a favorite charity to get the proceeds.

SWAG

There's no hard and fast rule for the incidental freebies that get given out at trade shows or packaged along with review copies, but a $10 to $20 value limit is probably a good rule of thumb. So keeping a *Fallout* bobble head on your desk is probably OK, but keeping an HDTV is not. Accepting an *Assassin's Creed* letter opener is OK, but taking World Series tickets from a publisher probably is not (yes, the latter really happened to a critic I talked to).

Also, I know game t-shirts are a staple in the industry, but please, *please* don't wear them to official reporting events. This is a pet peeve of mine. You're a professional for gosh sakes—when you're on the job, wear a shirt that wasn't provided free by Sony. Maybe you could even branch out to something with buttons and a collar, eh?

LIVING THE LIFE

Of course, whether you can live by these rules is largely a function of your financial situation, employer budget, physical location, and personal tolerance for selling out your credibility. But if you use these rules as a guide, you'll probably be able to look at yourself in the mirror without being disgusted. And that's the greatest gift of all.

Gamers Go Gaga Over GameSpot's Gerstmann-gate

Originally published on GameDaily, Dec. 6, 2007

AUTHOR'S NOTE

If you weren't there, following the news in the wake of Gerstmann's firing, it's hard to understand the sheer intensity of attention the scandal received in our little corner of the Internet. That intense coverage instantly converted Gerstmann (and the staffers that left GameSpot with him) into a cause celebre in the game journalism world.

That attention in turn gave the departing staff instant cachet when they eventually launched Giant Bomb, helping the site succeed where most newcomers failed. GameSpot parent CBS Interactive would eventually come full circle and buy Giant Bomb in 2012, leading Gerstmann to publicly reflect on what he called a "management team [that] buckled when faced with having a lot of ad dollars walk out the door."

In the years since Gerstmann-gate broke, I've had off-the-record conversations with some of the parties involved that give me reason to believe Gerstmann's firing may have been about more than just some *Kane & Lynch* advertisements. Regardless, the way the scandal played out in public will forever be an important part of the history of game journalism and how it's viewed by readers and critics alike.

A few months ago, when I ranked the top ten[91] video game journalism controversies,[92] I thought the list would stay relatively consistent for the near future. Turns out I was wrong. The week of controversy following GameSpot's sudden firing of Jeff Gerstmann last Wednesday has unquestionably jumped to the top of the list, and the public's impressions of video game journalism will never be the same.

While this isn't the first time there have been accusations of the games press being unduly influenced by game publishers and/or advertisers, it is the first time those accusations have seemed so credible and gotten such wide coverage. All the elements aligned to create a truly epic controversy:

- A long-standing editor of a major site, fired abruptly and without warning or public announcement.
- A plausible connection between the firing and a negative review of a major advertiser's game.
- The suspicious removal of the site's video review (later reposted) and the post-publication edits on the text review [93] of said game.
- A confused and disgruntled staff leaking information—on deep background, of course—to an eager press.
- An insanely popular webcomic calling the gaming community to arms. [94]
- A slow, post-Thanksgiving news cycle which allowed the story the space to break and expand.
- And finally, relative silence from the major parties involved, leaving the press to trip all over itself on rumors and innuendo.

It's that relative silence in the wake of the allegation that probably hurt GameSpot more than anything else. The powers-that-be at CNET seemed truly unprepared for the storm of attention and controversy that Gerstmann's firing would provoke.

Not that they necessarily should have expected any different. While there are a few game journalists with the name recognition and brand-power to demand their own following, most readers recognize the name of the outlet before the name on the byline (if they read the byline at all). Gerstmann was moderately well-known and liked in gaming circles, but he wasn't really a household name, even among core gamers. Under slightly different circumstances, the firing probably wouldn't have ranked more than a passing mention on most gaming news sites.

CNET's real mistake, as they'd probably acknowledge, was not responding quickly enough once the rumors of advertiser influence on the firing started swirling late Thursday night. Friday's brief, blanket statement that "we do not terminate employees based on external pressure from advertisers" was both insufficiently detailed and insufficiently disseminated to truly turn the tide of discussion. The firing wasn't even officially mentioned on GameSpot's site itself until Monday, when the newest denial had an entire weekend's worth of speculation and discussions to contend with (a lifetime in the Internet age). By the time Wednesday's one-two punch of a candid staff podcast and in-depth Q&A[95] started to really address the questions everyone wanted answered, public opinion had already gelled and the damage was largely done.

Of course, any response would have been too late for many readers, who had made up their minds as soon as they first heard the rumors discussed. The gaming community's ready acceptance of these allegations (and other, less credible ones) highlights a deep image problem that runs throughout game journalism.

Talk to many gamers, and it's taken as a base assumption the review scores are constantly "bought" via advertising, access, swag, trips, or even direct pay-offs to editors. The default reaction among many readers to any positive review they don't agree with is invariably, "I wonder how much [game publisher] paid them to write *that* one?" (or, if the review is negative, "I wonder how much [rival publisher] paid them to pan *that* one?").

Some healthy skepticism among the public is to be expected, but the wide prevalence of these views in the online gaming community seems staggering. Indeed, this controversy probably wouldn't have been able to get off the ground if the community hadn't already been pre-conditioned to believe the worst about game journalists by years of similar accusations. The best way for outlets to fight this problem is probably a borderline ridiculous level of transparency, which is where CNET largely failed in this case. The company's policy to not comment on personnel matters might be important from a corporate and legal standpoint, but it's woefully insufficient for a gaming community that is inclined to instinctively believe the worst and takes silence as acceptance.

Moreover, such rigid secrecy seems antithetical for a journalistic organization, which should be devoted to openness and truth-telling above all. With the speed of Internet rumor and discussion, corporations need political-style rapid response teams to quickly defend their reputation—journalistic corporations doubly so.

Even given the silence, the game press' overall coverage of the scandal was a little glib, to say the least. Some outlets seemed almost giddy as they reported on the anonymous rumors, reveling in the confirmation of their own widely-held beliefs and the downfall of a major competitor. In the absence of any hard evidence or comment on either side, outlets around the web played to the court of public opinion, deifying Gerstmann and vilifying GameSpot when more middle-of-the-road skepticism of both sides may have been warranted. (You can judge for yourself[96] whether my own coverage of the scandal at Joystiq was similarly slanted).

Perhaps the most striking thing about the coverage overall was its reliance on anonymous sources. In the information vacuum created by the general lack of official comment, those covering the scandal latched on to any bit of evidence they could, regardless of its provenance or reliability. Nowhere was this more apparent than the wide coverage given to comments from an anonymous Valleywag commenter and self-proclaimed "insider" going by the handle "gamespot."[97] While "gamespot's" comments do contain some potentially blockbuster details, there was absolutely no attempt on the part of the press as a whole to corroborate them or even confirm the identity of the poster. The phrase "a story too good to check" comes to mind. (Full disclosure: I linked to these same comments in a daily roundup of Gerstmann news.)

That said, I was genuinely shocked at the amount of original reporting the game press put into this story. Journalists that can usually be counted on mainly to reword press releases suddenly started digging for insider sources, looking for additional evidence, and generally pressuring the involved parties to comment on the record. In fact, I doubt GameSpot would have felt the need to issue the comments it did if the game journalism community hadn't kept the pressure on. The intensity of coverage may have gone a bit overboard at points (I'll admit to adding to the problem on that score), and that intense scrutiny may have been driven by a desire by competitors to stick it to "the Spot." But none of that diminishes the quality of the reporting on this story.

So what does this scandal mean for the future of game journalism? Well, for GameSpot, the damage will never be truly undone—there will always be a distinct segment of the audience that will question anything and everything related to the organization, fairly or not. As for the rest of the industry, the incident has likely served as an intense warning to avoid even a hint of impropriety in both reviewing standards and dealings with publishers and advertisers. If this whole debacle causes even one editor to be more open with their readers about their editorial process, then it won't have been for nothing.

Frozen Out

Originally published on GameDaily, Jan. 11, 2008

AUTHOR'S NOTE

The major publishers still occasionally use blackballing to try to punish outlets for coverage they don't like. Kotaku's Steven Totilo has been outspoken in publicizing his outlet's continuing problems with Ubisoft and Bethesda[98] on this score, after the site published leaked information about *Assassin's Creed* and *Prey* franchises, respectively. Totilo has also been upfront about the ways the site tries to work around this lack of "insider" access.

Kotaku also faced blacklisting pressure back in 2007, when the site published leaked PlayStation Home details before they were announced. Sony tried to lock Kotaku out of planned E3 meetings, but quickly backtracked after Kotaku published the blackballing threat,[99] highlighting the power the site had to generate bad PR for Sony among its readers.

That power is more diffuse now that the game journalism audience is spread among a constellation of different outlets, including thousands of rising Twitch and YouTube stars desperate to compete for attention and access. In such a world, the leverage in the blackballing battle may be back in the publishers' hands.

Ideally, journalists should be totally independent from the subjects they cover. As unbound, impartial observers, we should be able to report the facts and give our opinions on them without bias and without fear of reprisal.

In reality, though, things are never so simple. Like it or not, we journalists rely on the people and companies we cover for information and on-the-record quotes. If those sources decide to withhold that information for any reason, we're often at their mercy—"no source, no story," as they say.

In video game journalism, the codependence can run even deeper than in other fields. We rely on the companies we cover for the preview access and early review code that is the bread and butter of the industry. Piss off a game company, and you can say goodbye to that early FedEx'ed review code and hello to Best Buy on launch day.

And no one is immune. Take *Electronic Gaming Monthly*, one of the largest game magazines in the country. In the February issue, 1UP Editorial Director Dan Hsu wrote an editorial calling out three companies—Midway, Sony and Ubisoft—for withholding press assets as punishment for negative coverage in the magazine. According to the editorial, these publishers were a little pissed off by the magazine's "candid reviews" and "less-than-totally-positive previews." As such, Hsu says readers will "get little, late, or no coverage" of some or all of these companies' games. (None of the three accused companies responded to a request for comment as of press time. Full disclosure: I have written for *EGM* as a freelancer.)

> *Piss off a game company, and you can say goodbye to that early FedEx'ed review code and hello to Best Buy on launch day.*

The problem isn't exactly a new one, according to Hsu. "Sony's sports division and Midway's *Mortal Kombat* team have been on-again, off-again problems for several years," he told me in an exclusive interview. "They would say they're banning us, but then not really mean it, then do it again … so it's hard to say exactly when the official, definitive ban happened. But it wasn't very recently."

With Ubisoft, though, things were a little more clear cut. "They banned us shortly after our 1UP *Assassin's Creed* review appeared, but it wasn't just because of the review. They didn't like our last two previews of the game, which pointed out some of the design flaws that we were concerned about." Indeed, the short, post-E3 preview in the magazine's October issue gave the game the decidedly non-coveted "Game We're Most Worried About" award. While a more in-depth preview in December was a little more forgiving, it still took the game to task for what the previewer saw as slow combat, rough controls, and potentially repetitive gameplay. "[Ubisoft] basically said, 'That's it—we're no longer working with the 1UP Network in any capacity,'" Hsu paraphrased.

You might think withholding assets is a little counterproductive for a game company—after all, even skeptical coverage gets your game in front of readers, and there's no such thing as bad press, as they say. That may be true, but the widespread competition in the game press means publishers can usually take their exclusive access to a more receptive publication, leaving the blackballed outlet with little leverage.

"The press definitely has some power, but it's not like we're the only option for readers out there," Hsu admitted. "So on one hand, any bans mean roughly five million *EGM* readers per month aren't exposed to those games and coverage, plus several more million via *Games for Windows* magazine, 1UP. com, GameVideos.com, etc. But readers have many choices and the companies know that and can hold that over you."

That said, the pressure isn't quite the same as it used to be, Hsu said. "It's not like the cartridge days, where you could get final, reviewable code two months ahead of time," he said. "Nowadays, they can push the game code right up until disc manufacturing, so print reviews can sometimes be late regardless. So whether we get an early review disc or the final retail disc, that difference in time is less than what it used to be. So late reviews aren't as bad of a punishment anymore. The bigger punishment is not letting us cover the games, period."

This isn't the first time Hsu has publicly discussed ethical issues in the industry. An editorial in *EGM* #199 looked at the prospect of publications trading coverage for advertising buys. (See "*EGM* EIC Accuses Competitors of Pay-to-play Shenanigans" earlier in this section for more -ed.) Some readers have chastised Hsu and *EGM* for making too much of these issues, but Hsu felt he had to speak up in this case.

"I had to let our readers know why this coverage was missing from our print and online properties," he said. "I know some people are thinking I'm getting on my soapbox too often, too loudly, but I know I'm more vocal about these subjects nowadays. I think part of that is due to me being in a position to talk about such things. Maybe the other part of it is having the experience. Maybe I'm a grumpier old man now who cares less and less about what other people think."

But Hsu also wants to make it clear that, while these types of reprisals are a problem, they're not exactly a regular occurence. "Even though this issue is getting a lot of airtime right now, I wouldn't say this is a widespread problem—at least not with us," he said. "Of course, one time is one time too many, but the majority of the companies we deal with don't apply this sort of pressure all the time. Some do, some of the time, but it's not an everyday thing."

When the occasional company does turn the screws, Hsu relies on advice from those that came before him. "The thing that always guides me is something my first editorial director [Joe Funk] told me on the day I interviewed at *EGM* [in 1996]," he said. "I brought up an old *EGM* editorial where the editor said that Capcom has pulled advertising, but *EGM* wouldn't change its ways to win them back. I asked the editorial director about that, and how can *EGM* survive without advertising. How does the magazine deal with that pressure? He told me, 'As long as you write for the readers and not the companies, the readership will come, and the advertisers will have no choice but to advertise with you.'"

As of this writing, Capcom is currently a prominent advertiser in *EGM*. "Eventually, the companies all come back because they need to reach our audience," Hsu said. "I know that sounds cocky, and I don't mean it to be, but that's what keeps me going, even when things are looking bad and down for us. ... We are unwilling to bend on this. I'd drag *EGM* down with me or quit before we compromise our integrity."

Console Warriors

Originally published on GameSpot, June 8, 2008

> *This article is awful! The author is bias!*

AUTHOR'S NOTE

The console war specifics have changed since 2008, but the general reader cries of bias for or against one company or another haven't. On the one hand, I think the most fanboy-ish readers (who can often only afford one major gaming platform) are driven by their own biases and a fear of missing out. On the other hand, I think game journalists can often be blind to how they often follow the path-of-least-resistance conventional wisdom in the general tone of their coverage of various platforms and publishers.

It's an ungrammatical quote that should be familiar to anyone who's ever read a comment thread on a major video game website. The accusation can apply to a review, a news story, or really any article that the commenter doesn't personally agree with. The implication is that the author is being unduly swayed by some unseen factor (money, swag, advertising pressure, or even simple personal preference), and that their reporting or opinion is therefore not worthy of due consideration.

But while throwing up an anonymous accusation of bias is easy, answering the charge isn't always so clear cut. When I questioned members of the gaming press about what it means to be "unbiased," the answers ran the gamut.

"I think people are inevitably biased, and the best thing to do is just admit your preconceptions up front," said *Wired* Senior Editor Chris Baker. "I ... think that journalists covering games tend to get caught up in the horserace, just as journalists covering political campaigns do. Every game is evaluated not just on its own merits but based on what has come before in the console wars."

Many others agreed that subtle biases get introduced into gaming coverage for a variety of reasons. "Game press tends to go with the flow," said freelancer Matthew Sakey, "so if a trend of antagonism toward one platform begins, we often see it carried along by a sort of mob mentality."

Some blamed the hype-fueled expectations of the gamers themselves for putting undue influence on journalists. "In a sense, this is what happened with *Halo 2* and certainly with *Halo 3*," said the *Denver Post*'s Dave Thomas. "I don't know a single game critic who would put either of those titles on their top 10 greatest games. But the gaming community wanted those games so bad, was so excited about them, that not only were you sort of strong-armed into covering them, it also blunted your critical edge. ... It is an interesting case study in how fan enthusiasm creates something that looks like bias."

Of course, most journalists wouldn't admit to any personal bias in their own writing, when asked directly. Many echoed the sentiments of freelancer Kieron Gillen: "I view all the console manufacturers with about equal suspicion, and don't have an illusion that one corporation that exists to make a lot of money is somehow better than another one." Others followed the Harrisburg (Pa.) *Patriot-News*' Chris Mautner in insisting they were "more concerned about the individual artistic merits of a particular game" than the fate of a particular console.

There were a few journalists, though, who were surprisingly upfront and unapologetic about their personal system preferences. "Having owned all three consoles ... I felt that as a gamer, the PS3 offered much more of what I liked," said Epileptic Gaming co-host Robert Summa. "Our viewers know which systems the cast prefers and, to some extent, we actually play up on that. I don't necessarily dislike any of the other consoles, in fact I think each of them brings something important to the industry in their own rights. ... As I tell my viewers: 'I'm not a fanboy. I'm just a fanboy of the best system.'"

Not every journalist is on the Sony side of the fence, of course. "I don't like the PS3 and I don't have any desire to own one until the price drops considerably," admitted Gaming Target Managing Editor John Scalzo. "I'm a little sad to say that I sometimes get a little overzealous in reporting about the PS3's troubles compared to the other two consoles. But I'm not sure I see this as a problem because everything I'm reporting on as a PS3 problem is a verifiable fact. The games are being delayed. Developers are complaining about the development tools. The system isn't selling well. And it is too expensive."

> *I'm not a fanboy. I'm just a fanboy of the best system.*
>
> **Robert Summa**
> **Co-host, Epileptic Gaming**

Scalzo's comments reflect what many saw as a widespread anti-Sony angle that infected much of the coverage following the PS3's launch. "I do think the press on the whole came out of the 'next gen' gate with an angle against the PS3," said freelancer Tim Stevens. "After all of Sony's puffed chest proclamations of their complete dominance, and given how badly the company's initial E3 fanfare for the console backfired

... how could you not shake your head in bemusement at least a little at the immense cockiness the company's executives were exhibiting?"

Others saw the anti-PS3 backlash as a simple reflection of the feelings of gamers as a whole. "I think the *EGM* cover with the tomatoes all over the machine was a gutsy move and expressed a feeling that was almost palpable among gamers and journalists alike," said venerable game journalist Bill Kunkel.

Nintendo's Wii, on the other hand, is generally seen as getting an easier ride from the press on its way out of the gate, an attitude some say was all about expectations. "I think the general press reaction was based on surprise," Sakey said. "In 2005, my own opinion of the then-Revolution console was that Nintendo considered it an afterthought, something they 'needed' to produce to stay in the game, nothing but a distant second to the DS. I suspect many members of the press felt similarly until the control scheme was unveiled, and even then it wasn't until we saw early titles in action that the press was convinced."

Of course, the system's low cost and stratospheric sales were bound to have an effect on coverage, too. "When they put out a system that was reasonably priced and included a great piece of software, how could they *not* look good?" Kunkel asked rhetorically. "I don't expect this to change because who argues with success?"

These initial takes on the major consoles may be changing with time, according to many journalists, a trend that Sakey blames on changing facts on the ground rather than shifting biases. "I do think the press is losing patience with the fact that while the Wii may be revolutionary from a control perspective, but that you can count the number of really important games for the platform on one of Bart Simpson's hands," Sakey said. "Similarly, I think the PS3 is out of jail and will receive more complimentary coverage in 2008, especially if Sony is savvy when it comes to price cuts."

Stevens similarly sees the press softening to the PS3, and thinks that "most of the media now seem to be hoping for a come from behind victory for the console." Of course, the change in tone might come too late to change the initial impressions of each system. "The steady barrage of '2008 is the Year of the PS3' and 'the Wii is just a fad' articles are increasing all the time," Scalzo said, "but neither seems to have any effect on how those two systems are perceived by the public."

In the end, while coverage may occasionally be colored by personal opinion, most journalists try to be fair and balanced in their coverage of the never-ending console wars. "I think most of the people working in this business understand that there's nothing to gain from playing favorites," said Giant Bomb's Jeff Gerstmann. "All these supposed payoffs that we're all getting to fix review scores at major outlets don't actually exist—at least, not in North America. Most of the people in this line of work spend their work hours surrounded by every console and a game-ready PC. Unless they're sleeping with PR people or something … no one has any real reason to develop a bias in the first place."

Come and Get Your Beta Codes

Originally published on The Game Beat, April 30, 2010

If you currently have early, "Friends and Family" access to the highly anticipated *Halo: Reach* multiplayer beta, you probably fall into one of three camps.

1) You are actually "friends and/or family" with someone who works at Bungie or Microsoft

2) You are a journalist who has a legitimate work reason to have early access.

3) You got a beta code in a giveaway from someone in Group No. 2.

It's this third group I'm concerned with in this piece. Or, more accurately, why the second group is being used to facilitate the third group's early access.

If Microsoft and/or Bungie wanted to give a limited set of lucky gamers access to this beta (before the hordes of *Halo 3: ODST* owners get their hands on it May 3), they surely could have come up with a contest or random drawing of their own to facilitate it. Instead, they've handed heaping handfuls of extra beta codes to seemingly every game journalist on god's green Earth and given these journalists free reign to hand out the codes in whatever manner will attract the most page views, Twitter followers, Facebook fans, etc. (and trust me, a giveaway for access to an anticipated game like this has the potential to attract a *lot* of attention).

I'm certain there's nothing so tawdry as a journalistic quid pro quo going on for access to these giveaway codes ("Hey, Microsoft, for every five codes you give our readers, I'll guarantee an extra 1/10th of a point on the final review score"). In fact, I doubt access to these extra beta codes will directly affect the critical evaluation journalists eventually make about the game in the slightest.

Of course, there is a small chance that an outlet with access to extra beta codes might be less likely to antagonize Microsoft in the future, for fear of getting cut off from the lucrative giveaway spigot. But these outlets are likely already sufficiently afraid of losing access to press preview events, live press conferences, early reviews copies, and a host of other necessary information that Microsoft directly controls, so this concern is probably a bit overdetermined.

But think for a second about the image of the game press that this journalist giveaway system conveys to the readers. Throughout the week, anyone who pays attention to the game press has been inundated with tweets and blog posts and "news stories" featuring journalists hawking beta codes like a barker at the county fair. Even the low-key giveaways carry with them the idea that *Halo: Reach* is a game worth playing— after all, you can't really offer a contest for something without implicitly endorsing it as something that is desirable to win. Is it really possible to enthusiastically push beta access to a game one day and then credibly critique that game the next?

Appearances aside, I can't help but think Microsoft knows these kinds of giveaways have a subtle effect on the way a journalist sees a game and its fanbase. Sure, as journalists we might know abstractly that a lot of gamers are really excited about *Halo: Reach*. But in actively working to give away beta access, journalists are put directly in touch with the most rabid fans of the game, who will be clamoring for those beta keys via e-mail and comments and Twitter replies and all sorts of direct appeals.

By making journalists intimately aware with how much their readers want this game, these giveaways can't help but influence the way it gets covered in the future (and if you think a journalist is going to ignore the directly demonstrated passion of their readers, you're nuts).

None of this is entirely new, or really much different from what game journalists do every day. We often give up a bit of independence for access, be it to a beta code or a hard-to-get interview. We often give up our appearance of impartiality so we can get the Google juice from being the first one to repeat a hot press release verbatim. We often pay attention to the games we know our readers are already excited about rather than trying to expose them to hidden gems they might not even know they want to know about.

But I guess the implicit boosterism on display among journalists in these *Halo: Reach* beta giveaways struck me as a little less subtle than usual. The next time you wonder why game journalism is often seen as just an extension of video game PR, remember promotional "events" like this.

Should E3 be Party Time for Journalists?

Originally published on The Game Beat, June 12, 2010

> By the logic of the press corps, these White House social events have no real effect on the news narrative. I find that interesting. There are some very smart people in the the White House. It would seem that by now they would know their soirée press strategy has been a miserable failure. And yet they press on. I wonder why?
>
> **Ta-Nehisi Coates**
> **The Biden Beach Party** [100]

AUTHOR'S NOTE

The older I get, the less appeal the lavish parties that surround various game conferences become. Part of that is because an the prospect of an open bar and loud dance music is no longer appealing enough to force my aging body to stay up past 10 pm. But part of it is because I have more shit to do at conferences these days, and these parties are usually not conducive to getting things done. Networking is nice and all, but yelling over well drinks isn't always the best way to do it.

With E3 and its attendant array of late night press parties coming up next week, the above quote could easily be used as a challenge to the video game press as well as the political press. Just replace "The White House" with "big name game publishers" and the essential question remains: If these lavish parties really have no effect on how a company is covered, why do all these savvy game PR firms continue to waste money on them?

There are a few possible non-sinister answers, of course. Publisher parties aren't always just for the press—they're often for all the employees and developers and retailers and distributors and dozens of other people a party-thrower is trying to impress as well. Even when they're press-only affairs, these parties are sometimes the best opportunity for many journalists to play some games that are hard or impossible to try elsewhere at E3 (I distinctly remember placing my cheese plate on the floor and tearing into 30 minutes with a *Super Mario Galaxy* demo at a Nintendo party one year).

And even if there are no games at a party, the events are great opportunities to network with game-makers and executives in a casual environment, getting off-the-record information or even stealing away from the thumping music for a quick on-the-record interview. These parties are also the main place where journalists from competing outlets meet and chat with each other at the show, passing on tips about potential sleeper hits and helping to form the conventional wisdom that will shape what games and companies come out as the "winners" of the show (a concept that deserves a post of its own).

But even with these mitigating factors, some of these lavish parties are a bit hard to justify. I say this as a person who's gladly eaten endless smores and ridden a mechanical bull courtesy of Bethesda Softworks, left a massive dance party at Dodger Stadium with a free travel suitcase in tow courtesy of Sony, and gotten to see Queens of the Stone Age and The Who at exclusive concerts courtesy of Harmonix. And that's not even counting the dozens of open bars and re-warmed hors d'oeuvres I've had to endure on a publisher's dime since becoming a game journalist.

So I'm obviously not above dipping into the trough at these things. And if pressed, I'd probably offer up the same defense as political reporter Marc Ambinder: that the relationships between the press and their subjects "can be cordial, occasionally cozy, and they can simultaneously be professional and skeptical."

But part of me worries, as Glenn Greenwald does, that attending these kinds of parties "helpfully reveals what our nation's leading 'journalists' really are: desperate worshipers of ... power who are far more eager to be part of it and to serve it than to act as adversarial checks against it."

How Game Publishers Captivate Journalists with Junkets

Originally published on The Game Beat, July 29, 2010

EDITOR'S NOTE (published with the original): This article was originally commissioned as pitched (and written) by a major video game news outlet, then killed upon receipt because an editor thought it would "cause too many problems." I present it here as it was presented to that outlet.

AUTHOR'S NOTE

I write this a week after attending a lavish two-day *Fallout 76* junket in an extremely expensive West Virginia resort. I was lucky enough to drive myself to the event and pay for my own hotel room through my outlet's travel budget. The vast majority of the attendees did not need to, thanks to Bethesda's largesse. So this is not a problem that's exclusively in the past.

This April, a group of a few dozen game journalists flew off to a beautiful Hawaiian resort for a three-day trip. The occasion wasn't some sort of industry-wide retreat or group vacation, but rather a Capcom game preview extravaganza known as Captivate. There, these select opinion-makers of the game industry enjoyed some of the best accommodations Hawaii had to offer, many of them on Capcom's dime.

Ostensibly, the purpose of these kinds of events—known as junkets in the industry—is to write up early access previews of upcoming games and interact with the people who make them. But the fringe benefits of these publisher-sponsored junkets—which can range anywhere from free food and drink to flights and hotel stays to exclusive trips in military fighter jets and Zero-G suborbital planes—can draw controversy for their effect on the way games are covered.

"You can argue that you can continue to be impartial in that situation, but the company paid for your plane ticket and hotel room in an island paradise," said Ars Technica Gaming Editor Ben Kuchera, who does not accept paid travel from publishers. "They are paying for your food and your drinks. It is not the best circumstance for a sober, measured look at these games."

Of course, the journalists that accept these trips insist that the all-expenses-paid trappings are beside the point. "I won't lie, Hawaii was nice," said Destructoid Editor-in-chief Nick Chester, who let Capcom pay for his trip to Captivate. "I'd never been before! But really, I was there to do work, and I'd say I spent the bulk of the time watching presentations, playing games, and speaking with developers."

> *The money that a company uses to finance the travel and, to some degree, vacations of a few dozen of the country's gaming press is money that, ultimately, is coming out of consumer's pockets.*
>
> **Chris Grant**
> *Editor-in-chief, Joystiq*

For Chester, and many other journalists I spoke to that accept paid travel from game publishers, taking a free trip to a junket is the best way for them to inform their readers. "There's simply no way we could have been able to cover the event if Capcom hadn't covered the costs," Chester said. "We're in the business of delivering to our readers the information that they want—it's why they keep coming back for more. [If we hadn't attended] our coverage would have suffered greatly, and our readers would have been forced to look elsewhere."

Those that attend junkets also stress that a free trip doesn't guarantee a good review for the games on display there. "I'm about to give *Lost Planet 2* a 5/10 rating because it was a horrible experience," said *Maxim* Gaming Editor Gerasimos Manolatos, who had Capcom pay for his trip to Captivate. "It wouldn't have made a difference to me if it was the grandest party of all-time ... it could have taken place in my living room." [**EDITOR'S NOTE:** After this story first ran on The Game Beat, Nick Chester wrote in to note that he gave *Lost Planet 2* a 4/10]

All of which inevitably leads to one question: Why do publishers pay for these junkets in the first place? Capcom Senior PR Manager Melody Pfeiffer says the trips are more about securing a journalist's attention than their opinion. "Our annual event, Captivate, was first inspired by the idea of creating a full 'Capcom Experience' where press would have three days to spend playing our upcoming lineup, getting to know our producers and discussing our games with their creators," she said. "We didn't tell them that in order to be invited they have to write about everything they saw and in a positive way. This is up to them to decide, we just gave them the opportunity to do it."

But many journalists think there's more to a junket than getting journalists' attention. "Let's be logical here: no company gives you money for nothing," Kuchera said. "If your site has been given thousands of dollars worth of flights and amenities, there is an expectation there. It's not as sinister as a straight bribe, but PR will always position itself to try to get the best coverage of as many of their games as possible, and they spend money to do that."

And some journalists think that's money that could be better spent elsewhere. "Keep in mind, these events are very expensive," said Joystiq Editor-in-chief Chris Grant, who maintains an editorial policy against taking paid trips from publishers. "The money that a company uses to finance the travel and, to some degree, vacations of a few dozen of the country's gaming press is money that, ultimately, is coming out of consumer's pockets."

While many outlets somehow disclose when coverage comes as a result of a publisher-funded junket, Grant worries that gamers don't really understand what goes into the game previews they read. "From what I can tell... readers do not realize the nature and frequency of events like these and, even more disappointingly, most of them don't seem to care," he said. "It's not a matter of whether or not I trust my writers to remain impartial in the face of gifts and free trips; it's more a matter of whether readers can continue to place their trust in us if they know we accept those things."

Some journalists, though, argue that their readers' trust isn't such a fragile thing. "We are an enthusiast press, and as such, we work closely with publishers and developers," said Tom Chick, a freelancer who writes for Syfy's Fidgit gaming blog. "It's important that readers realize that, but it's also important that they know they can trust some of us. I spent two days in Hawaii looking at Capcom's upcoming game line-up. I really like *Lost Planet 2*. There is no causation between the former and the latter. That's where my reputation hopefully comes into play."

In the end, most who write about games acknowledge that managing junkets is a balancing act. "The fact is, we, the press, are there as guests," said GamingNexus Staff Writer Jeremy Duff. "And it is up to each of us individually to walk the fine line of being a gracious guest while still maintaining our responsibility to our readers."

Balancing Openness and Safety with Steam Spy

Originally published on The Game Beat, Sept. 16, 2016

What do you do when the public's desire for information about a developer conflicts with that developer's desire to control its own self-image? Does the calculus change when the developer says that information might actually put them in danger?

These questions came surprisingly to the fore in recent weeks when PC sales estimation site Steam Spy announced it would no longer be honoring developer and publisher requests to remove their games from its service. Site creator Sergei Galyonkin had honored such requests in the past, saying, "I firmly believe Steam Spy should be seen as a useful tool by developers, not as a threat." More recently, though, he told Polygon the he sees being complete as a "valuable lesson" to the public. "The point of Steam Spy is to be a helpful tool for game developers," he told the site. "Removing several important independent games from the service will hurt everyone else while not necessarily benefiting the publishers of the removed games."

Developers, like Paradox's Sham Jorjani, argue on the other side that Steam Spy's "flawed" sales reporting on competitors can do more harm than good, leading to unrealistic business plans based on fiction. But Galyonkin has never argued Steam Spy was a perfectly accurate accounting of a game's Steam sales. The site is very clear about its methods, which involve random sampling of publicly available data to estimate how many owners and players various games on the service have.

As long as this is made clear, it's not fair to blame Steam Spy for the way others might misinterpret its data.

Others argue[101] that Steam Spy's publication of this data can expose developers to undue criticism, and reveal sensitive financial data that companies would rather keep quiet. I'm somewhat sympathetic to this argument, but on the whole I don't think it's fair to make that Steam Spy's concern. The data they're using is public, surfaced by Valve itself through its user pages and publicly accessible API. Once the data is out there, it's hard to fault Steam Spy for aggregating it and publishing it (with clear caveats about how it should be used and any potential error). After all, even if Steam Spy agreed to hide a publisher's games, there's nothing to stop someone else from using the same data however they wished.

(Of course, I'm a little biased in evaluating these arguments, since my own Steam Gauge project[102] was the inspiration for Steam Spy.)

The most interesting wrinkle in this tale, though, comes from a developer which has argued in the press[103] that Steam Spy's reporting actually put them in danger. *PC Gamer*'s article about that allegation is vague about the specific threats involved, but hints that an unnamed developer is concerned about criminals looking at Steam Spy to find successful companies that may be ripe targets for corporate kidnappings in some developing nations.

Despite *PC Gamer*'s reluctance to name them, the source for these allegations is pretty clear. *Kerbal Space Program* developer Squad argued on Reddit last year that Steam Spy data exposed them to safety risks. "Basically, being based in Mexico, we aren't really crazy happy with the idea of everyone knowing potentially how much money we have made from *KSP*," a former Squad developer going by the handle Maxamps wrote. "We would honestly love to be like every other gaming company and celebrate each and every sales milestone with the community, but it is simply not worth risking the team's safety and integrity."

Mike Futter (previously of *Game Informer*) put an even finer point on it: "SteamSpy is putting lives in danger with its antics," he tweeted. "The *Kerbal* guys asked for removal because of danger in being successful in Mexico City."

Galyonkin himself argued on Twitter that Squad was being a bit hypocritical, since the developers didn't seem concerned about safety when they revealed their own sales data back in February. He also told *PC Gamer* that he finds the hypothetical corporate kidnapping situation set forth in their article pretty dubious. "I highly doubt that [gangsters in the developer's country] would be sophisticated enough to find [the game developer] on Steam Spy and estimate its revenue based on that data.... I don't want to deal with distinguishing between 'valid' causes for the game removal and 'invalid.' Can a single person do this, honestly? I am certainly not qualified."

This is a tough position for any journalist to be in (and I'd find it hard to argue Galyonkin's data doesn't serve a journalistic purpose). The public's right to access public information is a key tenet of journalism: as the SPJ's Code of Ethics puts it, journalists should "Seek Truth and Report It." Yet that same ethics code also urges journalists to "Minimize Harm" and to "balance the public's need for information against potential harm or discomfort. Pursuit of the news is not a license for arrogance or undue intrusiveness."

Personally, I find it hard to believe that Steam Spy's data would actually, materially affect the safety of anyone at Squad. We're not talking about troop positions or national security secrets here; we're talking about sales estimates. The fact that *Kerbal Space Program* is a success is hardly a secret elsewhere in the press, and having a more specific estimate of the number of Steam owners for the game seems unlikely to make them a *bigger* target for any potential criminals.

That said, in a case like this, I think it might still be worth simply erring on the side of caution and removing the data. Squad's location in Mexico City and its seemingly genuine fear over the issue (misguided or not) mean the potential harm from publishing the data probably outweighs the small truth-telling purpose from publishing data on a single game. Others may try to use the same excuse, of course, but I think it'd be relatively easy in most cases to judge if each case was a valid safety concern or simply an excuse to avoid inconvenient publication.

Regardless, I don't envy Steam Spy its position making a tough call on the matter.

Eurogamer and Microsoft Make it "Exclusive"

Originally published on The Game Beat, April 17, 2017

It's not uncommon for the biggest gaming news outlets to secure exclusive reveals for previews of big-name games, or even occasional exclusive early reviews of hot new titles. Hell, at one point *Game Informer* was securing a "World Exclusive" reveal of a new game on its cover practically every month.

Even considering that context, though, Eurogamer's exclusive reveal of the specs behind Microsoft's upcoming Xbox One "Scorpio" refresh this week (later released as the Xbox One X -ed.) was quite a coup. It's one that the site made the most of, too, spreading its coverage out across five separate stories and three separate videos on its Digital Foundry subsite (not to mention an interview with Digital Foundry's Richard Leadbetter on sister site USGamer). The interest from the public was intense enough to briefly bring down the Eurogamer servers Thursday morning, even causing collateral damage on other sites that share Eurogamer's server infrastructure. (Eurogamer was briefly forced to direct users to its Facebook Instant articles during the server trouble.)

That kind of server-melting traffic shows why it would have been somewhat crazy for Eurogamer to turn down Microsoft's invitation to see Scorpio up close at their Redmond headquarters last week. But agreeing to an exclusive of this magnitude also risks coming across as a mere mouthpiece for a company you're supposed to be covering with a kind of detached objectivity. The mass of approving tweets from Microsoft executives and official accounts suggests the corporation as a whole was pretty happy with the coverage it got out of the relationship.

Even assuming Eurogamer went in with the intent to be fair and even-handed, the mere appearance of any kind of overly cozy "exclusive" relationship can be damaging to an outlet. Can readers really trust Eurogamer to really bite the hand that feeds it such a traffic bonanza? Would Eurogamer's Scorpio coverage ever end up overly skeptical and/or negative, even if the hardware warranted it?

Take the quote below,[104] from Eurogamer itself, which I think betrays how Microsoft's exclusive invite may have left the site feeling like the lucky belle of the ball:

> *Microsoft's invitation to Digital Foundry to talk tech and exclusively reveal specs is a bold, brave move that at once highlights the platform holder's confidence in its new hardware, and continues its strategy of keeping users informed well ahead of time, as opposed to seeing carefully laid plans exposed via a relentless, inevitable trickle of leaks. ... I can't think of any example of access at this level so far in advance of the launch of new hardware...*

Then there's the question of why Eurogamer was chosen for the exclusive. Digital Foundry has a well-deserved reputation for best-in-class coverage of the kind of detailed technical minutiae needed to interpret the dense tangle of gaming hardware specs and performance, of course. By going through the site, rather than just issuing some dry "official" press release, Microsoft is in effect latching on to Digital Foundry's reputation in this area. The intent is to earn the reader's trust that the presented interpretation of the specs is at least somewhat independent from Microsoft's spin.

But Leadbetter's interview with USGamer gives some important insight on another reason Microsoft may have gone through Digital Foundry specifically:

> *The funny thing is that Microsoft knew exactly what my expectations were because I posted them in response to their E3 announce video last year. So with the GPU clock speeds in particular, they have delivered much, much higher frequencies than I expected - it took me by surprise and I think they got a kick off my reaction.*

In other words, Microsoft knew what Digital Foundry was expecting, knew they'd be able to beat those expectations, and thus knew they could practically guarantee some glowing coverage from Digital Foundry's captive and "exclusive" media audience. Other outlets could have easily come away from a similar reveal more skeptical—Kotaku's Stephen Totilo certainly seemed less impressed with the reveal in a recent tweet.[105]

Contrast the Digital Foundry exclusive with 2013, when Microsoft opened up its Redmond campus to literally hundreds of media outlets for a splashy Xbox One press conference and media day ahead of E3. Casting such a wide media net ensured a much larger reach Microsoft's news, but it also meant ceding a lot of control to outlets that would all be competing to have their own unique takes on the event.

After the overwhelmingly negative reaction to 2013's TV- and media-focused Xbox One rollout, Microsoft may have learned its lesson, leading to this more controlled "exclusive" reveal for Scorpio's specs. And with every other outlet essentially forced to link to and quote from Eurogamer's coverage to get the news out anyway, Microsoft's message probably had about the same reach it would have with a wider media event.

(Side note: While there's definitely been an undercurrent of "who cares about teraflops, where are the games?" blowback in the reaction to Digital Foundry's number-heavy exclusive, revealing the Scorpio specs now gets this kind of technical dryness out of the way ahead of what's sure to be a software-focused unveiling at E3. And, of course, there's a huge segment of the core gaming audience that care to the point of obsession about this kind of digital dick-measuring.)

To be fair to Digital Foundry, the site's coverage of the Scorpio specs often went out if its way to add caveats to the overwhelming praise of the system's performance. At one point, Leadbetter goes beyond the raw numbers to point out that, "what PS4 Pro has proved is that checkerboarding, advanced anti-aliasing techniques, temporal super-sampling and dynamic resolution go a long way in closing the gap between sub-native ultra HD resolutions and the true 4K experience Microsoft is aiming for."

> *[Comparing Scorpio to PS4 Pro] is really impossible... because there are no comparison points where it matters: software. On a pure specs level, Scorpio beats Pro in all areas but what Sony has shown is that its hardware can punch well above its weight. You look at Horizon Zero Dawn or Ratchet and Clank and these are awesome 4K games, regardless of the technical sleight of hand going on in the background. That said, in [multi-platform games], that extra four gigs of RAM in Scorpio ensures we get higher quality textures wherever they are available—and a lot of games do support that now.*

Leadbetter is also quick to point out multiple times in his coverage what he calls "the pretty huge caveat that we've only seen one demo running on the machine—and for the umpteenth time, software is everything." As Leadbetter elaborates in his USGamer interview:

> *This is the kind of fair-minded, context-filled coverage that shows Digital Foundry deserved to be on top of the list of outlets Microsoft would consider for such a major technical reveal. That said, Microsoft definitely knew what it was doing when it chose to funnel its Scorpio message through its own hand-picked media filter.*

ADDENDUM

The following pieces, originally written for and published on Ars Technica, could not be reproduced here but should be of interest to anyone interested in the kinds of issues covered in this book. Please use the links below to read them online:

- Source: *Nintendo Power* to cease publication (Aug. 22, 2012) (https://arstechnica.com/gaming/2012/08/source-nintendo-power-magazine-to-cease-publication/)

- Final *Nintendo Power* cover brings the magazine full circle (Nov. 20, 2012) (https://arstechnica.com/gaming/2012/11/final-nintendo-power-cover-brings-the-magazine-full-circle/)

- Stealth marketing: Microsoft paying YouTubers for Xbox One mentions (Jan. 21, 2014) (https://arstechnica.com/gaming/2014/01/stealth-marketing-microsoft-paying-youtubers-for-xbox-one-mentions/)

- Electronic Arts also paying YouTubers to promote games (Jan. 22, 2014) (https://arstechnica.com/gaming/2014/01/electronic-arts-also-paying-youtubers-to-promote-games/)

- Confessions of a 13-year-old Mario fansite creator (March 12, 2014) (https://arstechnica.com/gaming/2014/03/remembering-my-first-cautious-steps-onto-the-web-on-its-25th-birthday/)

- Steam Gauge: Do strong reviews lead to stronger sales on Steam? (April 23, 2014) (https://arstechnica.com/gaming/2014/04/steam-gauge-do-strong-reviews-lead-to-stronger-sales-on-steam/)

- Addressing allegations of "collusion" among gaming journalists (Sept. 18, 2014) (https://arstechnica.com/gaming/2014/09/addressing-allegations-of-collusion-among-gaming-journalists/)

- Twitch, Steam now require disclosure of sponsored content from users (Oct. 3, 2014) (https://arstechnica.com/gaming/2014/10/twitch-steam-now-require-disclosure-of-sponsored-content-from-users/)

- Activision using copyright notices to take down *Call of Duty* exploit videos (Nov. 24, 2014) (https://arstechnica.com/gaming/2014/11/activision-using-copyright-notices-to-take-down-call-of-duty-exploit-videos/)

- The spotty death and eternal life of gaming review scores (Feb. 15, 2015) (https://arstechnica.com/gaming/2015/02/the-spotty-death-and-eternal-life-of-gaming-review-scores/)

- How a journalist briefly got control of a major new gaming brand's domain (April 10, 2015) (https://arstechnica.com/gaming/2015/04/how-a-journalist-briefly-got-control-of-a-major-new-gaming-brands-domain/)

- Analysis: Kotaku, blacklisting, and the independence of the gaming press (Nov. 20, 2015) (https://arstechnica.com/gaming/2015/11/analysis-kotaku-blacklisting-and-the-independence-of-the-gaming-press/)

- How sky-high hype formed a storm cloud over *No Man's Sky*'s release (Aug. 10, 2016) (https://arstechnica.com/gaming/2016/08/how-sky-high-hype-formed-a-storm-cloud-over-no-mans-skys-release/)

- Why early reviews of video games are getting rarer and rarer (Oct. 26, 2016) (https://arstechnica.com/gaming/2016/10/why-early-reviews-of-video-games-are-getting-rarer-and-rarer/)

- So you think you want to go to E3... (Feb. 8, 2017) (https://arstechnica.com/gaming/2017/02/so-you-think-you-want-to-go-to-e3/)

- Sony's legal quest to remove its leaked developer's kit from the Web (July 20, 2017) (https://arstechnica.com/gaming/2017/07/sony-using-copyright-requests-to-remove-leaked-ps4-sdk-from-the-web/)

- *FireWatch* dev uses DMCA against PewDiePie after streamed racial slur (Sept. 11, 2017) (https://arstechnica.com/gaming/2017/09/firewatch-dev-uses-dmca-against-pewdiepie-after-streamed-racial-slur/)

ENDNOTES

1. https://web.archive.org/web/20031002093904/http://www.nerdsahoy. com/interviews/090103_gaben_hl2.htm

2. http://xbox.gamespy.com/xbox/halo-2/564301p1.html

3. https://web.archive.org/web/20041204083543/http://www.1up.com/ do/reviewPage?cId=3136245&did=6

4. https://web.archive.org/web/20041204091256/http://1up.com:80/do/ reviewPage?cId=2005815&did=2

5. https://web.archive.org/web/20041204065752/http://www.1up. com:80/do/reviewPage?cId=3136252&did=1

6. https://web.archive.org/web/20041109015341/http://www.gamespot. com/xbox/action/halo2/review.html

7. https://web.archive.org/web/20041109214544/http://www.g4techtv. com/halo2day/features/50249/Halo_2_Review.html

8. https://web.archive.org/web/20041109231930/http://www.ugo.com/ channels/games/features/halo2/review_1.asp

9. https://web.archive.org/web/20041109035722/http://xbox.ign.com/ articles/557/557509p1.html

10. https://web.archive.org/web/20041110082649/http://microsoft. gamerfeed.com/gf/reviews/520/

11. https://web.archive.org/web/20041109015341/http://www.gamespot. com/xbox/action/halo2/review.html

12. https://www.gamespot.com/reviews/astro-boy-review/1900-6105611/

13. https://web.archive.org/web/20050308134518/http://rogerebert. suntimes.com/apps/pbcs.dll/section?category=ANSWERMAN

14. https://web.archive.org/web/20051126014325/https://grumpygamer. com/7462425

15. https://www.kotaku.com.au/2007/10/dissecting_jacks_latest_tv_spi/

16. https://web.archive.org/web/20070420035734/http://www.joystiq. com/2007/04/18/what-i-know-about-violent-games/

17. https://web.archive.org/web/20080906091107/http://www.1pstart. com/did-the-virginia-tech-murders-rob-me-of-my-love-for-halo-2/

18. https://web.archive.org/web/20060820124649/http://www.maximonline.com/slideshows/index.aspx?imgCollectId=107

19. https://web.archive.org/web/20060820124649/http://www.maximonline.com/slideshows/index.aspx?imgCollectId=107

20. https://web.archive.org/web/20080317101851/http://www.gamedaily.com/articles/galleries/top-ten-pokemom-wed-like-to-eat/?page=1

21. https://web.archive.org/web/20090711120653/http://bitmob.com/index.php/mobfeed/Top-10-Bad-Things-the-Internet-Brought-to-Gaming-Journalism.html

22. http://www.smbhq.com/

23. https://www.ign.com/articles/2010/04/21/videogame-celebrity-trash-mags

24. https://kotaku.com/scandal-hits-call-of-duty-devs-what-we-know-update-5483492

25. https://web.archive.org/web/20060308174402/http://www.joystiq.com/2006/02/22/former-gizmondo-exec-involved-in-ferrari-enzo-crash/

26. https://web.archive.org/web/20100618223218/http://blog.us.playstation.com/2010/06/15/surprise-twisted-metal-coming-to-ps3/

27. https://www.rockpapershotgun.com/2010/07/23/no-starcraft-2-reviews-before-lunch/

28. https://www.rockpapershotgun.com/2016/08/17/broken-promises-of-no-mans-sky/

29. https://www.reddit.com/r/gaming/comments/4y6nyc/no_mans_sky_how_the_media_hyped_the_game_and_now/

30. https://kotaku.com/the-no-mans-sky-hype-dilemma-1785416931

31. https://twitter.com/sciencegroen/status/765648624600485892

32. https://ungaming.tumblr.com/post/149102772520/i-tweeted-a-link-to-this-article-on-the-bus-about#_=_

33. https://www.eurogamer.net/articles/2016-08-22-ps4-slim-leaks-online-first-pictures

34. https://www.youtube.com/watch?v=aM2CuIrluF0

35. http://letsplayvideogames.com/2016/08/review-playstation-4-slim/

36. https://www.youtube.com/watch?v=AFGAJtnky7A

37. https://www.wsj.com/articles/nintendo-begins-distributing-software-kit-for-new-nx-platform-1444996588

38. https://arstechnica.com/gaming/2016/05/why-nintendo-nxs-rumored-shift-from-discs-to-cartridges-is-actually-smart/

39. https://www.eurogamer.net/articles/2016-07-26-nx-is-a-portable-console-with-detachable-controllers

40. https://www.wsj.com/articles/pokemon-to-create-games-for-nintendos-next-system-1474371834

41. https://www.polygon.com/2015/10/26/9616468/halo-5-story-ending

42. https://motherboard.vice.com/en_us/article/bj54vq/playstation-steam-super-seducer-pua-game

43. https://www.rockpapershotgun.com/2018/03/08/super-seducer-review/

44. https://thenextweb.com/gaming/2018/02/19/slimy-seduction-expert-slips-worlds-sleaziest-game-onto-steam/

45. https://arstechnica.com/gaming/2018/03/dating-coach-game-super-seducer-barred-from-playstation-4/

46. https://arstechnica.com/gaming/2012/03/why-linking-developer-bonuses-to-metacritic-scores-should-come-to-an-end/

47. https://arstechnica.com/gaming/2015/02/the-spotty-death-and-eternal-life-of-gaming-review-scores/

48. http://www.quartertothree.com/game-talk/showthread.php?t=33997

49. https://web.archive.org/web/20081217013949/http://kotaku.com/347350/keighley-sets-mass-effect-record-straight-or-tries-to

50. https://web.archive.org/web/20090708023355/http://gamecriticsawards.com:80/judges.html

51. https://twitter.com/Quinnae_Moon/status/798668442853404672

52. https://www.washingtonpost.com/news/act-four/wp/2016/11/14/no-passionate-young-pop-culture-fans-did-not-cause-donald-trumps-victory/?utm_term=.1b9ca1589625

53. https://web.archive.org/web/20161224041116/https://twitter.com/NickCapozzoli/status/798203799974252544

54. https://waypoint.vice.com/en_us/article/a-note-on-trump-waypoint-and-why-we-play

55. http://venturebeat.com/2016/11/09/tetris-vr-and-escapism-why-we-play/

56. https://twitter.com/NerdGerhl/status/797095008662908928

57. https://c.opencritic.com/releases/BrashGames.pdf

58. http://archive.is/1179o

59. https://www.youtube.com/watch?v=sUwzpEE9KsI

60. https://xkcd.com/606/

61. http://seattle.bizjournals.com/seattle/stories/2003/06/02/story7.html

62. https://www.penny-arcade.com/comic/2006/01/20/the-partial-revolution

63. https://money.cnn.com/2003/08/27/commentary/game_over/column_gaming/?cnn=yes

64. https://web.archive.org/web/20030902121458/https://www.gamesindustry.biz/content_page.php?section_name=dev&aid=2161

65. https://web.archive.org/web/20040705175211/http://www.gamesindustry.biz/content_page.php?section_name=dev&aid=3645

66. https://web.archive.org/web/20040706003751/http://www.gamesindustry.biz/content_page.php?section_name=pub&aid=3669

67. https://www.gamespot.com/articles/nintendo-console-patent-sparks-rumors/1100-6105085/

68. https://web.archive.org/web/20160614220356/http://www.1up.com/do/blogEntry?publicUserId=5545444&bId=5233614

69. https://web.archive.org/web/20051128204324/http://www.1up.com/do/newsStory?cId=3141932

70. https://web.archive.org/web/20030620042019/http://www.planetgamecube.com/news.cfm?action=item&id=4344

71. https://www.theregister.co.uk/2001/01/10/sega_to_ditch_console_biz/

72. https://www.esquire.com/news-politics/news/a797/esq0706kloster-66/

73. https://web.archive.org/web/20060712003024/http://www.wired.com/news/columns/0,71290-0.html?tw=rss.index

74. https://web.archive.org/web/20070319004410/http://www.gamasutra.com/php-bin/column_index.php?story=8374

75. https://arstechnica.com/gaming/2006/08/4944/

76. https://web.archive.org/web/20071019002406/http://www.1up.com/do/blogEntry?bId=7748784&publicUserId=5519593

77. http://www.gamesetwatch.com/2006/12/anatomy_of_a_goof_xbox_360_sal.php

78. https://web.archive.org/web/20070520060954/http://biz.gamedaily.com/industry/media/?id=16197

79. https://arstechnica.com/gaming/2015/02/the-spotty-death-and-eternal-life-of-gaming-review-scores/

80. https://www.gamasutra.com/view/feature/1542/pr_and_the_game_media_how_pr_.php

81. https://web.archive.org/web/20120426074451/http://gillen.cream.org/wordpress_html/assorted-essays/how-to-use-and-abuse-the-games-press-and-how-the-games-press-wants-to-use-and-abuse-you/

82. https://arstechnica.com/gaming/2017/03/early-review-mass-effect-andromeda-is-dragon-age-inquisition-in-space/

83. https://twitter.com/Nibellion/status/843774560260575232

84. https://kotaku.com/the-future-of-kotakus-video-game-coverage-is-the-prese-1644297778

85. http://www.ign.com/videos/2017/02/23/our-mass-effect-andromeda-hands-on-impressions-unlocked

86. https://theconcourse.deadspin.com/god-help-me-i-dont-like-the-new-legend-of-zelda-game-1793718635

87. http://web.archive.org/web/20040213144919/http://www.rottentomatoes.com/games/

88. https://www.polygon.com/2017/8/23/16184068/why-i-worship-crunch

89. https://twitter.com/bombsfall/status/900381593453330432

90. https://www.youtube.com/watch?v=RDdk47stWGo

91. https://web.archive.org/web/20080216053429/http://www.gamedaily.com/articles/features/courting-controversy-part-1/70911/?biz=1

92. https://web.archive.org/web/20100302085328/http://www.gamedaily.com:80/articles/features/courting-controversy-part-2/70944/?biz=1

93. https://web.archive.org/web/20170810013210/https://www.engadget.

com/2007/12/05/comparison-shows-significant-edits-to-gerstmanns-kane-and-lynch-r/

94. https://www.penny-arcade.com/news/post/2007/11/30

95. https://www.gamespot.com/articles/spot-on-gamespot-on-gerstmann/1100-6183666/

96. https://web.archive.org/web/20171213132814/https://www.engadget.com/2007/11/30/rumor-gamespots-editorial-director-fired-over-kane-and-lynch-rev/

97. https://web.archive.org/web/20080102235152/http://valleywag.com:80/commenter/gamespot

98. https://kotaku.com/a-price-of-games-journalism-1743526293

99. https://web.archive.org/web/20070303064324/http://kotaku.com/gaming/top/sony-blackballs-kotaku-240860.php

100. https://www.theatlantic.com/politics/archive/2010/06/the-biden-beach-party/57821/

101. https://twitter.com/Muckbeast/status/768845821475520512

102. https://arstechnica.com/series/steam-gauge/

103. http://www.pcgamer.com/a-game-developer-believes-steam-spy-puts-its-employees-in-danger/

104. https://www.eurogamer.net/articles/digitalfoundry-2017-scorpio-is-console-hardware-pushed-to-a-new-level

105. https://twitter.com/stephentotilo/status/849978506213806080

ABOUT THE ETC PRESS

The ETC Press was founded in 2005 under the direction of Dr. Drew Davidson, the Director of Carnegie Mellon University's Entertainment Technology Center (ETC), as an open access, digital-first publishing house.

What does all that mean?

The ETC Press publishes three types of work:peer-reviewed work (research-based books, textbooks, academic journals, conference proceedings), general audience work (trade nonfiction, singles, Well Played singles), and research and white papers

The common tie for all of these is a focus on issues related to entertainment technologies as they are applied across a variety of fields.

Our authors come from a range of backgrounds. Some are traditional academics. Some are practitioners. And some work in between. What ties them all together is their ability to write about the impact of emerging technologies and its significance in society.

To distinguish our books, the ETC Press has five imprints:

- ETC Press: our traditional academic and peer-reviewed publications;
- ETC Press: Single: our short "why it matters" books that are roughly 8,000-25,000 words;
- ETC Press: Signature: our special projects, trade books, and other curated works that exemplify the best work being done;
- ETC Press: Report: our white papers and reports produced by practitioners or academic researchers working in conjunction with partners; and
- ETC Press: Student: our work with undergraduate and graduate students

In keeping with that mission, the ETC Press uses emerging technologies to design all of our books and Lulu, an on-demand publisher, to distribute our e-books and print books through all the major retail chains, such as Amazon, Barnes & Noble, Kobo, and Apple, and we work with The Game Crafter to produce tabletop games.

We don't carry an inventory ourselves. Instead, each print book is created when somebody buys a copy.

Since the ETC Press is an open-access publisher, every book, journal, and proceeding is available as a free download. We're most interested in the sharing and spreading of ideas. We also have an agreement with the Association for Computing Machinery (ACM) to list ETC Press publications in the ACM Digital Library.

Authors retain ownership of their intellectual property. We release all of our books, journals, and proceedings under one of two Creative Commons licenses:

- Attribution-NoDerivativeWorks-NonCommercial: This license allows for published works to remain intact, but versions can be created; or
- Attribution-NonCommercial-ShareAlike: This license allows for authors to retain editorial control of their creations while also encouraging readers to collaboratively rewrite content.

This is definitely an experiment in the notion of publishing, and we invite people to participate. We are exploring what it means to "publish" across multiple media and multiple versions. We believe this is the future of publication, bridging virtual and physical media with fluid versions of publications as well as enabling the creative blurring of what constitutes reading and writing.

www.ingramcontent.com/pod-product-compliance
Lightning Source LLC
Chambersburg PA
CBHW020723180526
45163CB00001B/85